Blessings on you. You
have meant a lot to
our family. John 14:6
Willis

BY THE WAY

A Farm Boy From Kansas, To Berkeley, To Bourbonais

Willis E. Snowbarger

authorHOUSE™

1663 LIBERTY DRIVE, SUITE 200
BLOOMINGTON, INDIANA 47403
(800) 839-8640
WWW.AUTHORHOUSE.COM

First published by AuthorHouse 05/09/05

ISBN: 1-4208-2542-9 (sc)
ISBN: 1-4208-2543-7 (dj)

Library of Congress Control Number: 2005900282

Printed in the United States of America
Bloomington, Indiana

This book is printed on acid-free paper.

Scripture quotations noted NIV are taken from the HOLY BIBLE: NEW INTERNATIONAL VERSION. Copyright © 1973, 1978, 1984 by the International Bible Society. Used by permission of Zondervan Bible Publishers.

Dedicated to my family and colleagues along the way.

TABLE OF CONTENTS

FOREWORDS

A word from my eighties

    A word on how to live and thrive

A word from a college teacher and dean

    A word from middle management

A word from one who hopes to deserve to be called Christian

    A word for friends and neighbors

A word for family

    My memoirs.

Willis E. Snowbarger

PREFACE

BY THE WAY has a double meaning. We use the phrase to mean "incidentally." It is those fortuitous random incidents, the micro, not the necessarily macro events that really make a life. The names, the surprises, the challenge of routine events yield a life of humor, improbabilities, achievement, and joy. You have heard it said, "The devil is in the details." True, but I have found that "God is in the details as well."

The phrase "The Way" or the "Path" is planted in the Scriptures. "The Path of the Just." The "Way of the Righteous," The "Way of the Holiness." God's directions, the journey, the "Way to live." Early Christians, guarding their conversations, inquired "Are you on the Way?" How far up the Way are you?" Before the great love chapter (I Cor. 13), St. Paul says, "Now I will show you the most excellent way" (NIV). The **WAY** is revealed.

Willis E. Snowbarger

CH. I AN AUSPICIOUS START

"The beginning is the most important part of the work." Plato

The America I discovered on August 24, 1921 was thoroughly rural, full of opportunity, and optimistic. Later we were told America was in a farm depression, that the plains should have been left to the bison and Indians, and that the entire future of the country was wrapped up in its cities. My parentage and the story of their arrival in central Kansas was told in *The Snowbarger Family in Kansas*. Of course, I was not conscious of that during my first several years but I was the beneficiary of the genes that had stirred my forbearers to leave Europe, start from scratch in a new country, and dream better things for their children. While this chapter covers the time frame of "pre-memoirs," I hope the following observations and commentary on these beginnings may be interesting and not extraneous.

The family, school, country church, the way of life, and the rural economy were all conducive to the upbringing of a boy like me. I was extremely fortunate. As the oldest son of an oldest son, my position in the family was ideal. None of my cousins enjoyed the doting I received from grandparents, uncles, and aunts. Only the first four or five grandchildren lived in this complete family unit before it began to break up, moving to other parts of the state. My blind aunt, Elsie, had nothing to do but to make over me. She lived one-half mile away and could walk over to our house unassisted. I was unaware of how thoroughly they all spoiled me, but I quickly learned how to make it work to my advantage. The reader may think this is imagination (and to a certain extent it is), but read a letter my Grandpa Sam Snowbarger wrote to me on February 7, 1930:

1

Willis E. Snowbarger

Dear Grand Son,

Your good letter at hand, and contents noted. Was so glad to get your fine letter. You are sure a mighty fine boy, and have a wonderful future, if you stay true to Jesus and I believe you will. Harraugh for your side! Of course, whatever side you are on is bound to win. That is the way that we always win, when we play the game fair. Never try to win in any other way for it is wrong and will not pay.

There may come a time when the other side will win. That will be your chance to show yourself (to be) a real little man. Take those who did win by the hand and congratulate them over their victory, and rejoice with them if they did it on the square. If they did not play fair, let them know that you are sorry for them. If you will do this you will always have friends.

Well, I am feeling fine, hoping to get home soon. Again let me say, I am proud of you, you are the oldest grandson I have, and you have one of the greatest mothers in the world, and a better father no boy could wish for. So you see there will be no excuse for you not making good. I am expecting you to set the pace for all the rest of my grandchildren since you are the first and the oldest. I assure you that I have great faith in you, and will not be disappointed . . . .

Your Grandpa Snowbarger

That is quite a load to throw on an eight year old! But I grew up with that, they believed in me and I believed I could do anything. Ray Sauer, an older friend at church, would often say, "My how tall you are; you remind me of Abraham Lincoln."

My parents were very capable people who chose to invest themselves in their children, their community, and other people. By staying with the family farm (although not having enough acres to make it economically viable), they were usually strapped for cash. After I became their trustee and sold the farm, collecting 9% interest, I owed federal income tax. My mother protested that I must have made a mistake. "We don't make enough to owe income tax!" No, they usually did not because, while they worked the land, they could not make the equivalent of 9% interest on the value of the land. But they were leaders in the community because of character, dependability, and identification with the needs of their neighbors. My father, Edward, was a veteran of World War I, graduate of Bresee College, a Bible school. When the Armistice was signed, he made his way home to marry his sweetheart and take over the timber claim farm his Grandma

Yust had hoped he could have. It was not until 1938, at a closed family auction, that he was able to buy the farm through his mother's bid. So in the first nineteen years of their life on the farm, they were renters and the property deteriorated. Nor was there modernization. Apart from the party line telephone, the house was very much as it was when built in the 1880's. My mother's *Autobiography* has vivid descriptions of the hardships that were the lot of the frontier woman, in her case, right up until 1942 when electricity reached Hayes Township. Edward had tried to buy more land. He had rented 80 acres from Uncle Oscar Werner, a professor of Education at the University of Nebraska, and, in the late twenties, he and his brother, George, bought some land in southwest Kansas.

The Kansas Farm

What they could not accomplish by increasing their income, they did through working as a family team. Edward, brother Wesley, and Sam combined their resources, equipment, horses, and labor essentially farming together. Later it was Edward, Sam, and brother Clarence. Still later, it was Clarence, Edward, and cousin Ralph. I believe George was included for a few years. They bought some machinery jointly and shared equipment, horsepower, and manpower to keep costs low. Large families made it unnecessary to hire any farm workers. At the end of wheat harvest, they would bring their records together and "settle up." To illustrate, I worked row crops, driving the tractor to cultivate corn and sorghum, because my hay fever rendered me worthless in wheat harvest. So I cultivated everybody's corn and remember to this day the undulations of all those fields.

We didn't like to keep hogs, so we did not eat bacon or pork. We ate chicken and beef which we raised. Likewise, we ate the kind of fruits and vegetables we raised. The economy has something to do with raising kids. First of all, children learned to work and so did all the neighbor kids. You can't beat the farm for a place to teach practical lessons about life all the way from sex, to the food chain, the need for work, discipline, obligations to animals and people, and the need to care for the soil and the environment. Kids learned that there were cold rooms and corners of rooms, no cash, disagreeable realities – you live with them. You can't quit in the middle of critical jobs even if you feel like it. Some authority figure has to take charge in a crisis and there were a few every day. Limits are all around you: you can't go to a grocery store today, you are snowbound this week, there's no one to play with. So you learn to make do. GI's in World War's I and II were noted for all the repairs they could make to vehicles and gun mounts with baling wire, pliers, and a screw driver. All frontiers taught the need for making common cause and cooperation just as surely as they taught competition. The last, the farmer's frontier, showed the need to work together to achieve better things in a community.

Edward, my father, doubtless had received the same admonitions that Sam passed along to his grandson (above). He was hard working, a good student, thoroughly dependable, a true Christian and churchman, a good steward, and a leader both at church and in the community. He served as Sunday School teacher, chorister, board member, district advisory board member, member of the General Board, and college trustee (for thirty-five years). He was the kind of person who would stand in there and take it. That included several very difficult decisions and situations. For example, the merger of Bresee College and Bethany-Peniel in 1940, several crises in the Kansas District, moving the church to a new building in Sylvia, the building program, and the calling of pastors. Things did not always go his way, but he was loyal to the decision of the body. And he always paid more than his share of the bill. In the community, he was active on the school board, the Co-op, Republican precinct committeeman, sexton for the Fairview Cemetery, township board, and the County School Reorganization Committee. He was assessor for the township for a term after our house had been remodeled and was proud of the fact that he assessed his property higher than any other in the township. (Volume II of *The Snowbarger Family in Kansas* details these facts about both Edward and Mary).

By the way, Edward had not only rectitude, but courage. After a certain pastor had received a poor vote, he told me, "I had no idea he would drop that many votes. If I had, I would have talked to the pastor and warned him." He was the more silent partner, allowing others to gab at the family gathering, following the conversations closely, then doubling over with laughter when something struck him as being funny. He was not reluctant about giving instructions about work to be done. He was just the strong, silent type. Like his mother, he may have been "handicapped" a bit when it came to expressing his emotions. In church, it was tears more than "Amens." We knew he was proud (or not so proud) of us but it was not because of hugs (at least not in public). He took leadership training courses, even teaching one in the home community. During his Bible School days and for several years afterward, he must have thought of himself as a lay preacher. He helped out with the music in many revivals and home mission projects and in one year, held a local preacher's license. But, he apparently concluded that he did not have a call to full-time ministry. His life centered in the church. There was no doubt or question about our attendance any time the church doors opened. In all the above matters, there was never an objection from my mother, Mary. They stood together in values, lifestyles, and priorities.

They were together on the matter of Christian stewardship. I am convinced that this principle, observed by children as it was lived out in the priorities of the home, taught more than any other about true Christianity. It was tough and humbling. Whether little or much is given the principle says "It was not mine anyway." I was only the steward. Proportional giving, modeling not preaching, meet the needs of others as we are able. "Against this there is no law." "The Lord giveth, the Lord taketh away. Blessed be the name of the Lord." My parents were also together on discipline of the children, spending priorities, rules of the home, healthy diet, regularity of schedules, doing well in school, and assignment of work to the children. Not only grandparents, but uncles and aunts, confirmed to us before we had any basis of comparison, that we had excellent parents. Edward and Mary knew their own shortcomings and we heard them call on the Lord for help as they commented on the Scripture lesson and in family prayer at morning worship.

My Parents, Edward and Mary

My mother, Mary King Snowbarger, was a remarkable woman. She lived to age 95 and was alert to within ten days of her passing. At my urging she dictated her *Autobiography*. To read it reminds me that, in many respects, life on the farm in the 1920's was not that different from life in the 1880's. Change was so much slower then. The details are in writing, so I recount only general impressions. Her love for Edward was deep, abiding, and mutual. She had done some advanced study in piano and had taught music, Latin, and German in the Bible School (later it was called Bresee College). She and I agreed that her level of completion was equivalent to an associate degree. Most of those going into business prior to 1920 had achieved a similar level through attendance at a business college. My father's level of completion was just a bit lower. Both were excellent students, so they had not reached an upper limit, only the customary level of schooling for their age cohort. But, no doubt, Mary could have gone higher in music, even as a member of an evangelistic team, if that had been her choice.

The King family (my maternal grandfather's and the Smith family (my maternal grandmother's) were Mennonites. Forbearers came from Germany, Switzerland, and Alsace Lorraine to Lancaster, Pennsylvania in the 1700's (perhaps as early as 1724). Many, if not most of them, were Amish. Migration to Ohio and Illinois resulted from the search for better and cheaper land, not to mention the needs of large families. My grandfather, Emmanuel Jesse King, put it plainly (of his father), "He has six boys to look after and keep them busy. I was the second of the boys; there was not enough work for us all. So it came my lot to go away from home and work for the other man." He did odd jobs like hauling coal from a railroad to their neighborhoods near Gridley, Illinois. He rented a small farm. When he was married in December 1885 to Magdalena Smith, they migrated to Kansas as a honeymoon of sorts. Relatives had moved there in July of that year, living between Larned and Belpre. They moved on an immigrant train, the men riding on the cars carrying livestock and possessions, women and children in coaches. About one month prior to their arrival on February 6, 1886, the Great Blizzard had struck Kansas. Hundreds of cattle froze to death. My grandfather's first job in Kansas was taking the hides from their carcasses (one way to salvage some value from the disaster). When he was well into his nineties he related this experience to me with excitement and crystal clear detail of the journey, Illinois friends he saw at the railroad stations enroute, and the sights and effects of the blizzard. It was not the best of starts. He farmed in Pawnee and Harvey counties and had a tree nursery in Reno County; but the only real estate he ever owned was 607 East 6th Street in Hutchinson, Kansas. At the end of his 96 years, he died with all his bills paid and his younger daughter, having sold the home to pay expenses, had less than $15 per surviving child to distribute to his heirs. I am sure that she paid some expenses herself so as not to embarrass him but that is "coming out even" in the end!

They called them "Man" and "Lena" (for Emanuel and Magdalena). Their story is told in *The King Family History* by Jesse Edward King, which includes material by Benjamin J. King and Esther V. King Anderson. They were not only pioneers of the Farmer's Frontier but also devout people who sought a "deeper life" and explored outside the Amish-Mennonite fold. My mother recalls attending a holiness camp meeting in which a "Bishop Eisenhower" was the preacher. She believed him to be a relative of Ike. They went to several different meetings of this sort, including the Beulah Camp in Wichita. When some of these people began to talk of starting a Bible School, Lena, my grandmother, was asked to be the cook. They packed up the family and moved with the younger children into the larger building on East Fourth Street in Hutchinson. They began to make things happen. Grandpa King was the handyman who, with his wagon and team of horses, got the groceries and was likely the only maintenance man the institution had. Later when a rescue mission for unfortunate girls was established across the alley on Third Street, Grandpa carried out similar duties for them. In the *Herald of Holiness*, an ad for the home lists him as "Manager." They were also pioneers of the "holiness movement." Tillman Smith, my mother's cousin and former president of Hesston College, assures me that the doctrine of holiness was their motive for leaving the Mennonites. The relationships within the extended family remained cordial. Lena's sister, Anna Smith King, played an important role in the early days of Hesston College. So all of my grandparents (Smith, King, Yust, and Snowbarger) as well as uncles and aunts played an important role in Christian education. This was in spite of sparse resources, even what would be called today poverty levels of income. They were not short on dreams, romance, courage, IQ, and the will to make things better for their children. And all the families were devoted Christians, who placed their ultimate trust in God who would guide them and see them through, regardless of the difficulty. It should not seem strange that a high percentage of my cousins are college graduates, that the in-laws, likewise, hold degrees, and that there are several college or university professors and administrators among the ranks. Except for her choice to marry and raise children, my mother was one of these professional types.

I remember having been with three of my great grandparents. David H. King had a long white beard and I saw him at a King reunion at Uncle Sam King's house in Hesston. His wife had died, leaving him alone with his young son, Amos. When Amos was able to fend for himself, David H. began his wanderings and came to be known as "The Gleaner." His diary for 1917 is partially filled in. The front page had a place for his address. He wrote, "No particular place." He details the places to which he traveled, in whose homes he was entertained, and where and how much he gleaned. He traveled with a team of horses and a wagon. He would harvest the wheat by hand as he found it in corners and fencerows after the binders or headers had finished the field. He got the owner's permission, threshed the grain in the farmyard, cleaned up the mess, and moved on. Several stops landed him with relatives, but he freelanced all the way from Texas into Kansas. At the end of 1917 he totaled his earnings: $750.00. There were undoubtedly many regular farmers who netted less cash for that year. One time he was out of touch with the family for several months. He had taken a trip by wagon back to Illinois to visit relatives and to repay a debt. But he returned to Kansas and lived out his last years in Hesston.

Great-Grandpa Yust was a Civil War veteran who pioneered in Kansas, homesteaded, and planted a timber claim (where I was born). He also started the German Methodist church, the public school in the community, and gave the land for the cemetery. Family referred to him as "der GrossVater." He died in 1937. His daughter, Emma Coleman, often invited our family to visit him in their home. His oldest son, Will, was a librarian at Rollins College. He wrote a biography soon after his father's death that provides an excellent account of the first settlements in Hayes Township, Reno County. I was fifteen at the time of his death.

Great-Grandma Snowbarger lived one-half mile from us in a small house next to her son, Sam (my grandpa). I knew her better than my great-grandfathers. She was short, wiry, and fairly quiet but interesting to observe. Her story is told in *The Snowbarger Family in Kansas*. Their home in Missouri was apparently filled with drama as she gave vent to her fiery temper, throwing dishes and furniture. But she was converted and sanctified in the early years of her move to Kansas. She was a charter member of the Pleasant Hill Church of the Nazarene and very regular in her attendance. She was fearful as she approached her time to testify on Wednesday night (everyone must testify). So she would stand and say (very rapidly), "Bless the Lord, Oh my soul and all what's in me. Bless His holy name." We all laugh at her impatience, when the family was not ready for church as early as she. She would start walking down the sandy road and the family would catch up to her, pick her up, and give her a ride the rest of the way. I always liked the story my grandfather told about her hoeing corn in Missouri. He went with his mother to hoe corn after the noon meal. At about two o'clock, she said, "Now, Sammie, you hoe this row, then that row, and finish with the third row. Then you can come in for supper. Mommie is going to the house right now." Sam did as he was told; then he went back to the house. Inside, he discovered that he had a new baby brother, Paul.

Something further must be said of U.S. Highway 50 and the section where I was reared. From Ocean City, Maryland to San Francisco, California, it is "the most central yet least traveled national route." It parallels or traces parts of the Santa Fe, Oregon, and California trails; the pony express, the Overland-Butterfield Stage routes, and the Santa Fe Railroad. William Least Heat-Moon dwells on this route in his *PrairyErth,* pp. 11-12. He traces it past the Captiol; Constitution Avenue; the National Archives; White House; Washington Monument; Lincoln Memorial; Hayfield, VA; Coolville, OH; Loogootee, IN; Flora, IL; Useful, Mo; Dodge

City; KS; Royal Gorge, CO; Deseret, UT; Eureka, NV; and Placerville, CA. He notes that between Washington and San Francisco there are only four cities: Cincinnati, St. Louis, Kansas City, and Sacramento. Westward bound, when you hit the Flint Hills in Chase County, Kansas, you have "arrived in the American West."

> **For the unhurried, this little known highway is the best national road across the middle of the United States . . . for the last couple of generations, the westering center of American population has followed 50, at times edging precisely along it like an aerialist on his wire.**

Our farm was just one-half mile off U.S. 50. It was ninety miles west of Chase County, which Heat-Moon called "the most easterly piece of the American Far West." We were on the plain that rose seven feet per mile toward the Rocky Mountain ranges. We were six miles from the transcontinental route of the Atchison, Topeka, and Santa Fe Railroad. My grandfather's farm, adjacent to ours, was purchased directly from the Santa Fe. We were west of the "Trans-Mississippi West." Willa Cather said, "Between that earth and that sky I felt erased, blotted out." Heat-Moon says,

> **But for the wooded vales, the trees have nearly disappeared altogether. To encounter treelessness of such distance has often moved eastern travelers – and sometimes natives - more to discomfiture than rapture . . . . The protection and sureties of the vertical woodland . . . are gone . . . . The land is . . . a world of air, space, apparent emptiness, near nothingness . . . .**

They must conquer agoraphobia. Our farm was a timber claim so there were trees but the normal vista was nearly treeless. I believe this setting, my association with the spirit of the Far West, contributed to my personality and outlook on life. It is neither conservative nor liberal; or it is both. To view the country for distances of twenty to forty miles was to see a special kind of beauty. In western Kansas, I recall counting the lights of twenty-one towns one night from my uncle's farmyard. The air was so clear, and, before electricity, the nights so dark, that thousands of stars and planets seemed ready to tumble out of the sky. I always said I am a Westerner at heart.

I went to Bresee Academy and College in Hutchinson, twenty-five miles from home, and lived with Grandpa King, Alvin Allers, and in dormitories from 1934-1940. But this Hayes Township community and lots of contact with family on all sides must have had a great deal to do with physical health, personality development, character, habits, and outlook on life. "The lines have fallen unto me in pleasant places; yea, I have a goodly heritage" (Psalms 16:6 NIV).

By the way, my mother kept a record of all the firsts in my life in a baby book. It is completely full and included childhood diseases up through mumps in the fall of 1938 when I was a college freshman. The shower gifts for my birth included six dresses, three petticoats, and two pink blankets. "Personal Characteristics" is filled in with "lovable, affectionate, diplomatic, strong will power, studious, musical, and religiously inclined" (my mother's writing). I first attended church at age three and a half weeks. I got my hand slapped within my first year for tearing a piece of loose wallpaper. Under "Favorite Occupation," food and eating fills all the space allowed. I cried at my dedication on October 16, 1921.

I sat on the piano bench with my music teacher mother about as soon as I could sit up. One of her horrible memories was my fall from the bench and a cut on my upper lip which bled profusely. As she feared, it left a permanent scar, but no one sees it except the one who has shaved over it for sixty-some years. She gave me piano lessons until she decided another teacher might do better. I took lessons from Ruth Lang Smith (who later taught at Bethany), Pauline Howard, and (at Bressee) Walter Burdick Larsen. He put me through the Robyn-Gurlitt materials so I would get the technique right even though it is better to have that at the beginning. Dr. Larsen was division chair at Olivet when I went there to teach. In high school years, I took up trombone and played in summer band in Sylvia and orchestra at Bresee and Bethany. I had enough keyboard, theory, and sight-reading that my mother could clear her conscience and I was prepared to enjoy choir in college and throughout my life.

The house where I lived was built in 1886 by my great-grandpa Yust, the homesteader. It was built on the timber claim quarter. At least twenty-five of the forty acres of trees that he planted survived and were a pleasant feature of our farm. The Round Oak heating stove furnished the heat for the whole house. My two grandmothers attended at my birth. I am told that, two and a half years later at the birth of my sister, I awoke and said, "I 'fot' I heard a noise." Not a lot of privacy. There were two large bedrooms upstairs with no heat. The kids slept under blankets, comforters, all we could find. A glass of water on the stand would freeze, but we survived. Getting undressed, warming up the bed, and then dressing in the morning were the times of serious discomfort. There was no running water, except for a hand pump in the kitchen. We took baths in washtubs. Then there was the "slop jar" pottie. There was the "milk house" by the windmill, convenient for cooling the milk and cream as freshly pumped water flowed around milk cans on its way to the stock tank across the driveway. We did not own a car for the first four or five years of my life. We drove horse and buggy to school and church. Again, cold weather was a challenge. Heavy coats, blankets, and oven-warmed bricks for the floor of the buggy were the best we could do. Without electricity, there was no fan for cooling the house in the summer.

Both parents worked at home day in and day out – night and day. We grew up in sight of one parent all the time. They had no respite from us until we were old enough for school. I am sure that cooking was not easy for my mother. She had to make do with what she had; it was still two weeks before she would go to the store. We learned to eat what she set before us. If we made faces or said a disparaging word, she would say, "Eat it; it's good; I fixed it!" We all learned to eat without being picky about food. Our fun and games were with our parents, as well as our times of learning to take responsibility and to work. It may have happened only once, but I listened to a three hour sermon by my grandpa while the two of us shocked oats together. That operation was taking bundles where the binder dropped them, and standing them on end so they could dry in the field. Both church and school reinforced the same patterns and values. So we were "programmed" as they would say now. These were major socializing experiences and we never wanted to be absent. There was no chance of going elsewhere. Grandparents, uncles, and aunts half a mile away were a big help to fill the time with pleasurable experiences.

We got a new 1927 Ford and made a remarkable trip to Arizona, December to February, 1928. That was a time when roads were not well marked, seldom paved, and some routes impassable in the winter. But, with Grandma King, we were off to visit the Herman Wolf family near Casa Grande. Aunt Laura Wolf was my mother's older sister. The mountain highways were really exciting (and actually dangerous). Once there, we did not plan to come back soon. They put me in school at La Palma but, after a couple of weeks, my mother thought the discipline was so poor that she kept me at the Wolf's home. I got to know several cousins. Nona and I stopped there on our way to Berkeley in 1947, and we have kept in touch with that family quite well through the years. My dad had to check up on a copper mine investment in Douglas, Arizona so we returned via the southern route. When we got to El Paso, we had a brief visit in Juarez, Mexico. It was quite an experience for my young mind to take in. When we returned to Kansas, I was placed in the second grade and able to keep up even though I had only a half year in the first grade, was out of school more than a month, and had just over three months in the second grade. For more on my one-room school experiences, see chapter V of *The Snowbarger Family in Kansas*, Vol. I.

When I was three years old, I wanted to go to Hutchinson to see my Grandpa King. No one else was making plans to go, so I set off on foot. I got to the hill east of our property (about one-third of a mile) headed for Highway 50 going in the proper direction. Some one missed me around the house, started searching, and spotted me before I got to the highway. That was the only time I tried that stunt.

In our home, matters of our spiritual life and relationship to God were the top priority. Dad would be up early, feeding livestock and milking. Then he would come into the house for breakfast with the family and "worship" before going into the day's work. This had been the pattern in the families of parents and grandparents of both my mother and my father. So there was no rush to get to work or school. Bible reading and prayer came first. There was a life and death seriousness about that because they prayed problems through. Many things were unmanageable in the human, but God was able! The prayers were often very specific so the whole family knew how serious matters were. Promises were quoted to God.

It was no surprise that church attendance was a requirement. The community of faith was essential. Fellowship, worship, and burden-bearing required assembling ourselves together. And it was urgently important that children be brought up "in the faith." It was not strange that my mother, an ex-college instructor, should find her work in the church with children (since they had an abundance of musicians). Whether in Sunday School or Vacation Bible School, her children always had to learn all the Bible passages and "Golden Texts." We did; and we have a large repertoire of Scriptures we can quote to the end of our days. Ditto for the great hymns and gospel songs. It was the college years before we interwove the meanings from these with life experiences and formal theology. But, it was not lost motion. It was the ideal curriculum taught by the ideal teachers – our parents and neighbors.

Folklore suggests that the fiery evangelists we heard, whose sermons were mostly stories woven together and designed to get sinners to move to the altar, actually deterred the work of the church by their excesses. I heard nearly all of them in our church or at the camp meeting that was held at the Kansas State Fairgrounds in Hutchinson. Their stories, unsettling questions, and hymns of invitation really were combinations that could and should be criticized. A group of professors at Olivet were discussing that culture after church one Sunday evening. After recounting some of our worst memories, one said, "But we are all here discussing the matter after a Sunday evening service we have just attended." We were survivors! The message of salvation and power over sin was the central message and we had, somehow, sorted it all out. There is a God of love, but he has requirements. After life comes the judgment and I must give an account. It is a terrible thing to be lost. Heaven is a wonderful place.

The kind of preaching for a decision was not debated so much in circles where I grew up because we all faced up regularly to death. Whole families went to funerals. And sometimes, death came to the young. My close friend, Norman Lang, died when his appendix ruptured at age twelve. That brought it close to me. Also the stories were not all extreme. One evangelist told of a horse named Selam. We had a horse named Selam (I think he had been one of Grandpa King's horses when he had retired to our farm). The story goes that Selam had gone blind and was no longer able to work. He required feed and attention so someone suggested they do away with him. But no one had the nerve to shoot him. Finally they decided to lead him to an abandoned well where he would fall in, and the men would fill the well with rocks, timber and dirt and the horse would be buried. Things went as planned. And the men worked a half day filling the well. When they paused to see how their work was coming along, to their surprise, old Selam's neck and head were just below the surface. A few more rocks and shovels of dirt and he walked out on his own power. The moral of the story was obvious: take life's unfairness, put one foot after the other on top of all the obstacles, and you too can come out triumphant over it all.

By the way, I made my own trip to the altar as a small boy and Christ forgave me of my sins. I would falter and fail and ask His forgiveness. I do not remember a lot of ups and downs, as do many of my contemporaries. Surely this was due to the guidance of my parents who advised me never to wait until Sunday to make things right. At night, under the stars, we would pray over the failings of the day. There was a difference between discipline and "sin." If it were willful and rebellious, we need to pray about that now. A more mature and comprehensive commitment to Christ came in my early college years. Meantime, I belonged to the family of God and became active in all the programs of the church for which I was eligible. I was part of a junior boys' Sunday School class that met in the coal room, next to the furnace. Bert Shull must have been driven to distraction, but he loved his boys. He taught with tears in his eyes.

Life for a kid on a farm twenty-five miles west of Hutchinson in the 1930's meant a lot of work. The trick was to make the work fun. We milked cows morning and evening. If we could get cousins from the city to come at milking time, we asked them to open their mouths and we would aim a stream of milk at the target. We liked horses. We rode them and drove them hitched to a wagon, hayrack, or implements in the field. We got our first tractor when I was twelve, but we kept horses throughout the 1930's. That was both fun and work. From the fifth through the eighth grade, I drove a buggy (pulled by one horse) to school. I would usually pick up two or three people along the 2 ¾ mile route. The horse would be put in the barn at school and I fed her grain at noon. That experience was both fun and responsibility.

As children we took our share of work responsibilities and felt like big folks when we could help. At four or five we would gather eggs and feed the chickens. We carried small sticks of firewood and corncobs for the kitchen stove. Then we could help in the garden, chop thistles out of the buffalo grass pasture, and begin milking the tamer cows. At about six, I took my own team of four horses to the field to harrow ridges between the rows of corn. When grubbing out old trees in the orchard, Papa sent me up to attach a cable about twelve feet up in the tree. Then, he asked me to stay up while he drove a two-horse team, first to rock the tree, then to pull it over. I rode the tree down. We spread gravel on the driveway, helped fix the barbed wire fence, and spread sorghum fodder in the pasture in the winter. I learned to drive the truck by taking the wheel in the pasture while my father scattered the fodder. We fed milk to small calves and drove the cows in off the wheat fields where they pastured in the winter. It was nice to have livestock around, but they had to be bedded, watered, and fed. We were extra hands and feet for Mamma during laundry, canning, house cleaning, and preparation for company.

As we got to the teen years, we were full-fledged workers. I usually milked four or five cows in the morning and evening. I worked regularly in the field cultivating corn and milo, preparing for planting, and harvesting. I became a part of the team for bigger operations like wheat harvest, silo fillings, sawing firewood with the buzz saw, mowing, raking and bailing hay, butchering a calf, and repairing and lubricating machinery. Shelling corn, shocking oats, and working up wood making it ready for the saw were tasks during which I could talk at length with Papa, Grandpa, and my uncles. I especially enjoyed cleaning up brush in the timber after we had trimmed out the logs. We had bon fires that burned for two or three days to rid the place of trashy limbs and leaves. A rainy day job was shelling seed corn. We had tossed aside the perfect ears of corn. When we could not work outside, we took off the irregular grains on either end of the ear, then shelled the perfect kernels with a small hand operated sheller. Talk about "laid back!" Story telling, jokes, and practical jokes were in order. Neighbor Irv Yates was very good with dogs. We asked him, "Irv, how do you train a dog?" "Well," he said, "In the first place to train a dog, you have to know more than the dog . . . ."

Trips to town were infrequent but they included visits to the grain elevator, D.J. Fair Lumber Company, the hardware store, and the blacksmith shop. Later, we even patronized the barber but parents did that job through most of the thirties. We also used the Santa Fe railroad to get to Hutchinson and to meet visitors. My grandparents were the hosts for evangelists who came to our country church for many years. In the forties that responsibility shifted to my parents. Neither hotels nor restaurants were close enough to be very useful in that situation. The cooking was fine; the privacy left something to be desired. I believe Dr. A.L. Parrott stayed at our house during three revivals at the church. Gary Hartpence stayed there during a weekend meeting. Our fun at school was at recess and noon breaks. We had swings, a slide, and outdoor basketball goals. Games were all out-of-doors because there was only one room in the school. My grandmother and father had both attended the same school I attended. There was no lunchroom, no restrooms inside, no gym – all eight grades and one teacher. The water pump was outside. We had races, softball, basketball, and "shinny." The latter was played with a stick that had a crook on the end (somewhat like a hockey stick) and a tin can (for a puck). Shinny was sort of field hockey but with all those sticks flying around, there were a lot of skinned shins, hence "shinny." We invented some of our games (and the rules too). The teacher was the only playground supervisor but she could not be everywhere.

I was in the first grade while two uncles were still in the upper grades. During one recess, a fourth grade bully grabbed my new cap which was apparently quite attractive. As someone pumped water, he held my cap under the spout, filled it, and slapped it back on my head. My uncles soon had him in tow and that kind of thing came to a screeching halt.

We also had programs in which every student had a part and the whole community turned out. The parents had nothing but school and church for their social life, so sing-alongs and refreshments were their fun too. We also had good competition in ciphering matches and spelling bees.

Discipline was strict at home, church, and school. The worst offenders got whippings but these were few and far between because most of the kids were promised by their parents, "If you get a whipping from the teacher, there's another one waiting for you when you get home." More than whippings, I remember a swat with a ruler across the hands (when hands got where they didn't belong, like untying a girl's belt or hair bow). One of my teachers wore at least a half a dozen rings, so she didn't need a ruler. Her slap had a real sting to it; I remember. Extra work or staying after school was the main form of punishment. Also some had to write on the blackboard 100 times, "I will not (fill in the offense) again." Fortunately what was considered wrong in one family was usually wrong for all the families. That made it easier to bear strict discipline and usually it was "for your own good." In other words, the teacher and the parents were right. On important matters it took a lot of time to explain their reasons. On questions more obvious, no explanation at all. Oh yes, and cleaning the blackboard and erasers was obviously a good form of punishment. Sunday School picnics and family reunions were favorite summer activities. Besides eating, bag swings, riding horses, marbles, and races were the order of the day. Older kids played softball. You were lucky if there were more than four or five of these occasions in a summer. In winter, a wood-sawing bee, a butchering, or corn shelling was an excuse for a big meal with several families together. In winter, the men and boys often went hunting for rabbit and squirrels. We had no chance to swim, roller skate, or fish without traveling quite a distance. So I had to learn these things as a teen and they were harder to learn at that age. Remember too, we did not have electricity at home, school, or church, so that makes a lot of difference: no radio, no running water, no fans, no electric lights, no forced air heating. No records or cassettes either. I think we read more books then and probably took more music lessons, memorized more Scripture and literature, and played more table games as a family than is customary today.

Dollars were very scarce in the 1930's. My parents took eggs, cream, milk, and chickens to town (often to the grocery store) and picked up a credit slip that they applied to the cost of groceries as they left. They only bought sugar, salt, baking powder, cornstarch, vanilla, spices, crackers, and medications. They produced their own meats, bread, vegetables, fruit, eggs, dairy products, and cereals. We always had enough to eat but very few dollars. So what's the value of a dollar if you don't have any? I found a list of "What things cost in 1918." The prices were not much different in the 1930's. For month-by-month needs we operated on a modified barter system so prices did not matter so long as a dozen eggs could be traded for a bottle of vanilla extract.

There were no "allowances" at our house. We all worked hard to take care of the land, the livestock, firewood, canning, and laundry. As children our main work was to get our education but we must also learn to carry our share of responsibility. We all wanted to be helpers but after a few times, the fun wore off and we had to be prodded. I was expected to get a supply of corncobs for the cook stove and wood for both cooking and heating. Sometimes cows had to be rounded up and driven back to the barn. So

17

instead of dividing up spending money with the kids, my parents divided up the work to be done and we were each "entrusted with a responsibility." Fortunately, we had few bills to pay because we had no water or sewer system, no electricity, no gas, and no cable TV. When we sold the wheat or corn crop, perhaps a calf, that income was carefully guarded because it had to pay tithe, taxes or to buy gasoline or clothing for the whole year. There were no monthly paychecks.

I have an interesting receipt dated December 14, 1934, which shows how my dad paid for my high school tuition. He butchered a calf and took three pieces of beef to the Bresee dining hall. Two of them were front quarter and one piece was hind quarter. The front quarter piece weighed seventy-eight pounds and was worth seven cents per pound. The hind quarter (seventy-five pounds) was worth nine cents per pound. He traded 180 pounds of beef for my tuition.

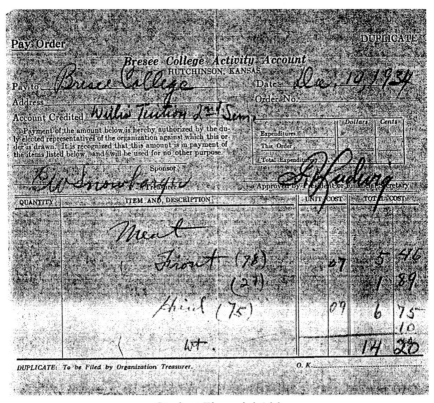

Student Financial Aid

Is life better now? I can't answer that. Jesus said, "Sufficient unto the day is the evil thereof." Or, every day has its bad aspects. And every age has its advantages. We had a happy childhood because our parents, grandparents, uncles and aunts, and cousins were close by. We were part of a good family, good church, and good school. Our clothing, shoes, and toys had to last longer than they do for my grandchildren. Apart from school we saw our other friends and cousins once or twice a week. We had to improvise a lot, like making a milk cart out of junk, inventing games, making a baseball bat, re-sewing the seams of a softball. We spent most of our time at home with wholesome work and play, but we were "bored" (like my grandkids are) a lot of the time.

As I entered my teen years, I was expected to carry a fairly heavy responsibility around the farm. I had learned to work. We did not count the hours I worked but I worked before and after school. I did well in school. I got several blue ribbons in district track and field meets, largely because I had a spurt of growth and stayed fairly well coordinated. I had memorized the Sermon on the Mount for a $5 prize offered by Alice Reed, my grade school teacher. My health was good; in fact, I have to attribute my lack of injuries in sport to the development of good arm and leg strength by work in the fields and lots of walking. I never carried excessive weight. In recent years, doctors have commented, "Your lungs and heart are those of a man thirty years younger than you." The diet, discipline, work, and healthy mental outlook are a heritage of youth for which I am thankful.

By the way, my family furnished the heredity and the environment that made adjustment to life outside the home easier and relatively painless. The authoritarian tilt of the times and the family was part of that. I have sympathized with those whose heritage is more egalitarian because I believe life is harsher for children moving into life outside the home from the more permissive environment.

As to a work ethic, I was very pleased when a neighbor said to my father in my presence, "I have watched as he worked across the road from my farm and I wish my boy worked as well as Willis." So there was not only discipline but also a pride in the discipline developing. I also watched my father's self-control and discipline. In 1933, wheat harvest was almost incidental, finished in one-half day. A little brother arrived on June 30th. Still my father took out a twenty-pay life insurance policy on me and paid the premiums until I graduated from college. Books, music, games, and social life in the home, church, and community, though limited, were all a part of wholesome personal development and formation of values and character. Bible knowledge games, Authors, Monopoly, puzzles, and homemade games (that my grandchildren still like to play) made for a happy evening and intergenerational competition and cooperation. Dominoes, checkers, and singing around the piano were normal to an evening (but not every day of the week). There was not as much age segregation then as now. All ages liked to play with little calves, newly hatched chicks, puppies, kittens, and, babies. After Grandpa King moved in with us, we enjoyed his "Edison" Victrola and the quarter inch thick records. Again, a good heritage packed with education and fun.

This heritage of history and geography of the plains, climate, family, value system, religion, and the daily, seasonal, and yearly schedule of operations undoubtedly left an indelible imprint on my character. It brings a sense of responsibility caught up in the lines of Hillaire Belloc's "Dunction Hill:"

He does not die that can bequeath
Some influences to the land he knows
Or dares, persistent, interwreath
Love permanent with the wild hedgerows;
He does not die but still remains
Substantiate with his darling plains.

Of course, I am taking myself too seriously! There is a hedgerow just outside my window as I write.

NOTES

Sources for this chapter are substantially those cited in Volume I of *The Snowbarger Family in Kansas*. In addition, Jesse E. King's *The King Family History* (1984) and Mary K. Snowbarger's *Autobiography* (1983) helped fill in my mother's side of the story. Various church records, baby book entries and family discussions have provided details.

CH. II TEEN YEARS

"He was born on third base and he thinks he hit a triple." Anon.

As I entered my teen years, my life took a dramatic turn. At 13, I went away to Bresee Academy in Hutchinson (25 miles from the farm). So, I lived with my uncle and aunt (the Allers) for one year, then, another year with my King grandparents before moving into the dormitory. I had finished the eighth grade in the one-room school, passed the county examination, and started the ninth grade in 1934. As they say, "You can tell a child is growing up when he stops asking where he came from and starts refusing to tell you where he is going." That is about where I was in the fall of 1934.

In place of the farm setting, I now lived in a city environment. After school, with a pack of my friends, we roamed the streets on our bikes, and visited in one another's homes. We threw ourselves wholeheartedly into the school programs. Choir, trombone trio, plays, athletics (including the YMCA where there was a pool), and part-time jobs (lawns, leaves, washing windows, even washing whole houses after a dust storm). That was enough to keep us out of mischief. I went home for most of the weekends. This was entirely different for a farm boy and quite exciting. I worked on the school paper, traveled with a male quartet, played trombone in church, played all the sports, and really lived it up. I wrote one play, "The Little Foxes," that we presented. I wrote a paper on the Bank of England, "The Old Lady of Threadneedle Street." At about sixteen, I started dating a succession of girls, but none for very long.

I often wondered what my calling in life was. Shouldn't that affect my choice of courses in high school, surely by time for college? Would it be full time Christian ministry? Preaching? I took notes on many good sermons. Maybe I would be a student minister. But I seemed more fitted for teaching. At that time teaching was a layman's role. In any case, I would prepare for Christian service wherever I found an open door.

I turned 13 on August 24, 1934 and assumed the serious work of adolescence. I was already a serious factor in the work force and was rather mature in my sense of responsibility. I had sensed a real lack of news and contact with the larger world due to the lack of a radio or a major newspaper. The Sylvia *Sun* only reported on who had dinner with whom last Sunday. But the normal restlessness of these years was tempered by the plan of my parents that I should attend Bresee Academy in Hutchinson rather than Sylvia High School. Having finished elementary school in seven years, thirteen seems to have been a tender age for leaving home but it worked out. For the first time it was practical for me to have a bicycle and roller skates, to have access to a swimming pool, a radio and other conveniences that required electricity - in a word: urban life. The comradery and combination of independence and supervision was just what I needed. These were happy days for me.

Even though I went home on most weekends, I look back and wonder how my parents could have let me go that way! In a sense, I never returned to the farm although I loved it. Likewise, I always wanted to be with my family. Years later when I contemplated a job on the West Coast I had quietly calculated that the salary had to be enough higher there than in the Midwest to pay for air transportation for me and my family to get back to Kansas at least once each year, or I would not take the job. The lesson: Parents have to turn loose of their children in order truly to keep them. I am also convinced that developments of these kinds are the best arguments for Christian colleges. I don't mind calling the colleges hot houses or transitional environments for young people to develop their own character and life patterns with more freedom than the home offered but with limitations and dominant influences that keep them from the catastrophes that accompany the fiery trials of adolescent years. In my own case, I had so much learning, socializing, and polishing to do that these years were vital in my development.

I continued working on the farm each summer and began to think of how I would manage things differently if I were in charge. I dreamed of using the natural gas in Grant County to pump irrigation water on the land my father owned there. (This is commonly done now but was not common when I pondered it.) I thought of other crops, different layout of the fields, other livestock breeds, grading the fields to avoid the perennial "mud holes" that drowned out crops year after year. But, it wasn't my farm, and I was not to be a farmer anyway. My mind was buzzing. I finally engineered an outdoor shower by the windmill. We placed a water tank on a platform about six feet high. The windmill could pump water into the tank, the sun would warm it (more or less), and upon returning from the fields, a shower was certainly better than the small washtub even if the water was really cold. And, I don't remember any provision for privacy! I guess we just passed the word, presuming we would not draw a crowd! I also built tennis court backstops and leveled the ground for a court. It was a "dirt" surface (not clay) and I spent far more time clearing and building it than playing tennis on it. There was scarcely anyone to play with me nor time to play, but maybe it is the thought that counts. After all, the summers on the farm were quite dull (after "he's seen Bresee!").

By the way, I mentioned the scarcity of dollars and a barter system of exchange in Chapter I. My parents never seemed to doubt that they could afford private school tuition for both high school and college for four kids. I vividly remember a "family council" in which my father explained that each of us was expected to complete a four-year college degree. Our task was to prepare for college, make good grades, and concentrate on college preparatory subjects, help out on the farm in the summers, and the parents would see us through with financial support. This discussion must have occurred in 1933 or 1934, so my youngest sister is probably right when she said, "I never heard of that arrangement." There was a stinger in it. It would hold as long as we did not get married before college graduation. We all met that condition. It is remarkable to me that my parents could make that commitment in the depths of the depression, owning very little property, scrambling to keep us in decent clothing, with no relief in sight. But they had decided their children's education was to have top priority. True, the dollar amounts were small then. Dollars were almost unavailable to any of us. And they were paying for the construction of the building I was to use for high school and college as well.

As their off-spring, we protested only mildly about the co-mingling of our funds (money from part-time jobs) with theirs. Rather, we marvel at the providential way in which all our needs were met. Uncles, aunts, grandparents all pitched in together and the accounts were paid on time. The college also played a part because nearly 100% of the students faced the same problems and all got part-time jobs to close the financial gap. In turn, we helped the college raise money and produced good will through weekend revivals. The entire context of college finance was shaped by very supportive people whose children were the chief focus of their own financial priorities.

I kept a diary for the year 1937 when I was sixteen years old. Somehow, it survived the moves, even a flooded basement, and is legible. It covered the last semester of my junior year in high school and carried over into part of the senior year, including part of 1938. It is not particularly remarkable except to show quite a disciplined young man. Going to church, time to study, a full slate of activities, home for the weekend, or a weekend meeting in which the quartet sang. There were a few capers better forgotten, basketball on the dirt floor of an unheated state fairgrounds barn, sixty miles per hour on a sled pulled behind the car across the ice-covered wheat field. I made $31 that summer and saved $20 of it. You can be sure that the $11 unaccounted for really went for tithe and necessities, perhaps a bicycle pedal and that kind of extravagance. I read this diary and marveled. My parents really had nothing to worry about. (That is not to say they would have wholeheartedly approved everything I did.)

Meantime, those years at Bresee (through the sophomore year in college) were remarkable for the faculty people I got to know and who shaped my outlook on the future. Administrators Sylvester T. Ludwig, R. R. Hodges, and Harold W. Reed all knew me like a son and there are now buildings named for each of them on a Nazarene college campus somewhere. My high school teachers also included Howard Hamlin, Paul Gresham, Earl Greer, Walter B. Larsen, and Florence Aller. In lower division college work, I had Kathryn Ruth Howe for history and psychology in addition to the above. Even though I had a home economics teacher for college chemistry, I passed the federal civil service exam for "Chemist" when I took it in 1942 without any further course work in chemistry. My curriculum for high school included strong components in English, math, history, and science but there were also four units of Bible and three of Latin. These units, not often included in a public school program, were both of value equal to, or greater than the standard requirements.

The co-curricular activities were varied and formative for me in my Bresee years. Religious activities were attractive from chapel, through Hutchinson First Church services, and meetings across the Kansas District. Compared to our small rural church with few visiting dignitaries, Bresee offered a wonderful and inspirational diet of spiritual blessings. College revivals were unmatched by anything I had previously experienced. In those days, no one, it seemed, prayed through in five or ten minutes. I remember numerous times when a group of young people would be praying for a friend until after midnight and we frequently prayed for a "clean sweep," meaning that every student had gotten victory and was saved. The list of speakers for the year was a "Who's Who" of the church. We saw the church at its best. In Dr. A. F. Balsmeier, Superintendent of the Kansas District, who lived on the corner of the campus, we saw one of the real heroes of the church. In the 1930's, he literally planted a Nazarene church in nearly every crossroads in the state. The students prayed and worked to help him in that effort.

We had literary societies very much like those I later found at Olivet. (With S. T. Ludwig, R. R. Hodges, Earl Greer, Walter and Naomi Larsen, Wendell and Viola McHenry all from Olivet, on the Bresee faculty, I should not have been surprised.) The societies were the basis for literary, artistic, and athletic competition. By sign-ups at the beginning of the year, you were either an Olympian or an Adelphian (later we used Greek letters). Each society was to provide one variety program per month, thus, giving performance experience to many who were not taking private lessons and otherwise presented in recitals. Six-man football, softball, basketball, tennis, and ping-pong gave the men an outlet for exercise. It was mostly all intramural and we had no gym. So indoor basketball was played at the nearby state fairgrounds. Opportunities for team play, leadership, socialization, and character development abounded. On extremely limited resources (almost no budget), Bresee gave me great opportunities. I took a crack at almost everything: music, drama, athletics, publications, and, later, leadership roles. During my last four years at Bresee, Harold Reed was my president. I could not know then what role he would play in my future career.

By the way, during these Bresee years, my parents were able to buy the farm on which I grew up. This was possible through a provision of my Great-Grandpa Yust's will that (at his death) called for a sale among his children with closed bidding. Some of the uncles and aunts did not bid because they knew that Edward wanted the farm and would buy it from Katie (my grandmother) if she were high bidder. Three equal bids on round one meant that there was a second round, and Katie bought it. Now Edward had to find the financing to buy it. That was not easy but he was successful. In 1938, nineteen years after their marriage, my parents were able to plan for renovation of the buildings. Actually, they hardly saw how they could meet the payments for the land. They had seen to it that Grandma Snowbarger was reimbursed.

Then, surprise of surprises, a wildcat oil well was brought in on Grandpa Snowbarger's farm in 1940. It was just across the road from our farm. In the next few years, oil wells were drilled and produced on our farm and my parents were able to build a new barn, do a major renovation on the house, and payoff the debt. In 1942, rural electrification came to our township so major conveniences came to our rural home. By that time the wartime shortages and restrictions also were realities but, by 1947, my parents had paid off the college debts for their first two children, modernized the farmstead, and paid off the debt on the farm. Almost that quickly, the oil production ceased but it gave my parents a more secure future.

Although I was making a new, urbanized life, the cords were not cut with my life on the farm. Many weekends and summers found me at work at the usual responsibilities there. Your work is never finished on a farm. At one time or another, Papa or Grandpa S. would give me ten acres to plant and claim the crop for one year as my own. Whether corn, wheat, or watermelons, I found that you scarcely ever make a killing - you just try to come out ahead. It did help. I heard all the first hand experiences with the Roosevelt farm program. It certainly did not treat my family fairly. Acreage cut backs when so many people needed food never squared with their thinking. The depression caught both my parents and grandparents owing for land and not having the money to pay as planned. Grandpa lost his second quarter. Papa could only pay interest (no principal) on his land. I observed how his creditor was so pleased to get the interest that he bragged to everyone about it, to my father's benefit. We could not get our watermelons on the market early enough so that my best price was one-quarter cent per pound for the first truckload; and it went down from there onward.

I got my right index finger in the buzz saw on a weekend wood-sawing bee but fortunately, it repaired itself completely. We went to Dr. Bauer in Sylvia who looked at the shredded, bloody mess. He tested each joint, and then found a pint jar of a yellowish liquid. He said, "Here, let's put it in here," as he plunged my poor finger into the jar. It burned like fire. Then he said, "Let's do it again." In it went for a second dip. There being nothing to sew to, he just wrapped it up and gave instructions for re-dressing and back to school in Hutchinson I went. Nona, my new girl friend, was put to the acid test when I asked her to change the dressings for me. I carry the proof of the treatment with me wherever I go, but I still have my finger and it works.

During those years, I got the experience of planning and presenting NYPS programs at church. Young people had a Sunday evening service for one hour prior to the regular church service. We led singing, sang specials as solos or ensembles, led in prayer, and made talks before our peers. Preparing these programs, participation, and taking leadership, was excellent experience. And it happened every week, so we got into a rhythm of responsibility. This experience prepared me for public appearances in weekend revivals and a traveling quartet that represented Bresee College in churches. We took over the whole service, leading the singing, special music, fund-raising, and one of our preacher boys would bring the message.

According to my 1937 diary, I discovered girls at about fifteen or sixteen. There was a succession of them. Dates were to a program on campus or to church. There was no transportation, so a date to church meant walking nearly one mile and a half (one way). Neither my date nor I had money for an ice cream cone so that was understood. As I will tell later, this shopping around largely came to an end in 1938 when the Horger family came to Bresee. I often wondered how I could appraise my own personality and character development. That was a primary element of the achievements of my life before and during the days at Bresee in the 1930's. By precept and limited experimentation, I had learned that honesty and truthfulness were good policies and the only way to live. You don't have to tell all you know, but what you speak, imply, or lead people to believe should be true. I had learned the value of hard work, developed the discipline to finish a difficult task, and had a reputation for dependability. I understood my duty, especially at that stage, was to be my best possible achievement in school. I had a sense of responsibility toward my family, the church, my school, and those around me. I knew the value of money and property and had observed many object lessons in Christian stewardship.

I had committed my life to Christ and was earnestly seeking His will for my life. I understood and practiced teamwork as a necessity for accomplishing most worthwhile tasks. I had nearly always succeeded in the tasks I undertook and had a high degree of self-confidence. But I had not assumed that I could climb the heights without the help of God and many other people. I believe I had an appropriate humility about my own ability and accomplishments. I had also observed members of my family show their care for others, whether friend or friendless, the value of life, and the need to share with those less fortunate. At this stage, I think my responsibility was largely focused on individuals rather than on the needs of society at large. I was both interested and committed to the work of the church, taking my own role and potential as a gift to be invested where and when needed. Bresee experiences cemented my church relationship so strongly that it was not interrupted, even when attractive offers from other groups would have advanced my career. I was part of the church when it was "a movement." Like my father, I was especially careful to discover any "call to preach," and felt none. There was certainly a call to serve which I accepted and did not waiver from.

I will interpose here a paragraph on early connections to Olivet Nazarene University that I have discovered only since my retirement from ONU as I had time for family history research. I had been aware of S. T. Ludwig's connection with Olivet and have mentioned above several other Olivet alumni who were my teachers and club sponsors at Bresee. I discovered a card written by R. R. Hodges in 1916, while he was a student at Olivet, to my father and uncle (Edward and Wesley). He said, "We have a very fine school here. You boys may want to finish your education here." The photo on the reverse side showed the new grand piano on the Olivet Chapel platform.

Was there a relationship of early Nazarenes in Kansas to Illinois Holiness University? It turns out that there was! Dr. P. F. Bresee's efforts to organize the Church of the Nazarene in the "Central District" were quite extensive. He visited the Midwest on several occasions and either started, or worked with the founders of, several Nazarene churches. The first district assembly was held in September, 1905. I am relying on Mark R. Moore, *Fifty Years and Beyond: A History of the Chicago Central District*, which has much more on his topic. My point is that, prior to the Pilot Point union in 1908, the region between the Rocky Mountains and the Allegheny Mountains was one large mass with scattered churches in Kansas, Nebraska, and on back to Illinois and Indiana and all of this was Chicago Central District. It included Calgary in Alberta, Canada. Nobody knew how far south it went and in 1908 that perspective changed as the Oklahoma-Texas Nazarenes looked to plant churches in Kansas as well as receive established congregations like Hutchinson First Church. This regional alignment is not unlike that of the accrediting associations. The North Central Association covered a territory that stretches from West Virginia to Arizona. It is the association that covers Southern Nazarene University, MidAmerica Nazarene College, Mount Vernon Nazarene College, as well as Olivet.

My insight is this: Olivet, the University for the vast Central District and Bresee College, always known in those days as "the Bible School," were not competitors. Bresee graduates might well seek a degree at Olivet, their sister college. Prior to 1908, this would have seemed very natural. Bethany was not the exclusive choice for Kansans in 1916. At least as late as 1915, there was a trustee from the Kansas District on the Olivet University Board of Trustees. So, while our family had no direct connection with Olivet prior to my moving there to join the faculty in 1949, it well might have been my father's alma mater. Both Bresee and Olivet were begun as independent holiness institutions and later were adopted by the Church of the Nazarene.

NOTES

My written sources for this chapter are a diary I kept for the entire year 1937 and early 1938, the Bresee yearbook, *The Comet*, for 1934-1943, and a few notes, letters, and pictures. These sources jogged my memory.

CH. III WAHNONA

"How do I love thee? Let me count the ways." Elizabeth Barrett Browning

You should meet Wahnona! She is my sweet heart! She is my "better half." For sixty-two years she was my one and only. We were husband and wife for fifty-seven years. It was God who said, "It is not good that man should be alone." Woman sometimes means "whoa man" to a young farm boy and I have needed restraint. But, in the stilted talk of my adolescent years, I needed a life companion. That's what I got in "Nona." (The spelling of the name is Indian, according to her parents – pronounced "Wah," not "Wy.") Someone to share the ups and downs, to enjoy our successes, to bear burdens, to brace for the tough times. She was always there and could be counted upon. Of some contemplated change, she would say, "Have you prayed about that?" Of a disappointment, she would say, "I believe God has something really good for us on down the road." You share a lot in a half-century! I want you to meet the Horger family of Texas.

I will start with Nona's grandfather, Jacob Travis Horger, son of Donald Asbury Horger. This German-speaking family came from Canton Zurich, Switzerland to South Carolina and got a land grant from George II in 1735. Other Horgers may have gotten grants in return for Revolutionary War service. Travis was born in Newton County, Texas near the Louisiana border. After marriage, they moved to Corrigan but, to get to a drier climate, they later migrated to Hondo, Texas (west of San Antonio) in 1895. Their youngest son, James Caughey (Nona's father), was born two years later. J. T. joined the Methodist Episcopal Church, South, at age seventeen and tells his own story of entire sanctification in a volume published in 1927, *Fundamental Revelation in Dramatic Symbol.* Whether in a Baptist, Methodist, or Nazarene church, he led the singing, was Sunday School Superintendent, and exhorter. He tells of Methodist pastors who experienced and preached holiness. While in Hondo he was busy in camp meetings as well as in the Methodist church. But he joined the Church of the Nazarene in San Antonio in 1915 and Rev. W. L. French conducted his funeral. He was a Bible scholar, good musician, and lay preacher. He made his living by working with leather--a shoemaker, and he repaired harnesses. Under Grover Cleveland, he was Postmaster of Hondo, so he must have been a Democrat.

James Caughey Horger was named after a Methodist evangelist under whose preaching William Booth was sanctified. While Caughey was preaching in Great Britain for four years, British Methodism was made stronger in the proclamation of sanctification than the American church, according to Timothy Smith. So Asbury and Caughey are the middle names of two of J. T. Horger's sons. Nona's father's military unit at Texas A. & M. was ready to sail for Europe just as the Armistice was signed ending World War I. He finished his bachelor's degree in engineering in 1919 and got his first employment in Dallas with the telephone company. He attended the Brooklyn Avenue Methodist church where he met and married Velma Frazier, Nona's mother. While they were very active in the Methodist church as a young couple, James and Velma became dissatisfied and, following the suggestion of his father, they became a part of the First Church of the Nazarene in Dallas (Oak Cliff).

Now for the Frazier side of the family. Velma, Nona's mother, was born in Ector, Texas. Her father, William Bartlett Frazier, was born in Tennessee of Irish and English descent. Her mother, Maude Huffacher, was born in Kentucky and was one-fourth Cherokee. (That would make Nona 1/64 Cherokee.) William Frazier was sheriff in Bonham, Texas for a number of years before moving to Dallas, where he joined the police force. Velma's mother died when she was twelve and she was unhappy at home thereafter. Nona recalls seeing her Grandpa Frazier in uniform, especially when they would go to the zoo. Velma was converted in the Presbyterian Church in Dallas, but was attending the Methodist church when she met James Caughey Horger. They were married on May 29, 1921. Both were very active in church work as Methodists and even more active as Nazarenes.

Nona was born in Dallas, February 5, 1923. Her father was seriously considering full-time Christian service and decided to go to Central Nazarene University, Hamlin, Texas in the fall of 1923. When he got there to take courses in religion, they were short of qualified faculty. So he taught science and math courses in the high school while taking courses in the college division. Velma finished her high school work while they were there (1923-1929). James was listed as "Acting President" in 1924-25. He edited the "proceedings of the First Annual Convention of the Hamlin District Young People's Society of the Church of the Nazarene, March 28-30, 1924." Nona's brother, James Caughey, Jr., and sister, Frances Edell, were born in Hamlin. So the family of young children was introduced to the rigors of low pay as well as the joys of the faculty family at a Nazarene college until the Hamlin institution merged with Bethany-Peniel College in 1929. They also saw the depth of commitment their parents had to the work of the church and to Christian higher education.

James found that he loved teaching and loved young people. To teach he needed to do graduate work. His experience included not only teaching but some time as registrar and business manager. Velma now had her high school diploma. She loved to read and was good in mathematics and spelling. Together, they decided to move to Norman, Oklahoma to give James the opportunity to take graduate work in zoology leading to a master's degree. Due to the depression and the demands of supporting a family, he could take only a course or two at a time at the University of Oklahoma. He was employed by the University to have charge of the supplies and to maintain the cars and trucks used by the department for field trips. Nona remembers the opportunity she had to accompany her father on some of those field trips to the Arbuckle Mountains. During all of this time they lived in Norman, Gladys Cherry lived with the Horgers after the death of her mother. She was Nona's cousin and only two years older than Nona. She was like a sister to the Horger kids. She rejoined her father in 1938 when the Horger family moved to Hutchinson, Kansas, but Nona and Gladys continued to feel like they were sisters.

Nona's father joined the faculty of Bresee College in the fall of 1938. The family had an apartment in the large, three story, frame building moved to the campus for use as a women's dormitory. On many weekends, James enjoyed driving a student ensemble to a nearby church for a school service or a revival meeting. I was just beginning my college work and ready to explore a relationship with his fifteen-year-old daughter. She was a junior in high school. I first took note of her as she rode her bike around the semi-circular drive at the college one evening. I really took note!

Nona finished her high school work in Bresee in the spring of 1940, just as Bresee was merged with Bethany-Peniel College in Oklahoma. The young president of Bresee (1936-1940) who brought the Horgers to Hutchinson was Harold W. Reed, he later was our president at Olivet.

Again, the Horger family faced unemployment due to the merger of Nazarene colleges. This time James took a job in Richfield, Kansas that included his serving as Principal of the High School, basketball and baseball coach, and science teacher. In 1941, he took a position at North Texas Agricultural College (now University of Texas at Arlington). With the build up of war industries and the pressures for expanded production, his engineering training was needed at North American Aviation nearby so James worked there until the end of the war. In 1943, they moved back to Dallas.

Nona's heritage from her family include a rich church and religious background, athletic prowess from her father, musical interest and lessons, mathematical and scientific aptitude, and a rich heritage in education. Her elementary and junior high education was done in a university town full of opportunity. She was accompanist for the high school choir. She had rich musical experiences in a good public school (music was to be her college major). She was active in athletics and had a good record in mathematics, English, and the social studies. Activities in church also qualified her for leadership when she got to Bresee College. Reverend A. Milton Smith was her pastor both in Norman and later in Dallas. Smith, J. Erben Moore, and Charles Strickland were her pastors through formative years.

What I am saying is this: I married into a family and a heritage that was as devout, as sure of what they believed, and one that followed the same ethical principles as the family in which I grew up. My parents dearly loved Nona. The Horgers gave me full acceptance and love. After the War, Uncle John inquired if I would be interested in taking over his funeral home business. Sometimes, it is more or less a joke when we say, "You married the whole family." Our marriage had the tremendously strong advantage of unanimous support from a large network of genuine Christians who believed in us and encouraged us at every critical point in our lives. Sharing a common church background solved a multitude of potential problems. Standards of conduct, the ethics of doing business, raising children, priorities in life - so many things depend upon the strong agreement of the partners in a marriage. This all became clear through dating and visiting in the homes of our in-laws over a period of nearly five years before marriage - that's time enough. And there are no regrets.

Nona was a jewel! No one who knows her doubts her Christian testimony. She bore the burdens and pressures of life on a limited income, remade clothing bought on sale, subordinated her career, and did a lot of volunteer service. She has done more than her share in rearing two children of whom we are very proud. She has given me heroic support in my responsibilities. We have a happy home and beautiful family. As I write, I can think of so many friends and colleagues who could not make the statements I have just made. The rest of Nona's story is intertwined in the chapters which follow.

NOTES

Eggen, Leora Horger. *The Horger Family.* (1670-1989), unpublished.
Fuller, Gene, et. al. *Hallelujah March: 75 Years of the Church of the Nazarene in West Texas* (1908-1983), 1982.
Horger, Jacob Travis. *Fundamental Revelation in Dramatic Symbol* (1927).

CH. IV COLLEGE

"Character, Culture, Christ"

In the fall of 1940, Bresee College merged with Bethany Peniel College in Bethany, Oklahoma. I had finished two years of college at Bresee had some excellent teachers, now I was off to finish my degree. Some Bresee constituents and students opposed the merger fiercely. The wisdom of the church that supported the college dictated a pull back due to the Depression.

Nona and I joined a load of Bresee students, boarded "Old Betsy" (the bus), and made the trip to Bethany to receive their welcome in May, 1940. The example of our parents in accepting the inevitable and following the leadership of the church helped us to be open-minded. Others among our classmates could not be so generous. Some of them went to Northwest Nazarene College. Many Kansans went to Idaho and Oregon in those depressions years (Frisks, Vails, Hobsons, Sauers). Some left the church of the Nazarene over the Bresee-Bethany merger. We were welcomed with open arms. I joined the Bethany Class of '42 as a junior and was elected as class representative on the Student Council. Nona's parents were merged out of a job for the second time in their Nazarene higher education experience. She attended Bethany but could not afford private music lessons. Of course, she was a freshman so a major was not all-important. Unofficially she became a history major. It was not until she had the security of my Navy subsistence allowance that she could commit to a music major and hope to complete it.

So we got to Bethany but neither of us had any money, a car, or a chance to get home unless we could hitch a ride. I remember my dad giving me a $10 bill in September for spending money until Thanksgiving. At least the church was on campus; no three mile walks to take your girlfriend to church! And we got our freedom from parents. We were on our own. I had one on-campus job that made me the envy of the men's dorm. Bud Robinson Hall had hardwood hall floors. Each Saturday morning, I had the honor of cleaning and waxing these floors in this girls' dormitory. Between calls, "man in the hall" quite often there was a screech! Later, I sold shoes on Saturdays for Montgomery Wards, Bakers, or Burts in the City.

I was active in athletics, especially softball, basketball, and track. We ran the hurdles down the village street before it was paved. I actually held the record in 110 yard high hurdles for several years. That was a case of being pressured to run (even though I had never run that race before). I don't believe I ever ran that race again; I remember my time but it was so poor that I do not choose to record it here. We had class competition but also had an all-star team that played teams from an industrial league in basketball. I did not make the trip to Olivet in January 1942 but played as a substitute when the Olivet boys came to Bethany in February. I remember being put into the game shortly before half-time. I was so pumped that I pulled up at about twenty-five feet, fired a shot, and it went over the top of the backboard. I guess we were not ready for intercollegiate competition after all. (Cecil Crawford tells the story of this home and home exchange in *The Olivet Story*, pp. 79-83.) Nona was active in dorm, athletic, and music organizations. We both sang in the A Cappella Choir under Chester Crill. She became his accompanist for his lessons and recitals given by his students. With Everette Walden and Raymond Hurn, I continued playing in a trombone trio we had begun in Bresee. I was on the *Arrow* (yearbook) staff as Sports Editor. I ran for student body president (unsuccessfully) in 1941. Both Nona and I served on the student discipline committee as E.C. Hall began to use students on committees.

As at Bresee, we had our meals served family style in Bud Robinson Hall. Each of us rotated to become head of the table to which we were assigned. That responsibility taught us etiquette, and responsibility for the pleasant atmosphere that should surround the meal. Most memorable was the practice of arriving early for the evening meal. We often stood around the piano in Bud Robinson Hall parlor, singing and listening to some volunteer who played the instrument. We all entered the dining hall at the signal, stood for grace, then were seated waiting to be served. You don't have to be wealthy to have a nice meal. The contrast with present day desecrations of good food on college campuses is quite extreme. There were not always seconds, no soft drinks, not always a salad. When B.M. Hall, the Business Manager, had a successful deer hunt, we all ate venison. Much of the food was donated or came in payment of someone's bill. We used to bemoan the lack of school spirit. Actually, we had a wonderful sense of community, caring, and, even with all its shortages, that community had lots of things that were not to be found when individually we went back to our own homes. We walked nearly everywhere we went; our clothing was barely adequate. There was no air conditioning. But in many ways, these were the best years of our lives.

Oh yes, and the rules were quite strict and were enforced. But, most of us expected that from the discipline we experienced at home. And, again, most of us had more freedom than when we were at home. We had space in which to grow up. My roommate in 1940-41 was Raymond Hurn. I had an endless supply of popcorn. There was no way one could prepare popcorn in the dormitory without advertising it to everybody. So we spread newspapers over the bed and piled it on the newspapers. Without butter or margarine, we resorted to hair oil on a few occasions to get the salt to stick. Ray was busy courting, preaching in weekend revivals, and trying to finance a car. By year's end, he and Madelyn had decided to get married so I was looking for another roommate for my senior year. Ray was to be my "best man" in January of 1943. I always think back to their first date, when the four of us had traveled from Hutchinson to Sylvia to see a high school play. We had to get Madelyn's parents' car to make that trip. Through high school and college I had some outstanding young men whom I counted as good friends. Whether in athletics, music, drama, quartets, or work I got to know lots of fine men who contributed to my life more than they know. I also dated a remarkable number of young ladies. More than you would guess, considering the fact that Wahnona was practically my one and only after 1938. (There were some minor intermissions.)

The Class of '42 was a remarkable group of young people. Now, having had our 25th, 45th, 47th, 49th, 50th, and 51st reunions, one can make a better evaluation of the talent and quality of people who chose a Nazarene college in those years. Draft notices and the war made college attendance uncertain for the men, but a remarkably high percentage were able to finish college, after the war if not on schedule. Most were successful in their chosen careers and model citizens in their communities. Some achieved recognition far beyond their college aspirations. Pastorates, faculty positions, business leaders, school teachers, politicians, health professionals . . . our class gave a good account of their stewardship! You might have thought they were from Lake Wobegone: "all above average!" They were. We announced the reunions for the class of '42 and friends. As our numbers dwindled, the registrants were more and more "friends," but they continue, through our 60th!

We came to Bethany at a time when the College was attracting several additional strong faculty members. Dr. A.K. Bracken was near the conclusion of his presidency and they really did not have a single academic dean. In fact, the business manager was second in command ("first mate" in the *Arrow*). Dr. L.T. Corlett was referred to as "Ship's Pilot," E.C. Hall as "dean," and Willis Dobson as Registrar in the yearbook. Mrs. Mattie Bracken, Fred Floyd, and Alline Swann were mainstays but they were all lacking Ph.D. degrees at that time and were needing reinforcements. Dr. C.E. Grothaus, with his Ph.D. in Chemistry, came in 1940. Earl Greer and Vernon Snowbarger came from the Bresee faculty and were eventually to earn doctorates. Mendell and Gertrude Taylor, Delbert and Carol Gish, John Peters, and Chester and Alice Crill added lots of talent and three more doctorates. E.C. Hall, Willis Dobson, and Fred Floyd later got their doctorates. My upper division teachers were experienced teachers of doctorate quality in this small Nazarene college.

When I got to the University of Oklahoma, they told me of many history graduate students from Bethany – "all excellent students," they said. Of equal importance to the students (in my opinion), Bethany First Church had just called C.B. Strang as pastor. With all this new talent, we were about to experience a "quantum leap" for the college (although we had not heard that expression at that time.)

The library was pitiful but to the student, the question is, "Have you read the books that are there?" In later years, I marveled at how accreditation teams examine the number and quality of books, scarcely asking if they are used. Well, I read just about all the books they had in the history section. I studied quite diligently, participated in most of the activities they organized for us, and we organized a few more for ourselves. We were fully involved in college life and the life of the church and the mix was rewarding. We got our money's worth. I tried three times to enroll in American literature but never succeeded; there was always something else that had a priority in my schedule. Otherwise, I got everything needed to teach history and social studies in secondary schools. I had minors in philosophy, speech, education, and English (almost). I had left music and psychology along the way even though a teacher or a relative had tried to persuade me to major in those fields. I quit math after six hours because I did not want to teach it; ditto foreign language. I took more economics and political science later because I needed those courses. But Bethany really met my undergraduate needs very well.

Worship in a large church was also challenging and enriching. I had pursued my degree without a certain calling in mind. When I decided that I did not have a call to the ministry, I fell back on teaching as a wonderful service vocation. Since I did well in school, why not continue to do what I did best? It would have been presumptuous to think of teaching in college, so I prepared to teach in high school. Thinking and praying through this decision was left up to me. And the compulsions of living close to the financial edge meant I had better decide. As time passed, I decided as necessary, always keeping as many doors open as possible.

Ultimately, I decided to major in history, taking the necessary teacher training courses to qualify as a teacher of social studies and history at the secondary level. Beyond that, I would take minors or additional course work in as many fields as possible. Debate and drama were two areas relatively new to me. They were very helpful. When I graduated I had a long list of books that I knew I should read. And they were all over the spectrum, not just in my major. Whatever was to become of me, I knew that I was open to Divine leading and I had discovered a huge, big world out there that I wanted to know more about. As a second, fall back position, I could go back to farming. I had learned that I could review every course taken in the previous year while I drove the tractor down the rows of corn or milo. I could sing, orate, and recite poetry and scripture learned in school. It was not a bad prospect but the world was to open up still more with unheard of options.

Making the transfer of colleges successfully, being elected to student council, and graduating summa cum laude was a tremendous boost to my self-confidence. The War and the draft hung over our heads during the last semester at Bethany, but I believed that, given the chance, I could have competed with anyone. Application for, and being awarded, a scholarship at OU for graduate work played a part. You would have to see the context of home, church, and community to fully appreciate the giant leap taken from my eighth grade experience to the end of the college triumph I celebrated. Honestly, I felt nothing but a determination to make the most of the opportunity given to benefit my neighbors and the Kingdom of God. I did not expect special favors although I would apply when that was the appropriate way to knock on a door. I was not pushed by family or faculty to achieve more. But I was encouraged when I proposed an idea for something more challenging. And, as will be clear in the next chapter, I was learning that God's will may be expanding before me as I push gently on the door to something that seems desirable.

This period in life is one of major decisions. I had decided to be God's boy (man). I had decided to be a teacher, the best in the world. Now, I would decide who would be my life's companion. And Wahnona concurred. We had known one another for five years and dated regularly most of that time. Our break-ups were not fights. We could not afford to get married yet. Both of us thought we should get our degrees. We did not have money and jobs were hard to come by. I would go out with other girls but the conversation would drift around to Nona. They knew we belonged together. On a choir trip as we pulled away from a rest stop, I had just gotten on the bus and couldn't spot her, so I called out "Where's Wah Wah?" That expression haunted me through the rest of my college days. Some of the girls told me off when they thought I wasn't treating Nona right. Well, it was not someone else deciding for me. I loved Nona and she was the only one for me. In the spring of '42, we set the wedding date for August 1942. Another major decision made. And about all of these major decisions, I can say they were good, correct, and there have been no regrets. If my children and grandchildren arrive at age twenty-one saying the same, I would be so happy. The role of the Christian college in all of this is major and I believe will be for our offspring.

Admittedly, my environment was very sheltered for the first twenty-one years of life. I saw many things from the seamy side of life but was safely insulated. Only a few of my friends smoked cigarettes, went to the movies or pool hall, went to wild parties. I was never close to a scrape with the law. Most of my friends were church goers as were my teachers. My parents always knew where I was until I went away from home to school. Then, there were administrators "*in loco parentis*." Some people feel that such close control over children will surely make for rebellion later. It did not in my case. Some of my classmates may have had a time of rebellion, but for most it was not for long and not serious. I account for rebellion by the difference either in personality or in the spirit of the home that sheltered them. The experience of class reunions forty and fifty years later lead me to conclude that I was neither harmed nor held back by the sheltering and that children and young people benefit by such set limits. During the war years, I heard Harry Emerson Fosdick quoted as saying, "I do not try to persuade my sons to be Baptist. That is their choice to make." As pioneers of a new denomination, my parents made it clear that they wanted their children to be Nazarenes. They did it in such a genuine way, with their money, time, prayers that we respected them highly and did not want to do less ourselves. We wanted to keep their investment working. It may not work for all, but for Snowbargers, "Vive le hothouse!" I have seen many of my college friends at reunions and alumni gatherings. But I also bumped into one in a New York subway; another at a Western Pacific anchorage (Ulithi), one on a street in Seattle, and on and on. These friendships were deep and enduring.

I found gaps in my studies. I wish I had studied Greek Civilization more. American Literature was missing after high school. I took political science by correspondence while in the Navy. But, I was strong in theology and Bible. Our curriculum was structured, leaving little time for electives. Current students sometimes meet distribution requirements with less than fifty hours of credits. As my record shows, I filled in the low spots in time to do top notch work in the best of graduate schools.

CH. V WILLIS GOES TO WAR

"The years go fast at Oxford, the golden years and gay,
The hoary colleges look down on careless boys at play.
But when the bugles sounded war they put their games away."
Winifred M. Letts

Dinner at Bethany-Peniel College on Sunday, December 7, 1941 was routine as we neared the end of the first semester of the college year. At about 1:30 p. m., as I strolled across the campus to my dorm room, someone, called out the window, "The Japs have bombed Pearl Harbor!" I kept walking and thinking, "Where's Pearl Harbor?" It seemed that part of my education had been overlooked. Later, my graduate professor, John D. Hicks, related that he had exactly that reaction when he heard of the attack. (He suggested that the build up and importance of that naval base might be a good subject for my doctoral dissertation.) It took the news reports of the next week and the report of the President to the nation to make the import soak in. Suddenly, the lives of all of us were pulled up by the roots. Some of my classmates were in reserves and were unable to finish college as planned. All of the men were required to register with draft boards. The ladies saw their plans upset or at least made very uncertain.

I lacked one semester to attain my B. A. degree and was scheduled to graduate on May 27, 1942. We were planning an August wedding (after all, I wouldn't be twenty-one until then). Many young men have trouble concentrating on schoolwork while they wait for the tidings to come. Fortunately, I kept my composure and did my last semester's work well. Then the letter came. "Report on May 27." I wrote the draft board, "Please grant a thirty day delay; May 27 is Commencement Day." I started a pattern that lasted a lifetime. When you have a request, you don't need an advocate or an attorney, just ask reasonable persons. They delight in granting your requests if it is in their power to do so. My request was granted.

During June, 1942 I had a chance to investigate the possibilities open to me in the military services. I made a trip to Hutchinson in a farm truck with my Grandpa Snowbarger and went to the post office building while he attended to other business. Unable to find "Air Force Recruiting" on any of the directories, I stuck my head in an open door and asked, "Where is the Air Force Recruiter?" The man answered, "There is no Air Force representative here; you would have to go to Wichita." Then he asked, "What's wrong with the Navy?" I was in the Navy Recruiting office. I had no objections so I let him explain what programs they had that I might qualify for. He suggested naval officer's training. When he asked about my educational attainments, I told him that I had just graduated from college. "But it was not an accredited college," I told him, not wanting to mislead. "I don't see where it says the college must be accredited," he came back. (Another lesson: assume that my work was equal to that of others; it is his problem to tell me that I do not qualify.) "It won't hurt to apply," I concluded. The only drawback was that I had to agree not to marry until I finished my midshipman training.

Riding the twenty-five miles back to the farm, I told my grandfather of the plan. I would have four months of training at Notre Dame University, be commissioned an Ensign, U.S.N.R., then be assigned to a ship. What seemed to get his attention was that I would be an officer. He reverted to a familiar form: as we worked or traveled together, he often preached to me and I listened. His sermon topic this time was "humility." I was amused, but it was appropriate.

I was ordered to appear for a physical examination in Kansas City, Missouri on July 9, 1942. I made the trip by train, passed the exam and returned to my farm home to await further orders. While in Kansas City, at the Power and Light building, a television camera and monitor at the entrance gave me my first appearance on TV and my first idea of what it was all about. That trip also was the first of many experiences at Kansas City's Union Station.

The summer of 1942 dragged on. There was to be no August wedding. Farm work and improvements on our house took up the time. But, it was "hurry up, and wait," the pattern of military life for the next three years. It was a relief to get my orders to report to Notre Dame U.S.N.R. Midshipmen's School on October 5, 1942. (That is nine months of lag in mobilization after the Dec. 7 attack, plus one month due to my request for delay. Mobilization takes that kind of time for bases, ships, and planes to be built as well as to identify and train the personnel required.) I made one trip to Arlington, Texas, to visit Nona and her family. Otherwise, there were three months of boredom after being pronounced physically fit.

As I prepared to leave home, my father mused sadly, "If we had really finished the job in the last war, you fellows would not have to go now." I tended to feel that every young person needed to feel that he or she had a part in the watershed event of a lifetime. So I was ready and anxious to see how my role and schedule would unfold. In our farming community, everyone of draft age registered, and nearly all relocated. Those without children went into military service if they could pass the physical examination. (My mother had a list of the names and addresses of every Hayes Township serviceman and spouse and kept it updated.) The rest moved to Wichita or elsewhere to work in defense related factories. Only the older men stayed to tend the farms (always a few exceptions). Those rural communities would never again be the same. Interestingly, I went on active duty the same day my uncle, Alvin Aller, reported for active duty.

Meantime, a V-7 Orientation center at the University of Notre Dame was being organized and staffed as a Midshipmen's School. Our class of 1,300 was the first. We went in as "apprentice seamen," the lowest rank. After thirty days of a combination of boot camp, classes, and other stress producing indignities, 1,100 of us were sworn in as Midshipmen, the rank held by students at the Naval Academy. This screening period was called orientation. All of these experiences are recorded in *The Capstan*, a yearbook, which has pictures of all of us. A "V-7 program" had been operating at Notre Dame running six weeks, giving officer candidates with civilian experience and maturity, a quick preparation for service as naval officers. It seems that they tried to squeeze the six-week effort into four weeks for us. Boot camp was rigorous enough, but, when you add five classes a day and five problems each per night, it pushed some past the breaking point. Below the highest echelons which were filled with naval academy graduates, the instructors in the Midshipmen's School were reservists from V-7 or other Midshipmen's schools. Under the circumstances, they did a remarkable job but that was certainly not our first impression of the staffing.

Part of the experience was Notre Dame itself. It was then a men's college. Football was not just for the team; the grass was worn off between the dorms as all residents played the game every afternoon. Everywhere we went, we were in our military formations. We marched to the dining hall which we shared with the students. We saw the athletes eating on the elevated section where they had meals. Same times, but not the same menus. We were welcomed by the administration and students and marched into the stadium end-zone for every home game. I saw Heisman Trophy winner, Angelo Bertelli, play against Otto Graham of Northwestern. The game against Michigan was standing room only. Midnight mass on Christmas Eve in the beautiful, gold-domed chapel was unforgettable. I went to the balcony so as not to expose my ignorance of the liturgy. It was my first experience knowing Roman Catholics and it was generally a positive experience. Much later at a planning session for an educational conference in the 1970's, I had dinner with Father Theodore Hesburgh, the President who made Notre Dame a real university. He is a great man.

The weather on the southeast coast of Lake Michigan was all that it was cracked up to be. It got as low as -22° and the wind whipped across the campus without fail. Calisthenics, stripped to our skivvies, including push-ups on frozen ground, as we prepared for war in the tropics, seemed unnecessary. Seamanship began with the matter of straightening out the language: Food was "chow," you put your feet on the "deck." Stairs were "ladders," walls were "bulkheads," equipment was "gear," and you didn't need to go to the toilet, you were looking for the "head." And everything was "on the double," then the inevitable wait. Seamanship was also navy customs, "rules of the road," handling sailing vessels, mooring, anchoring, orders to the helm and engine room, tying knots, signaling, and Navy traditions. How to become a leader of men, Navy rules and regulations - that and more in the 793 pages of the 1940 *Bluejacekts' Manual* had to be mastered. This was one of the courses that ran through the four months and infiltrated conversation out of class.

The other courses included Navigation, Damage Control, Ordinance, and Gunnery, all of which seemed worth studying since some of us would very soon be commanding officers of LST's or other small ships and none of us had any knowledge of these subjects from college courses we had taken. None of us had spherical trigonometry but we tried to do the problems assigned in Navigation. After total frustration, they finally told us, "We have books of tables made up for solving these complex problems. We'll show you how to read the tables." Thanks a lot! Similarly, we studied buoyancy, center of gravity, and righting moment in Damage Control. But few of us had studied the physics underlying the problem's solution. Ditto Gunnery and how to correct for the roll and pitch of the gun platform, the effect of humidity or upper level wind on the trajectory of a projectile. But most of us would play a part in solutions to those problems under battle conditions within the three years to follow. So we were a studious lot; our lives and those of our shipmates depended upon it. For relaxation, I sang in the Glee Club.

When we finished on January 28, 1943, that class broke up and, though I knew some of those men better than most of my school mates in previous years, I only saw one or two of them again. Harold Sponberg (Gustavus Adolphus, '42) was president of Washburn University and later Eastern Michigan University. He was a prince of a guy and we visited at one or two educational conferences before he died of a heart attack. I went to Chicago for a weekend at the Palmer House with Bill Snyder (UC Berkeley, '42), great guy! Herb Spencer (Butler, '42) was a wonderful young man. Everything was arranged alphabetically so my battalion was Shu- through Z. They were truly the best and the brightest! Highly motivated and pushed to the limit for four months, they were ready, just a little cocky, and anxious to "get it over with." Dressed in the tailored dress blue uniform, I was ready for the wedding.

We were the English, history, philosophy, art, music, and business majors of our institutions. We came from UC, Harvard, Yale, Carleton, Texas, Princeton, Cornell, Kentucky, Kenyon, Columbia, and Bethany-Peniel. If we had been math or science majors we would have been in another program. In many respects, we were the ideal candidates for leadership of naval reservists and draftees. We were "ninety day wonders," the line officers to operate the fighting ships of the navy under the overall command of the graduates of Annapolis whose training had been more leisurely and thorough. The naval academy men were excellent, in some respects superior in their training, but we reservists were closer to the reservist enlisted men and draftees. We "interpreted" the rules and orders to make them palatable to civilians in uniform. Together, we got the job done, although not always within the regulations in the *Bluejacket Manual*.

OUR WEDDING

I was ordered to report to the Twelfth Naval District (San Francisco) on February 8 for transportation to my ship which was in the South Pacific. So we set January 31 as the date for our wedding. Most of the wedding party was in Bethany, Oklahoma which was about equidistant from Sylvia and Dallas. Ration stamps for gasoline were hard to come by, so the Horgers and Snowbargers met half way to allow this wedding to happen. Dr. C.B. Strang said it was the most beautiful wedding ceremony he had ever performed. The bride's attendants wore white dresses and red jackets and carried red roses. The men were in Navy blue (for a red white, and blue scheme). Weddings during the school year were few and far between in those days. Since neither Nona nor I was enrolled that semester, college authorities had no jurisdiction or they would have had serious problems in permitting the wedding. Given our long courtship, I am sure no one had any serious objections. Johnny Douglas took pictures with light available on his 8mm camera which was a novelty at that early date.

I wrote a letter to my parents clearing the use of a wedding ring for Nona in the ceremony. They did not object. Nona gave me a wedding ring after the ceremony; it was still controversial in the church but going abroad in the Navy, we both thought it was good that I wear one. We borrowed a car from Marvin Peterson. After a reception at Uncle Vernon's house we went to the Golden Pheasant restaurant in downtown Oklahoma City for a big dinner alone. Not knowing what to expect from the college crowd we kept our whereabouts secret. In fact we returned to the Boyer's Court Motel on the east edge of Bethany for the first night. There were no shenanigans from our friends. We had been on a tight time schedule for the travel and arrangements but everything worked out to perfection.

We went to the farm for almost a week with my family before we had to catch the Super Chief for San Francisco. At the same station where my mother had seen her sweetheart off to training for World War I almost twenty-six years earlier, they saw us off. (She cannot have known how thankful I was that she did not shed a tear.) I had learned that there was a three to four week delay in getting transportation from the West Coast to the battle zone so we decided it was worth Nona's trip to California so we could be together there. That was our honeymoon. When I purchased my tickets to go west, no one advised me that the Super Chief was all Pullman. So we had a problem. I had tickets and was traveling under orders but the train had no coach cars or empty berths and was Pullman only. They compromised and allowed us to board and sit in the club car (in the dark). "Sometimes there is a cancellation along the road," the conductor explained. We got to La Junta, Colorado and they had a crew change. We risked being thrown off but, in the nick of time, an upper berth became available. Although it was designed for only one person, we were newlyweds, "We'll take it!" So after sitting up one night, we were able to sleep the second night.

Off to San Francisco and West

Arriving in San Francisco, we were met by Stanley and Thelma Abbott (from Sylvia) and Ray and Eula Merle Simpson (Bethany friends and newlyweds themselves). They had a room for us at Hotel Herbert, on Powell about a block north of Market. The cable car went up and down Powell so it was an ideal location. Ray had a car and I had some gas coupons. We rode the cable car, Ray's car, and walked. In the next two weeks we saw Fisherman's Wharf, Telegraph Hill, Market Street, the Embarcadero, the Praesidio, Golden Gate and Oakland Bay bridges, Treasure Island, Alcatraz, Berkeley, Palo Alto, and a range of restaurants and hotels. We went to San Francisco First Church where Elwood Sanner was the pastor and we saw Claude and Crystal Yates (also from Sylvia). I met Lieut. Bud Smee there for the first time; I was later to work with him on the General Board. The entertainment highlight was the Gershwin Festival at the San Francisco Opera House and we were able to get standing room only tickets. Paul Whiteman, his orchestra, Bing Crosby, Dinah Shore, and several other musicians made this an extravaganza performance in a beautiful auditorium.

The routine was that I reported to 12th Naval District headquarters, would be told that there was no transportation, and be asked to report back in two or three days. Then we were on our own. Before that scenario changed, we ran out of money so I had to ask my parents to wire money. I had never before been where I couldn't cash a check; and I almost couldn't get the money that had been wired to me. My naiveté and the look of innocence probably helped. Meantime, the tension was rising. Some morning when I reported, the news would be different. That morning was February 24, 1943 and it meant that we had to swing into action. After a tearful farewell, I got Nona on a bus to Modesto to spend some time with Ray and Eula Merle Simpson before she returned to Kansas and Texas. Nona's entry in the diary tells it all: "Willis was detached and ordered to be on 6:30 train for Port Hueneme. We were broken-hearted." The honeymoon was over.

For us, the worst part of the war was the separation. I was to be abroad fifteen months this time. I couldn't say anything substantive in my letters as to my activities, location, or special events. When we next saw one another, we had to get reacquainted. I could never fully recall or explain my experiences or itinerary; Nona and my folks could at least keep me posted on their activities though there was a time lag. On one occasion we were at sea continuously for fifty-nine days. Through supply ships, we got only a small amount of mail. When we returned to port, I got fourteen letters.

At Port Hueneme (near Oxnard, California), I boarded the liberty ship, *John B. Floyd*, with a group of Seabees. These were construction specialists, headed for Guadalcanal where the American forces were in the mop-up phase of that historic battle. The ship had four holds intended for cargo. They had installed bunks, five and six high, and you could sleep in shifts but the ventilation was totally inadequate. The liberty ship was a factor in winning the war because Kaiser shipyards (and others) could turn them out so fast. But they made very poor passenger ships.

We topped off fuel and supplies in San Diego harbor and headed south and west. The huge ground swells off the West Coast continued three or four days. They reminded me of the hills of Texas around Abilene. The ship rolled continuously even when the water was glassy. They decided that they needed an officer to stand night watch in each hold. I stood at the top of the ladder as one after another of the sailors (all land lubbers) came running for the rail. Some of them did not make it in time and regurgitated on everything and everyone below. After an hour of that, I joined the parade to the rail. The stench and poor ventilation made life miserable below decks; on topside, it was great as we sailed past Christmas Island, Samoa, Fiji and finally arrived at Noumea, New Caledonia where the *U. S. S. Washington* was based. We had been on that liberty ship continuously for twenty-four days and we were all glad to get off. We had taken a rather circuitous route because we had no escort vessels and could not be sure where Japanese submarines were operating. I was learning the geography as we went. I could not send a letter during that entire trip. So the good-bye in San Francisco was indeed sad for Nona. I knew what was happening (or not happening): the folks at home could only imagine.

U.S.S. WASHINGTON (BB56)

Upon graduation from Notre Dame Midshipman's School I got an assignment that was the envy of every Annapolis graduate! A fast 45,000 ton, battleship that carried the flag of Task Force 64, Rear Admiral Willis A. Lee. It had been commissioned in 1941. The *U.S.S Washington* had been in the Pacific about five months before I reported (roughly the time of my training). In support of the landings on Guadalcanal, the ship had been very successful in the Third Battle of Savo Island, November 14, 1942. BB56 sank outright the enemy battleship *Kirishima* as well as assisting in the sinking of several enemy cruisers and destroyers. There was no damage to the Washington and no casualties. The *U.S.S. Alabama* was damaged in the same battle and got the publicity through the antics of her Captain, but the *Washington* performed to perfection. Pride and morale were very high on March 21, 1943 as I reported in. Mopping up operations on Guadalcanal continued and we operated in the Solomon Islands to be sure remaining Japanese got no supplies. So, I got acquainted with "the slot," as they referred to the waters off Guadalcanal; it was also called "iron-bottom sound" for all the sunken ships, both American and Japanese.

53

I wondered then, "Were any of the Japanese there Christians? Nazarenes?" As two or three Japanese prisoners of war were brought aboard our ship for questioning, their small size, fright, and humanity kept this question in my mind. It was not until 1994 that, through a missionary reading book by Alice Spangenberg, *Oriental Pilgrim* (NPH, 1948), I discovered that Shiro Kano, a former student of Eastern Nazarene College, was killed by shrapnel on Guadalcanal on January 19, 1944. What a waste! While telling the story of war, I do not want anyone to think it is pleasant. It is a horrible way to solve any problem. But, we humans have not found ways yet to avoid some war. Strangely, it now seems to me that God was "making all things work together for good" in my life. This ship, the separation, military experience, and responsibility were to add a rich dimension to my growth and development. In this chapter, I will concentrate on my own experiences and tell about Nona and her life in Dallas later.

For my first five months in the Pacific, our tasks were very much on the fringes of the war. That is not to say we had no function or were out of danger. I had been there less than a month when Admiral Yamamoto's plane was shot down in our general area. He was the most respected among Japanese military leaders. Our ship had a complement of 2,100 men, slightly more than standard. I am sure they were using it for a training facility so as to be able to man the many new ships under construction. I was a member of the 3rd Division, which was responsible for the fantail of the ship and Turret III, a sixteen-inch, three-gun turret. Projectiles and powder were stored three decks deep under the main deck. In action, turret officers are stationed in the turret where hoists bring up the ammunition and guns are loaded. There was a lot of redundancy so that, if there was damage to the ship, the crew of one turret could keep on firing even though remote signals were the normal basis for training and pointing the guns. I actually fired those guns in training exercises in which the targets were sleds towed by other ships at great distances from us. The range of those guns was almost 40,000 yards (twenty miles).

These exercises, care and upkeep of the deck area assigned to us, and training of the crew as many of them sought advancement in rank – these were the activities that occupied each day at sea. We also had responsibility for two seaplanes and the catapults to launch them. Rod Milddleton, my division officer, and Ed Robie were my superiors in the division. Both were graduates of the Naval Academy and were very glad to have me in their division, very supportive. I stood watches both in the turret and in the computer room (below decks) where we input the wind direction and speed, barometric pressure, and gyroscopic information to correct the signals of bearing and range to a target. In addition, I stood regular watches on the bridge as assistant officer of the deck.

Under delegated authority, the O.O.D. took charge of the ship (the driver, so to speak,) so that the Captain could tend to the business of the organization, personnel, and operations of the ship. I was promoted to Lieut. (jg) on March 1, 1944. It was about that time that I was approved, and took my place in the rotation, as Officer of the Deck underway. That meant that I gave orders to the helm and engine room, and reported on all important developments to the Captain - me, a farm kid not yet twenty-three. When Middleton and Robie were on watch, I also reported "Division III all present and accounted for," received, and passed along the "orders of the day" to about sixty men.

My training was really intense and incorporated the skills needed for the big ships to operate in the fast carrier task force and the strategy of island hopping. Both of these developments were the result of Nimitz, Halsey, and MacArthur rethinking the demands of a war in the Western Pacific. I had learned it on the job without the need to unlearn the traditional naval dogmas. I was at the forefront professionally. As more junior officers were assigned to our division, and the role of the battleship in the task force was more and more to throw up a protective shield of anti-aircraft fire to protect the carriers in the center of the formation, I was named assistant air defense officer. My battle station was shifted to the tower. With Commander H. W. Seely (the ADO), we were to direct the fire of five-inch, 40mm. and 20mm. batteries. Our job was to assure that every "bogey" approaching the formation was in the sights of our guns, and they were ready to open fire when the target came within range. In this we did not fail once. When "General Quarters" sounded, I was always able to get to my battle station within twenty seconds, whether to the turret or the top of the tower. In shore bombardments, Air Defense assisted in spotting our rounds, helping to coach the gunners on to the target. I was assisted in preparation for this assignment by watches in the gun directors for the anti-aircraft guns and Combat Information Center (CIC). Here we tracked all unfriendlies using radio reports, radar, and reports of lookouts. So I knew the system from top to bottom.

We were in the New Caledonia or the New Hebrides areas during early 1943 until June when we headed for Pearl Harbor for improvements in radar, some new anti-aircraft guns, and scraping barnacles in drydock. That was a pleasant six-week interruption of the boring routine in the tropics. The tropics had their own pleasant diversions. In Efate Harbor (New Hebrides) our recreation included swimming off the ship in very deep water or snorkeling in the coral reef area around the anchorage. Ashore, at an enlisted men's recreation area, Bob Feller demonstrated his pitching style. He was a sailor and at least a thousand Navy personnel, standing on the level, were there to catch a glimpse. Near the recreation area, there was a native village (off limits to us) but some of us stole a glimpse there too. I got pistol practice at a dump in Noumea (New Caledonia). I checked out a .22 pistol mounted on a .45 frame and the tin cans were the targets. On board ship, there were movies every night. Once in a while, there was one that was good, but there was nothing else to do and it could be hot below decks. An evening on the fan tail was always pleasant. Our Annapolis friends took some of us sailing once. "Divine Services" were held regularly aboard ship and were well attended. We stopped off at Fiji one time and I was fortunate to get to go ashore. I bought some silver trinkets there. Of course, in Pearl Harbor and Honolulu there were lots of things to do. We got a car and drove around Oahu, ate a Japanese dinner in a Japanese home, went to Waikiki beach many times. The Moana and Royal Hawaiian hotels were the centers of activity. We watched with everyone in the Harbor and cheered every submarine as it returned from the Western Pacific.

A History of the U.S.S. Washington, 1941-1946, details the story of our engagements and areas of support. It has pictures of shipboard routine, the wardroom, activities, and our mascot, Coxswain Zero. Officers had two-man staterooms; the junior got the upper bunk. We got our pants and shirts cleaned and pressed in the laundry. We were comfortably informal in our "undress" kakis, open collars, and overseas cap. These were not olive drab, but a nice tan. Officers got allowances and then paid for their own meals that were prepared and served in the wardroom by the mess boys. There was always coffee on the sideboard. With the regular hours, good meals, and plenty of exercise, I leveled out to a steady 180 pounds which I maintained throughout the war years (in fact, until age 40). When we went back to Hawaii, we instructed the committee to buy all the fresh fruits and vegetables they could find and not to spare the cost. As I remember, our allowance was $40 per month but the usual charge was $35 or less. Of course it was more in Hawaii or the States.

We had great conversations and games in the wardroom. I was surprised to find that less than 40% of the officers on the *Washington* smoked. The big surprise came when we got to Pearl. Nearly 99% of them drank liquor. There were some unexpected personality changes in some of my friends when they got liquor under their belts. Many spent spare time reading. I had several books that I fully intended to read but somehow I lost my concentration and was unable to stick to a book. I read Hemingway's The *Sun Also Rises*, but only dabbled in several other books. I always admired our Chief Engineer who never went to the Officer's Club or out on the town. He stayed aboard ship, reading about the various systems on the ship and improvements that were being developed. (I do not mean to imply that I imitated him.) Perhaps he was a workaholic but he became a model of professionalism to me. He would earn his advancements by reason of his knowledge and skill, not by dancing with the Captain's wife. Much later, Zenith's slogan, "The quality goes in before the name goes on," summed up a value that I wanted for my life and I had a disdain for all short cuts to recognition or promotion. I developed an aversion to self-promotion.

What did we do to help win the War? While I was aboard, we participated in "The Consolidation of the Southern Solomons," "The Gilbert Islands Operation," "The Kavieng Strike (New Ireland)," "Bombardment of Nauru Island," and "The Marshall Islands Operation" (including the bombardment of Kwajalein Island). After the bloody attack on Tarawa (in the Gilberts), they decided more bombardment was required at Kwajalein. When ordinary bombardment shells did not silence the fortifications, we moved out to about 30,000 yards, loaded armor piercing shells, and fired an arching trajectory that had the shells descending almost perpendicularly on the target. It worked. American casualties were light and the campaign was short. Using battleships and cruisers to throw up a protective shield of anti-aircraft fire to protect the carriers seemed to work to perfection while I was aboard. (That is, until the Japanese resorted to the Kamikaze attacks near the war's end.) The tactic of having our own patrol planes flying cover and picket ships (destroyers) deployed at about sixty miles in the direction of an expected attack meant that we usually had ten to twenty minutes warning of incoming bogeys. There was battle damage to some of our ships, but none to the *Washington*, nor to our carriers. Many of the enemy positions on New Guinea and in Micronesia were bypassed and left to "wilt on the vine."

After the Marshall Island campaign, we returned again to Pearl Harbor and I persuaded one of the pilots on board our ship to take me on a tour of the Islands. Pilots needed flying time to keep their skills sharpened. Seaplanes were scarcely used when we were operating in a task force. So we went up and the pilot put the plane through every acrobatic exercise in the book. That wasn't what I had in mind but I humored him and eventually we got a nice view of the Islands. My motion sickness tendencies were barely under control. When we landed in the channel near Ford Island, an LST had just entered the harbor and left a healthy wake. My pilot touched down on the edge of the wake and we chugged in touching only the tops of the waves. I swear, we bounced fifty feet off the first wave, perhaps twenty-five off the next one, etc. It was a horrible landing. I was sure that the struts were coming up through the floor of the fuselage. I lost it! I was sick as a dog for about three hours. He laughed at me and said, "If you mess up my plane, you have to clean it up." When we returned to the ship, I had mail; my orders to flight training! I was so green I couldn't eat lunch.

I had applied for naval aviator's training perhaps two or three months earlier. That's how bored I was with the South Pacific routine. Now I was selected. Since I was an officer, training was much more lucrative than for cadets. I got an extra 50% pay while learning. And, you may recall, I was looking for the Air Force recruiting station when I put my head into the Navy Recruiting office in the summer of 1942. So I was to report to the Dallas Naval Air Station in June 1944. That's where Nona was, with her parents.

The *Washington* returned to Bremerton, Washington for extensive overhaul and repairs. I called Nona and she took the Union Pacific to the Seattle area, interrupting her school year. The administrators gave her permission to do her work, attendance rules were waived, and she could return at semester's end and take her finals. We got an apartment in Port Orchard and we were reunited after fifteen months apart. The ship's crew was given thirty day leaves (in two shifts) so there were one-half or less of the total personnel aboard at anyone time. Those of us being transferred were held on board for those sixty days to keep the ship in some semblance of order while the navy yard crews did their work. At times, I got only one day in four off but they gave me the unusual privilege of bringing Nona aboard for the evening meal in the wardroom. On those days she sometimes watched me as I stood my Officer of the Deck watch. We were to inspect the sailors to make sure their uniforms were neat and clean. We cleared them as they faced us; they saluted and were gone. Nona would spot a hole in the heel of a black sock and, too late, call it to my attention. It was strange having a lady aboard. Of course, she would have to take the boat alone back to our Port Orchard apartment. And she had to get back to Bethany alone, because I was not detached until the ship was in San Francisco and ready to go back to the Pacific theater of operations again. She took her finals and was one semester closer to her degree. Before she got to Seattle, I went ashore twice with three other officers from the *Washington*. The first time we went to Hotel Washington and ate dinner in their huge dining room. There were not many people there and I said, "I know that girl," as I pointed across the large room. "She is Marjorie Nell Robertson (I don't know her married name)." The guys urged me to go over and talk to her, but just back from fifteen months in the South Pacific, ashore for the first time, I was uncertain and I had never met her husband. One of my buddies said, "Well, I'll go and talk to her." As he spoke, she turned my way, looked cautiously and unbelievingly. Sure enough, she was the daughter of my parents' best friends from Bible School days. As kids, we were together many times. Her husband was stationed at Sand Point. We tried to get together when Nona was there but couldn't make it. Four days later, we had dinner at another restaurant, and emerged on the street while it was still daylight. As we walked down the street, a female voice behind us said, "Willis, Willis Snowbarger." My friends could not believe it. "Are you one of those who has a girl friend in every port?" When the lady caught up to us, it was Gracie Morgan. At Bethany, two rooms shared a bath, so four people were "bathmates." That was the relationship of Gracie and Wahnona. My friends carried me high. It was great when Nona arrived and I could go to dinner with her.

The next stop was San Francisco and I was alone this time. With plenty of money now, I enjoyed a night in the St. Francis Hotel. I met Warren Craddock as he boarded the *Washington*. He was the son of Harry Craddock, long time business manager of Bethany Nazarene College. That contact, fleeting though it was, meant a lot to the Craddocks. Then I was detached from the *U.S.S. Washington*. That is a sad kind of order. It was a great ship and being detached was a horrible feeling. I made my way alone back to Bethany and Sylvia for a leave before reporting to my next assignment.

Those fifteen months on the battleship brought about the fastest learning and most rapid changes in my personality in my life to that time. I knew that I could function effectively on a small fraction of the information thrown at us so quickly in Midshipmen's School. There was time to master the additional facts, regulations, and skills of seamanship. I was amazed at how much I had already mastered. I had become more decisive, more self-assured. More mature and now able to face men old enough to be my father and give orders. I understood the organization, my role in it, and the need for discipline and promptness. The spirit of "can-do" was instilled.

I believe that I developed a presence and leadership demeanor in that stint aboard the *Washington*. We were comfortable with the routines; we were an unbeatable team. I knew what I would do in crisis - I would do my job well. I could calm those around me. The *Bluejackets' Manual* and *Division Officer's Guide* were just that: guides. There was a lot of justification for the full slate of regulations, but dependence upon so many reservists and the carrier task force mode of operation made many of those rules and practices unworkable or unnecessary. There were life and death situations and experiences that demanded adherence to the rules and the orders given. But, we could take things a day at a time and largely go by common sense to be safe and accomplish what was expected of us in the team effort. Men would comply with reasonable orders. (Only after the war did I get all those stories of "catch twenty-two.") On a long night watch wearing headphones, we could talk about these things (officers with enlisted men). I also knew that I could keep alert without sleep and do my tasks for a period of about forty-eight hours. I was comfortable with the chain of command. I had respect for Captain J. E. Maher and Executive Officer Arthur E. Ageton. I wanted them to look good. The divisional organization, ranks, petty officers, training role, it was all good and fair. We could make it work well both in emergencies and in port. Regular Navy and reservists got on well together.

DALLAS, NEWPORT, AND THE EAST COAST

From the *Washington* on May 5, 1944, I was assigned again to the 12th Naval District, which, of course, didn't need me. One of the guys, noticing that I had not had leave, said, "Oh, well, give him forty days leave," the intervening time until I was to report to Dallas Naval Air Station. So, I made my way via Los Angeles to Bethany for Commencement and, with Nona, made a trip to Kansas. While there, we bought our first car, a 1936 Chevrolet. It was very nice and we were fortunate to find something that we could afford. We then headed to Dallas via Bethany. We picked up Nona's things and got to Dallas on June 10 giving ourselves time to find an apartment before I reported for duty at Dallas Naval Air Station on June 15.

We were near Nona's folks so everything was relatively easy to cope with there, except for the heat. It was 100 at least one day. The day we moved into our apartment, I told Nona, "This is worse than the South Pacific!" (It was; but it was undiplomatic of me to say so.) It was just an eight-mile trip each day to Grand Prairie to the training station. We had a little time to spend with Dean and Roxie Wessels and Vernon and Adana Bugh, although neither couple was married at that time. Miniature golf at Wee St. Andrews was the best of our recreation, but, at least once, we went swimming with Dean and Roxie in Lake Dallas. (Even though Nona forgot to bring her swimming suit.) Nona nearly always beat me at miniature golf. We had rented the Gilbert's apartment for $10 per week, but for some reason moved to another small apartment later. With the first location in Port Orchard, Washington, that was the third home for us in less than eighteen months of marriage.

I have to tell of the removal of an impacted wisdom tooth at Dallas NAS. It contrasts with the butchery at Notre Dame when the first one was removed. The Dallas Navy dentist agreed to do it after hours on the base so there was just one dental assistant, the dentist, and me. After studying the tooth, the doctor said, "I will split the tooth and it should come right out. Cup your chin in your right hand and rest your elbow on your knee." With one blow on the chisel, it was done! Each half was lifted out. He had finished in less than half an hour and there was no swelling! That guy was an artist.

The flight school experience lasted until I was detached on July 18, 1944. By that time, the Battle of Saipan and the Battle of the Philippine Sea had occurred. The Japanese suffered defeats that all but obliterated their carrier fleet. There was no need for more naval aviators and word of this was circulating through our class as early as July 1. Nobody got a second chance on anything; quite different from earlier flight training classes. Eventually, about 80% of my class was sent back to the fleet or to new construction. The situation justified the decision to cut back the training of aviators, but individuals were devastated. I experienced unexplained stomach upsets and loss of weight (six pounds). I could not accept failure; but it was not really failure. Before getting on to the next assignment, let me describe a new dimension of learning.

The pattern at the Naval Air Station was ground school in the morning and flying in the afternoon. All communication was to be in block printing, something I had never done since first grade. With the prospect of dealing with government forms the rest of my life, this was very good for me. The same can be said for learning Morse Code. The Midshipmen's School paid passing attention to this but the prospect of needing to send messages from a one- or two-man plane made mastery a necessity. The procedures for voice radio communication also had to be mastered. Navigation in the air puts one on his own and is slightly different from surface navigation. Aircraft recognition, aerodynamics, aircraft design and parts, instrumentation, take-offs, landings, and rules of air traffic can be taught in the classroom.

Then in the afternoons, you do it. We trained in the Stearman N2s bi-plane, the same kind that General Eisenhower and thousands of others learned in. There were two open cockpits each with controls. The student took the front cockpit. After the first or second ride, the student did all the flying with prompting from the instructor. As time went by, the plane was put through acrobatics at safe altitudes (up to 10,000 feet). Eventually, the plane was put into a stall. The student was to pull it out of the resulting tailspin. The procedure was to kick opposite rudder and push the stick forward, putting the plane into a dive, regaining airspeed, then pull the stick back (now a few thousand feet lower) . . . leveling out. Navy landings are different as we were trained to make a tight circle at one thousand feet to simulate a carrier landing. We don't drag the plane in for a two or three mile approach, but after more like a one-half mile approach, set it down.

After 11.7 hours in the air, I was given 2.6 hours of check flights – a total of 14.3 hours. I had completed primary flight training but did not solo. On the final check flight, the instructor cut the power and said, "You have lost power, make an emergency landing in that pasture." All went well until we touched down. Then we went into a ground loop and skinned about three inches of paint off the underside of my left wing. The report simply showed ↓. The check pilot apologized saying, "I saw that you were not correcting for crabbing into the wind and should have saved you but I didn't." He was unhappy because he had to write up an accident report. But there was no second chance for me either. We had been becalmed for more than a week and my instructor had not had a chance to teach me about crosswind landings. I did not recognize the wind factor so a rather simple thing that I immediately understood caused me to fail on the first (and last) try. So, back to the Fleet! I never returned to flying but I would have loved to start again with a crosswind landing. Under normal circumstances, I am sure that I could have been a good carrier pilot.

One additional thing that the application for flight training brought to me was that I took and passed a rigorous physical examination. This self-knowledge was one of the assurances I carried into later life. I was given an unusually strong physique with all the skills of perception, balance, and coordination required for the most demanding occupations. For top offices and responsibilities good mental and emotional balance and certain physical powers and coordination are necessary. Stamina, resilience, and toughness depend upon these endowments and certain self-assurance and risk-taking follows from knowing that the body will not let you down.

It was an inconsequential failure that marred my naval record but that too was a positive experience in that I learned from it. Within a week I was reassigned to the pre-commissioning and training crew of the *U.S.S. Duluth* (CL87) at the Naval Training Station, Newport, Rhode Island. We made the trip in our car, stopping in Rushville, Illinois (where we got a rebuilt generator); Peru, Indiana (where we discovered a tire about to go flat in front of Alvin and Florence Aller's home); Sandusky, Ohio; Chambersburg, Pennsylvania; and, after brief stops at Gettysburg, Philadelphia, New York, and Narragansett, Rhode Island, we got to Newport on July 25, 1944. Such travel in wartime is guaranteed to be risky but except for one more flat tire, it was uneventful. It was fortunate that the need to get ration board help to replace a tire occurred in Peru, Indiana where an uncle and aunt lived. All told, we lost no more than five or six hours due to car trouble en route.

Newport is the summer playground of the rich and famous. To be frank, we knew very little about it. With about two summer months there and two more months based there later, we grew to like it. We got a small one-room cabin (our fourth residence) and proceeded to enjoy.

One afternoon we were walking along a creek bank that meandered along the back yards of the mansions. I guess we were trespassing. Beautiful landscaping and magnificent houses! Suddenly, we were close to a back patio and there was Doris Duke. We were so embarrassed but she smiled and waved to us. We were on our way!

Along with about twenty-five or thirty experienced officers and petty officers, I was responsible to work out an organization for a crew to man a new light cruiser just being completed in Newport News, Virginia. As time went on we got an influx of seamen, many of them inexperienced draftees. Our schedule was quite predictable, so when we had a weekend off it was feasible to get to New York City or Boston. In many ways, this was just what Nona and I needed to be away from family and to have some thoroughly enjoyable time together. We could see the Atlantic from our cabin. A trip to Boston was rich. We visited Don and Ruth Frye (cousins) there; he was also a naval officer taking work at Harvard. Ruth had mastered the subway system so she showed us around like a professional guide. Saturday evening, we topped things off with a dinner at Ruby Fu's Den.

Our car was a standard shift and had developed a problem. The shift would not stay in high gear but if you would hold the shift lever down, it would stay in high. Driving with one hand was not really safe, so I took some baling wire and tied it back. We were driving in Boston and (at night) driving back to Newport. The simple way was to slow as we approached a traffic light in order to hit the green. (No interstate highways then.) So we stayed in high gear (the shift tied back) and, ahead, the yellow light came on. On the right there was a service station so we turned in and drove across the corner turning right; onto a dead end road! I hit the brake, killed the engine and untied the shift. We got back on the highway and on to Newport, but it was an extra thrill producer. This was the car Nona later drove to Norfolk, Virginia, getting to the Holland Tunnel in New York City at about 4 p.m. The officer made signs to her and she thought he meant to slow down. He meant for her to speed up. We couldn't afford to have the car fixed so shortly before leaving for the Pacific; I sold that car for $35 to some shyster in Virginia. Service men in such a situation were targets of people like that when we obviously had no choice. He got a car worth $600, probably spent $50 to get it fixed, and resold it for $700. They were not making any cars for the market in those days.

Nona and I made a trip by train to New York City, September 9-19, 1944. We stayed in the Ritz-Carlton ($7.50 per night to us). We saw many of the usual attractions and also visited briefly with her brother, J. C., who was at Columbia University in a naval officers' training program. We heard Fred Waring and his Pennsylvanians, saw Times Square, Radio City Music Hall and the Rockettes, the Statue of Liberty, the Staten Island ferry, Grant's Tomb, and Riverside Church. On the Times Square subway, someone called out, "Snowbarger!" It was Elgin Purdy, in the Navy then, but from Kansas City and Bethany. We later knew him as a fine member of K.C. First Church. But once again, on the opposite coast, my cover was blown.

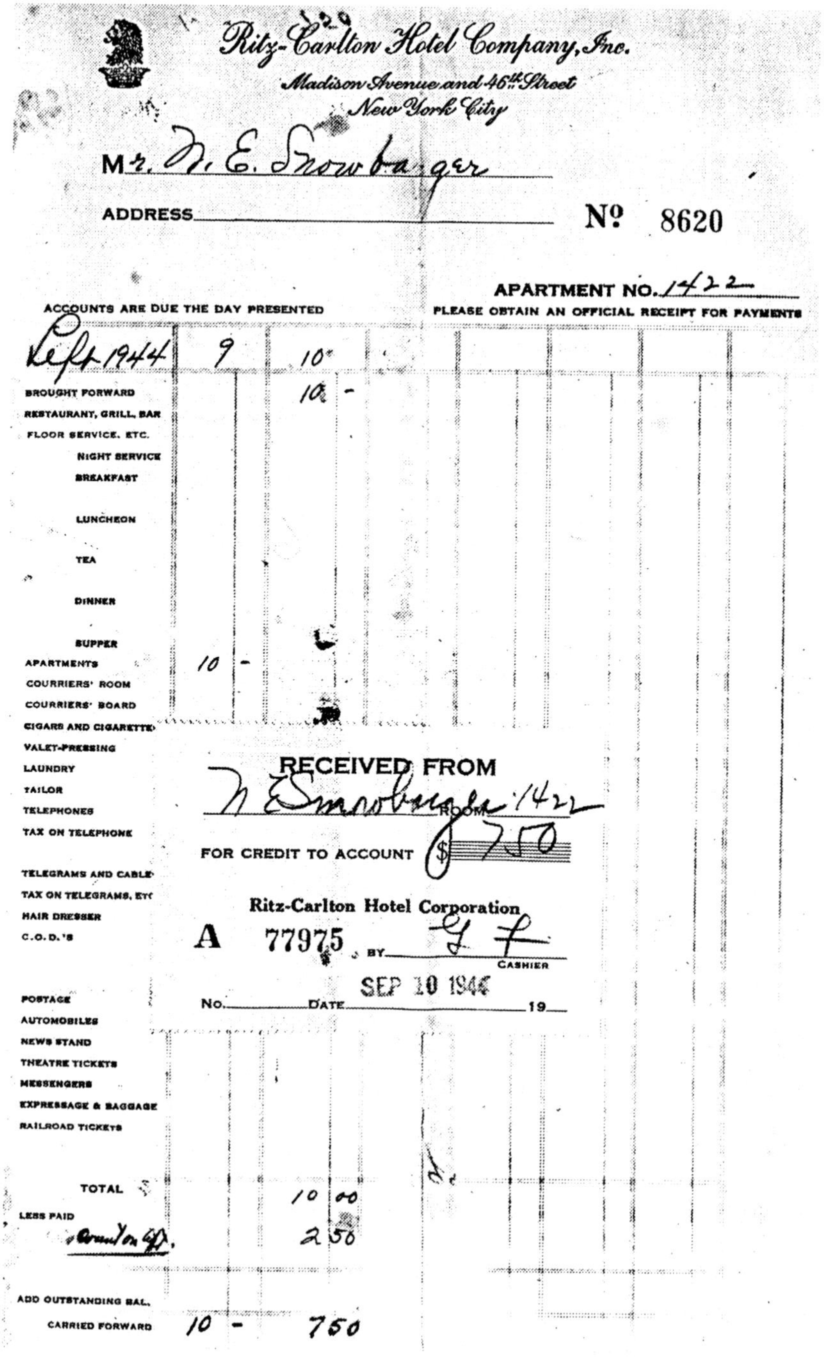
Ritz-Carlton Hotel Company, Inc.
Madison Avenue and 46th Street
New York City

Mr. N. E. Snowbarger

ADDRESS

№ 8620

APARTMENT NO. 1422

ACCOUNTS ARE DUE THE DAY PRESENTED

PLEASE OBTAIN AN OFFICIAL RECEIPT FOR PAYMENTS

Sept 1944	9	10
BROUGHT FORWARD		10 -
RESTAURANT, GRILL, BAR		
FLOOR SERVICE, ETC.		
NIGHT SERVICE		
BREAKFAST		
LUNCHEON		
TEA		
DINNER		
SUPPER		
APARTMENTS	10 -	
COURRIERS' ROOM		
COURRIERS' BOARD		
CIGARS AND CIGARETTES		
VALET-PRESSING		
LAUNDRY		
TAILOR		
TELEPHONES		
TAX ON TELEPHONE		
TELEGRAMS AND CABLES		
TAX ON TELEGRAMS, ETC		
HAIR DRESSER		
C.O.D.'S		
POSTAGE		
AUTOMOBILES		
NEWS STAND		
THEATRE TICKETS		
MESSENGERS		
EXPRESSAGE & BAGGAGE		
RAILROAD TICKETS		
TOTAL		10 00
LESS PAID		
a/c on 43		2 50
ADD OUTSTANDING BAL.		
CARRIED FORWARD	10 -	7 50

RECEIVED FROM N E Snowbarger ROOM 1422

FOR CREDIT TO ACCOUNT $ 7 50

Ritz-Carlton Hotel Corporation

A 77975 BY G F CASHIER

SEP 10 1944

No. DATE 19

What $7.50 Will Buy You

Another New England tradition was brought to us through the Training Station. They arranged for an authentic New England Clam Bake on the base on August 23. It was three days in preparation and we watched as they got the large rocks very hot, threw on a layer of seaweed, tossed in the cloth bags with a dozen clams, a lobster, onion, sausage, a potato, and an ear of corn in each, then covered it all with more seaweed, and let it steam. In the evening near the water's edge, we were all served a bag, brown bread, watermelon, and coffee (all for $2.50 per person). A wonderful memory of New England in the summer time!

To top it off, a real hurricane struck the New England coast just before I caught the troop train for Norfolk, the night of September 15. Nona and another navy wife drove out the next morning. They had trouble buying gas because the electricity was out and gas pumps were electrified. I had to ride the troop train with our personnel. I worried about Nona driving that distance not only because she was not that experienced as a driver, but they were two young girls traveling alone. They stayed overnight at Wilmington, Delaware and made it in good shape.

Wahnona stayed in Norfolk a few days, but, because I was to be in and out of port during shakedown and training, we decided that she should get back to college before it was too late (in September). She took a train back to Bethany. In mid-December she rejoined me for a couple of weeks. We had at least one additional apartment there (that would be number five). The big event was our overnight boat trip up the Chesapeake and Potomac to Washington, D. C. We had two days and one night in Washington before returning on the boat. We took in all the sights in Washington: Lincoln and Washington monuments, the Capitol, Smithsonian, Library of Congress, Pentagon, Lee's Mansion, and Arlington. We thoroughly enjoyed it all and decided we would return when we had the chance. Again, Nona was able to earn her fall semester's credit and to participate in many student activities. It was tantalizing to know that I was in the States, but on a very uncertain schedule. At any time, we might have headed rather quickly for the Pacific. By the time she should register for second semester, it was clear that I would not be stateside much longer. So Nona was to become a graduate with the Class of '45.

U.S.S. DULUTH (CL87)

Commissioning and manning a new ship was an interesting experience. Everything had to go by the book. Everybody was stiff and formal, not knowing the others well. Few of us had met the Captain. Safely in a U.S. harbor, all the rules of the peacetime Navy were in force. It was a different service than that we who were experienced in the war zone had known. One had no reputation to fall back on but it was a new beginning for everyone. The ship was totally up-to-date but unproven. The immediate task was that of provisioning and equipping it for a "shakedown" cruise. The personnel all had to be assigned and to learn their roles for housekeeping and for battle. Only a part of that could be accomplished on shore in Norfolk.

Our Captain was Donald R. Osborne, Jr., an Annapolis man who had most recently been in the Bureau of Personnel (BUPERS) in Washington, D.C. Like others who had previously had sea duty in their younger years, Capt. Osborne had looked forward to having command of a fighting ship in wartime. This was his chance and he wanted everything ship shape. Before going to sea, we did exercises in Chesapeake Bay. Those of us previously qualified for Officer of the Deck underway took our turns under the close observation of the Captain. He had to know his key officers well. He put us to the test in the safety of the Bay. When it came my turn, he threw the lifebuoy overboard, the signal for "man overboard" drill. The crew was aware that from the sighting of the buoy, to reporting to the bridge, through the whole rescue, it was a time test. How long would it take to get the man (buoy) back on board? The answer was "About ten minutes." And that was not good.

In task force operation, the situation was handled by calling (on voice radio) the nearest following destroyer (which would be on the outside perimeter of the force), requesting them to pick him up. Thus, you would not disrupt the formation nor endanger the other large ships near you. So I had to go back to my Rules of the Road in Midshipmens' School to remember all the orders required to meet the Captain's expectations when we were operating alone. "Stop all engines!" "Left full rudder!" (The man was over the port side; we didn't want our own propellers to chop him up.) Notify the Captain. Have the Boatswain's Mate Call over the speaker system, "Man Overboard portside," the signal to throw over lifebuoys to the victim. "Hoist the Man Overboard Signal." Call away the port motor whaleboat (when manned lower it into the water). It was quite a picnic for everyone except me. By turning to port, I was headed for the shore (not far away). The boatswain's mate and signalmen did fine. The motor whaleboat crews had barely been named. It was not a bad performance except that it seemed an eternity before that whaleboat got to the man (buoy). Everyone watching was determined not to fall overboard!

In the Navy you didn't make excuses, you just "got it done." But I took it personally. I was "pulling leather" as they say in the world of rodeo! I didn't get bucked off, but I was made to look bad. All but one key part of the team did very well; but the division responsible had not organized the boat crew. It was a good test even though it was artificial so far as winning the war was concerned. A new crew probably had other blind spots and lapses to be discovered and corrected. Obviously, I remember this as a blot on my record. It is quite possible that no one else thought of it that way. Six months later when we stopped over in Hawaii, the Captain arranged an interview for me at Admiral Nimitz' headquarters. It was a privilege to see the underground, secretive situation room. Nothing came of the supposed job but perhaps the Captain did not blame me for the man overboard debacle after all.

We took our shakedown cruise October 25 to November 23 going to the Gulf of Paria. This is a body of water off the coast of Venezuela. It was possible to run anti-submarine nets between the string of islands that surround the gulf making it safe for us to run tests and tryout our equipment. We had speed runs, fired all our guns, and made sure that the ship was able to operate as designed. It was also good training for the personnel as they became familiar with the equipment and installations. A checklist of items that needed to be corrected was kept and the company that built the ship or the Navy yard was required to correct the problems before we left for the war zone. Port of Spain, Trinidad was the only place for liberty. I got ashore at least once. We got to drive around the Island a bit. The asphalt lake and some beautiful beaches were the principal attractions. There was limited shopping in Port of Spain. Early birds were able to buy some nylons for a wife or girlfriend, but they were sold out when I got there. On the return to Norfolk we stopped briefly at San Juan, Puerto Rico and at Guantanamo Bay, Cuba.

We went through a twenty-four hour General Quarters on the way back to Norfolk and ran straight through a hurricane off Cape Hatteras on November 21 and 22. In General Quarters, everyone is at his battle station with watertight doors all closed. This severely limits the ventilation. I had my turn as Officer of the Deck and had to make my way from the turret aft on the ship to the bridge. With limited ventilation and terrible pitching and rolling, I was green with seasickness but I made it to the bridge to take my turn. The others looked me over and said, "Go on back to your battle station." I went back, hanging on for dear life as green water swept over the main deck. We experienced heavy seas as we went into the storm. Then after a calm in the eye of the storm, we had to come out on the other side. Coming out was just as rough as going in. We stayed in General Quarters for the twenty-four hours and had an unusually thorough shakedown!

After an Admiral's white glove inspection and various repairs and adjustments, the *Duluth* proceeded to Newport, RI for precommissioning training of crews destined to serve on similar ships when they were completed. This lasted from December 12, 1944 to March 1, 1945. Now we were the "old salts," helping the recruits learn about light cruisers as we paraded up and down Long Island Sound. We took six different crews of 200-300 men for a week of such training. That permitted another trip to Boston and another to New York City on a weekend. I was assigned to a ten-day catapult school in Philadelphia since I was to be the chief catapult officer. That gave me another stopover in New York City and New Years' Eve in Philadelphia (alone). I stayed in the Bellvue-Stratford Hotel, another prestigious address. The Officers' Club there was staffed by high society gals. They were nice to talk to but their ideas seemed stilted and unreal to a kid from Kansas. It was nice to see "the city of brotherly love." It was my first time to see the New Year in with the crowds of a big city. I watched from the safety of my hotel window.

On March 2, 1945 the *Duluth* went to Norfolk and on April 7 we left for the Panama Canal Zone, taking gunnery practice at nearly every designated, barren island en route. I had actually been out of the war zone for a whole year, although most of it counted as sea duty. We got to go ashore in Panama City and the transit of the Canal was a nice experience. But, once we were again in the Pacific heading west, things got a bit more sobering. We had only a short stop over in Hawaii before heading for Ulithi in the Western Pacific.

During our trip west through the eastern Pacific, Captain Osborne loved to call an anti-submarine drill to test the readiness of the watch. He had decided to select a team of only four or five to stand Officer of the Deck watches underway. The remainder of the gunnery officers was assigned to four-hour watches on the anti-aircraft batteries. My watch station was in a gun director for the five-inch battery. These guns were also used for the anti-submarine drills. The instructions were, when a submarine was reported on the starboard side, we were to train out on the beam, elevate to zero, load and fire. To those of us who had been in the war zone, this was total foolishness but we complied. Within ten seconds, we could get off a round - harmless because we were not with other ships. In task force formations it would never be done because of risk to other friendly ships. Its only value was to be sure the watch crews were alert.

I was the Third Division Officer with about sixty men and two other officers under me. It was similar to the Third Division on the *U.S.S. Washington*. We had two six-inch turrets to man as our battle stations. We had two seaplanes to launch and recover and we were responsible for the fantail of the ship for upkeep and mooring. At some point, I was switched to Combat Information Center, a nerve center where all voice radio, radar, lookout information came in and where a plot of that information was kept. We tracked our own combat air patrol, friendly ships, as well as bogeys for the information of the Captain and gunnery officers. By the time we were to Ulithi, my battle station was in CIC where it remained the rest of the war. I suppose my experience on the *Washington* was greater than that of others, our six-inch main battery was never fired, and probably the Captain gained a new appreciation for CIC as he eased into the Task Force mode of operation. In any case, we had 100% effectiveness - no bogey ever got into our formation or within range of our anti-aircraft guns without our giving the officers warning and the guns being on the target ready to commence firing. We had no damage from enemy fire on the *Duluth*. The Captain gave me his personal congratulations.

The *Duluth*, was not the happy, confident ship the *Washington* was. We had wonderful people. They were able and we knew our jobs well. But no one seemed to be able to gain the trust or respect of Captain Osborne. We all felt that we were under suspicion, failing, or about to be reassigned. It is one thing to keep people on their toes; quite another to build a "taut ship." The Captain should have relaxed, but he became a bundle of nerves.

He was later relieved in Tokyo Bay and the new Captain Samuel W. DuBois put everything back on a more normal set of watches and assignments. We had a great crossing when we returned from Tokyo to Bremerton. I was back in the rotation as Officer of the Deck. Osborne couldn't relax because the relaxed, reservist navy must have struck him as all wrong. He had ordered the ship to scrape the paint and shine the bright work (door knobs and kick plates) the very day the surrender of the Japanese was announced. That order was foolish, struck all the draftees wrong, and was rescinded the next day. He wanted the Navy of the twenties (when he had his first command) as well as a WWII fighting ship. His junior officers knew he couldn't have both. If he realized this he dared not to admit it. He must have been a nervous wreck.

Arriving at Ulithi in the western Caroline Islands, there was a sight not to be matched anywhere in the world. A huge anchorage, made safe from submarine attack by coral reefs and safety netting. It seemed to have a diameter of thirty miles or more. Most of the Pacific naval forces were there; tankers, sub-tenders, minesweepers, supply and ammunition ships, carriers, battleships, cruisers, destroyers – all of these and more. Then a blinker message came from the far side of the anchorage. It was for me from Lieut. Charles Browning. I invited him over to the *Duluth* for dinner, because he could get a boat easier than I could. He came and we had a wonderful visit. He was a good friend at Bethany. What a joy and who would ever expect such a contact six thousand miles or more from home! Vernon Hodges, a friend from Bresee and Bethany days, was a meteorologist but I missed when I tried to contact him in Hawaii. He was on Kwajalein but we did not go that way. Seeing friends in far away places unexpectedly has continued, even more so in connection with my education career and the college and church connections.

The *Duluth* was in Ulithi about one week, then was assigned to a unit operating off Okinawa and later was attached to the Third Fleet under Admiral Halsey. The Admiral wanted to hold position in order to launch air strikes in support of our troops on Okinawa when, in spite of adequate warnings, he took us straight through a terrible typhoon. Being in CIC, I heard all the voice radio messages from picket ships warning of the severity of the storm. Now we were in it, losing men overboard, frantically warning of the need to change course. But Halsey wouldn't listen. A day or two later, the papers in the states were talking of carriers with the corners of their flight decks draped down, the "suburb of *Pittsburgh*" sighted (sixty feet of the cruiser's bow that broke off), carrier flight decks swept clean of the planes. It was a horrible mistake. The air support was not given. Men were lost, and several ships were out of action completely for some time. The *Duluth* was among the ships requiring attention. The *Pittsburgh* and its bow were returned to Guam. I had seen the buckling of deck plates on the *Duluth*. They were finally stabilized during the storm by brave men (especially those on the bow side of the buckle) who welded angle irons across the buckles securing them to both sides of the damage until the decks were stiffened. There were creases on the outer shell of the ship as well. One could see that one more wave with the right angle and intensity could have torn off our bow too. They had one or two floating dry docks in the port of Agana and were able to make us seaworthy in about three weeks.

Meantime, we got to see the state of the war first hand. Guam had been retaken almost ten months earlier but there were still Japanese soldiers who had not surrendered. There was an occasional sniper, a prowler near the trash barrels, and the tracks of those trying to subsist off the leftovers. Also, you would think that the whole island would sink because of the acres of tanks, jeeps, artillery, fuel dumps, trucks and amphibious craft that covered the island. Here were the materiel and supplies that would support the attack on Japan. We also saw B-29's loaded heavily and taking off for runs on Japan. We got back in action supporting the last battle for Okinawa. All that we saw and heard about Iwo Jima and Okinawa said the Japanese would be desperate but never give up in a fight for their homeland.

Far from a concern for Japanese lives, they would fight to the death and to the last man. This is important intelligence to consider when the

71

atom bomb was finally tested. We fully believed then, and I do today, that the estimate of 1,000,000 American casualties in an assault on the Japanese homeland was conservative. From past experience, that would likely mean an additional 2,000,000 Japanese casualties. This would mean that the dropping of two atomic bombs, shocking the Japanese into surrender, saved not only the American lives, but hundreds of thousands of Japanese lives as well. It's a horrible numbers game, but the hindsight of those who did not experience the war seems to look only at part of the calculation: that which actually happened, not the alternative which was avoided. Whether in war or other tough decisions, I have been repelled by those who can only express outrage or denunciation. To me, fairness always requires a careful weighing of the real alternatives based on knowledge available at the time to the decision-makers. The Japanese had an alternative on December 7, 1941. They made a bad mistake. Harry Truman got no indication but that they would continue to fight to the last man even when the cause had been hopeless. It had been hopeless for more than a year on September 2, 1945.

Near War's End

To close out the war, the *Duluth* and her task force were back near Okinawa, dodging three more typhoons, and, after the Japanese surrender, taking up station under the airlift route of occupation forces. Along the route from Okinawa to Japan, a U.S. ship was stationed about every twenty miles. Should a plane go down, we were ready to rescue survivors quickly. Our forces would accept the surrender and take over the military installations in Japan to be sure that order was maintained. The marine contingent from our ship was among those that took part in this occupation. We continued to be alert to the possibility that some Japanese units had not received the order or a submarine had not accepted the defeat. But the surrender was so complete and orderly that two weeks after the documents were signed, the *Duluth* was in Tokyo Bay and the first liberty party went ashore on September 16, 1945. It was my good fortune to be in that party;

my bad luck to be the senior of those officers not invited to go with the brass.

As senior officer among the junior officers, petty officers, and seamen going ashore, I was in charge and given orders to keep the men "together." There were two hundred of us and, as we reached shore, the streets were thronging with Japanese people. We observed heavily damaged buildings but stores were open. How do you keep these sailors together? I gave orders that the men were to stay together as divisions with their own petty officers. The petty officers were to make sure that every man got back to the boat dock by 4 p. m., the time the boats were to return us to our ships. I could not recognize many of our men from the sailors from other ships so the small group approach seemed to me the only way to comply. Well, all but four of our men were at the boat dock and returned the way we had planned. The other four had to hitch a ride with a boat from some other ship and all of them got back by about 19:30. But our Executive Officer was mad!

I got to go ashore at least one other time. We saw Tokyo. I headed for the Imperial Palace and saw the outside grounds close up. We found the Imperial Hotel, built to be earthquake proof by Frank Lloyd Wright. I roamed around in it unimpeded. We dropped in briefly on a Japanese drama; standing although we were offered seats. I shopped in a department store. Everywhere the Japanese were in awe. We thought that perhaps the military might be inclined to harm us but they were most respectful (one does not know what went on in their minds). The second time ashore, I took a train to Yokohama, their naval base. It was flattened. I sifted through rubble and got a few trinkets. Damaged and half-sunken ships were there. I got some fans and lacquer items there. On the train, I sat by a boy reading a book in English. I tried to talk to him but he was unresponsive, perhaps because he did not wish to venture into conversation, or maybe there was hatred. There were some stories of Japanese naval officers surrendering their swords to the first Americans they saw who would come to their homes. I did not encounter such an officer. MacArthur was very definite that there should be no "liberation" as in Europe; Americans were to behave themselves as gentlemen. I believe we made him happy on that point. I am sure that is why the Executive Officer of our ship was so unhappy about the freedom I gave our men. I still think I made the best of the situation.

On September 21, we got a new Captain, Samuel W. DuBois. On October 1, we left Tokyo for Okinawa to pick up some passengers, and on October 5, we began the trip back to Bremerton, Washington, to participate in Navy Day activities. I was returned to the O.O.D. rotation; in fact, the ship's character and morale changed overnight. We had an enjoyable crossing.

Even in August, 1945, our training officer wrote an article about the G.I. Bill of Rights. Especially on the trip home, we all talked about readjustment to civilian life. Some liked the security of the Navy and wanted to stay in the service. We talked about keeping up our National Service Life Insurance and got the advice of our shipmates who had experience in the insurance business. I wrote to Kathryn Ruth Howe, Fred Floyd, and one or two others for advice on graduate schools. Because I thought it was proper but not expecting much help, I also wrote my father. To my surprise, his response was prompt and went like this: "I was at a district advisory board meeting and saw Harold Reed. I shared your letter with him and he said . . . ." The point is that through my letter to my father, I got advice from the one who would be my employer upon the completion of my graduate work. I not only got his advice but I made a contact for future employment by consulting with my dad.

Once in the U.S. we were released according to a point system and I had lots of points. Others had more. I was detached on November 2, and reported to the Great Lakes Separation Center. With thirty-two days of accrued leave, I was released from active duty on of December 9, 1945. I took a Great Northern train from Seattle, a beautiful route. The train was crowded and we had to fight for a sandwich as we passed through a western station stop. It was a happy trip, however, because so many of us were on our way home. We arrived at Great Lakes on November 5 and I started for Sylvia on November 7 - a free man. I was officially authorized to wear four battle stars on my Pacific Theater of Operations ribbon and given my "Certificate of Satisfactory Service." I was still in the naval reserves and was to keep in touch with the service, but a chapter of my life was closed.

Naval service was a very important component of my life. I knew it at the time; I thought of it many times later. The lessons included:

1. **Knowing myself, strengths, weaknesses, interests, abilities,**
2. **An openness to try new things and meet new people, assuming the best in others,**
3. **I knew I would hold together in the midst of crisis,**
4. **I developed a spirit of "can do;" the impossible only takes longer,**
5. **I learned the chain of command, span of control, and organizational wisdom that many never learn,**

6. **I learned to give orders with clarity, without timidity,**
7. **I gained experience in working with ordinary "grunts," and appreciating everyman, not just the bright, privileged, and elite,**
8. **I was no longer regional in my approach to things; I was American with a global outlook,**
9. **I was a gentleman: you don't chew gum in public, eat while walking down the street, you greet people you meet, you dress neatly, use correct table manners, you keep your word, you don't cut the line,**
10. **Great things happen when you make a request or apply. Just ask,**
11. **I learned to lead, work out solutions to problems with resources on hand, and organize people to accomplish a goal on time.**
12. **On the negative side, as well as positive, military experience may have accentuated tendencies towards perfectionism and an impatience with incomplete or shoddy work, both my own and that of subordinates.**

John Keegan, the British historian referred to the Second World War as "the largest single event in the history of mankind." Tom Brokaw says "The Greatest Generation," long silent on the subject, is now saying, "Whatever else I did in my life, I did that. I had a part in something that was larger than our ability to understand it." No way would I have missed that great event which has turned the world upside down and inside out.

NOTES

I have relied on Navy documents (orders, travel requisitions, letters of promotion), letters saved by my mother, History of the *U.S.S. Washington*, *The Capstan*, (Midshipmen's School at Notre Dame), *A Short History of the U.S.S Duluth*, and various shipboard newsletters. Fletcher Pratt's "The Fighting Machine: The Story of the U. S. Battleship *Washington*," *Harpers*, (March, 1945), pp. 359-368, is a flattering but accurate work. "The Biggest Decision" by Robert James Maddox in May/June (1995) issue of *American Heritage* (Vol. 46/Number 3) has pictures and a narrative of Tokyo at the end of the war just as I saw it. Since I later studied naval history and international relations, these fields of study undoubtedly influence my interpretation of the experiences I relate. My naval career also influenced my choice of these studies.

CH. VI WAHNONA'S WAR YEARS

"Separation"

There is a beautiful ceremony built into weddings centering on the unity candle. We did not use that in our wedding ceremony. It was not so common then. Upon reflection, I always have a problem after the center candle is lighted. Usually, the individual candles are extinguished and only the single candle remains to give light. I don't think so! Of course, it is the union we celebrate but what is extinguished is not so clear. Ambitions, hopes, aspirations may continue to be quite individual. In Nona's instance, her letters to my parents while I was away contain clues to her anxieties quite different from mine but natural and laudable. She is entitled to her space and her goals even though my career was to dominate in the beautiful life we shared together for more than fifty years. I celebrate the musician, artist, homemaker, teacher, mother, and devoted Christian she was.

From San Francisco in February, 1943, she took the bus to Modesto where Ray and Eula Merle Simpson were stationed. After two or three days, she boarded a train for Sylvia to spend some time with my folks before making her home at 501 West 10th, Dallas with her folks. She was somewhat bored but worked at the church office, saw Adana and Roxie Ann Moore occasionally, and wrote lots of letters. At first my letters were a long time in reaching her and came in bunches. Later, she got them quite regularly and they were only five or six days enroute. Her letters were varied and newsy but mine were censored and devoid of detail. She surely suspected that we were in Hawaii when I sent her a package or two and bought myself a watch (which I later learned she intended to give me as a surprise).

She had intended to lay out of school during spring semester, 1943, but when she discovered she was pregnant, she had to assume that the hiatus might be much longer. She was fearful that she might have to sacrifice her organ lessons and music degree. That was a serious concern because she was very intent on completing these studies. We had talked about the importance to her of preparing to support herself (and possible children) should something happen to me. That was to be our "insurance policy." More than that, she was to have a life! She was talented. Her contributions were needed. The pregnancy did, in fact, threaten those plans. It took a month or so for her letters to reflect her solution to that kind of challenge. She was back to the premarital argument for going ahead with the marriage no matter the uncertainties of wartime. If my life were taken, she would have a reminder of me in the form of our offspring. She put everything in the Lord's hands; He would work it all out to His glory. That would be all right with her. No more concern for school. She was consumed with plans for the baby and that meant keeping herself in top condition. She would follow doctor's orders carefully.

In a letter to my parents on May 25, 1943, Nona wrote of a visit to the doctor. She had various aches and pains including headaches that worried them all. Apparently, on one trip to a shopping center she almost had trouble. Doctor said that she had almost miscarried. She appeared to be five months along (instead of three and one-half). "There's nothing to worry about except twins," the doctor said. But one month later (June 28), she wrote, Dr. Green has acted so indifferent and nonchalant about my case that I am becoming concerned. I found at my last interview that he has also been quite worried all the time but was handicapped to do anything because it was too early. I had gained 7½ pounds in those three weeks . . . ." Nona had felt movement but it was too early for X-rays to show anything. The doctor thought "my trouble is an excessive amount of water." So, he ordered a restriction on the intake of water. The rest of an eight page letter was about farm life, layette, baby clothes and diapers. The pregnancy was still on track, so far as Nona knew.

In a letter of July 7, 1943 (just nine days later), Nona wrote the following:

[Dr. Green] never had liked the way things were going . . . . There just wasn't anything to be done up until now . . . . It was time that we did something and the only thing we could do was to interfere and take the baby. He sent me to a maternity specialist to get his diagnosis and it was the same. He said we could let nature take its course but it wouldn't be but a matter

of two or three weeks until the water would break anyway and that the baby, nine chances out of ten, would be deformed. Both doctors thought it best to go ahead and take the baby.

Nona continues.

I can't tell you how disappointed and heart-broken I am. I'm sure you understand. I thought everything was all right and had made complete plans for everything. If Willis were only here - the Lord knows best but I can't keep from being disappointed and heart-broken. I'm in the hospital now waiting for Dr. Green. They will break the water and everything will proceed like a normal birth. There isn't any chance for the baby to live, of course . . . . I won't mention it to Willis until after the baby has been delivered and I am doing well . . . . But, pray for me please, because it's so hard to give it up when I've planned on it so much.

Mother Horger wrote on July 9 at Nona's request and told how with three doctors present, the membrane was punctured at 6:30 p. m. on July 8 and twin girls were delivered about noon, July 9. She said, "The babies were normal but the excess amount of water was causing Wahnona to be too large and the Dr. said it was pushing against her heart and eventually would cause heart failure." Nona already had constant pain near the heart. In her letter of July 13, she said "It did turn out to be twins. I'd given almost anything to be able to keep them. I didn't see them but they told me they were perfectly formed. I'm proud of that." Doctors assured her that the problem was unlikely to reoccur.

Nona immediately felt better and in the same letter of July 13, spoke to Velma of the likelihood that I would want her to return to school in the fall. This would put her back on the schedule we had planned before marriage. The change to a music major and a one semester sabbatical placed her on track to graduate in May, 1945. That was just one year later than the fast track for music majors. I got letters from Dr. C. B. Strang and Dr. S. T. Ludwig after she returned to Bethany assuring me that she was there, doing well, but missing me. She entered into activities, made high grades and was elected to Phi Delta Lambda and Who's Who in American Colleges and Universities. The recovery was fast and complete. Parents, in-laws, and friends gave remarkable support to a twenty-year-old who faced and overcame a tremendous challenge without any help from an absent husband.

When I received the news there was nothing to be done. Over the years we have sometimes second-guessed the decision. There are so many things done during pregnancies now that were not done then. This was before ultrasound. X-rays only reflected bone structure, hence the wait that doctors felt necessary. Couldn't they have just drained some water? Could one twin have been taken and the other (with normal water) have been saved? Why? My division officer censored my mail so he learned of the shock and was very helpful to me. Nona was right; she had put the entire pregnancy in the Lord's hands. Now He had given her plans back to her.

Nona had almost an additional full year of college work completed before my return to the States in March 1944. The college administration gave her the same consideration given servicemen so she could join me in Seattle for the month of April. She had to do her work and return to take her final exams. But she salvaged her full credit for the spring semester. She made that train trip to Seattle from Bethany only a few weeks after a naval officer's wife had been killed on a similar train trip. I was unable to accompany her on the return trip to Bethany even though I was ordered to the Dallas Naval Air Station and given leave so that I could be with her at Commencement time in 1944. By this time she was a seasoned traveler.

I have given the story of our stay in Dallas and in Newport, Rhode Island in the summer of 1944. That included travel to Boston and New York City. Nona returned to Bethany alone by train to resume schoolwork in September of 1944. That was a tantalizing semester because my ship was in and out of port on the east coast through all of the fall semester. She joined me in Norfolk, Virginia, for almost two weeks at the end of November and first part of December. That's when we had the fabulous overnight boat trip to Washington, D. C. She returned to Bethany to finish the semester and enrolled for her final semester. While I was still in the States, my assignment to the Pacific and leaving for the war zone meant that it was only good judgment for Nona to complete her degree and earn her B.F.A. in May, 1945 as she did. I was not able to be with her for her graduation; it came after V-E Day and things were moving toward the end of the Pacific war ever more rapidly. Nona lived again with her parents, worked at Republic National Life, and served as organist at Central Church of the Nazarene where Curtis Smith was pastor. By the end of the summer 1945, Japan had surrendered. I was still not back at home until the middle of November, 1945. Nona's widowhood was finally over.

Her Navy experiences, the separation, her pregnancy, and extensive travels, meant that upon graduation at age twenty-two, she was far more worldly-wise than most of her classmates. But she was the same, sweet girl I married more than two years earlier. And now we were ready to pursue our dreams together.

NOTES

Letters of Nona to my family and yearbooks from Bethany Peniel College are the primary sources for this chapter. Nona's mother also wrote one letter to my folks and one to me.

CH. VII GRADUATE SCHOOLS

"Knowledge is proud that he has learn'd so much;
Wisdom is humble that he knows no more."
William Cowper

The desire of every reservist on September 2, 1945 was to get home as quickly as possible and take up plans for life as a civilian. Little did we think of the terrible displacement of people and jobs that war's end necessarily brought. Gone were so many wartime jobs. Where were the peacetime jobs to be found? The products of wartime factories were spewed all over the world. No longer needed. Those workers did not want to move but their jobs were about to disappear. Could the economy absorb eleven or twelve million ex-servicemen? We hardly gave it a thought on the way east from Tokyo. One fellow did crow, "I will make $6,000 per year!" Those inclined to stay in the Navy seriously questioned his optimism. Sounded like a lot of money then. This reminded me of the little two bedroom house we looked at in Concord, California in 1948 that cost $10,000 and we could have had veteran's financing but decided against it. Still the terrible inflation we have suffered should not confuse our thinking. Where were we all to be occupied upon our return home? It was the GI Bill of Rights that was both imaginative and a sound investment that provided an answer. It was an educational and training program that has repaid its cost many times over through the higher taxes paid by returning veterans over the forty years that followed. Governments do not generally invest so well!

Some few veterans were discharged on points of service in time to enroll for the fall semester 1945. Most, like me, were not back in time to resume studies until spring semester 1946. I was at the University of Oklahoma

83

showing my documents to a veterans' adviser named Williams. As he looked them over, he exclaimed, "Man, you could go all the way through to your doctorate with this program!" He was so impressed that it struck me as an incredible opportunity. Incredible that the country would invest so much in me. All of my professors had struggled to get their doctorates. I was not all that sure I would go past the master's degree. Surely, it was presumptuous to head for college teaching; I had not even taught in high school yet. The federal government paid the tuition and required fees to the university and gave us the books and required materials needed to pursue our course of study. They also paid the university an additional capitation grant so that this great influx of students would not break the institutions who had to expand services and facilities. Educational institutions typically charge students less than the cost of instruction, so we jokingly say, "It is a case of how many students can you take at loss until you start to turn a profit?" The last entitlement period gave me the additional wonderful sum of $105 per month for subsistence. (I believe it was somewhat less during the first year.) It was a real case of "pennies from heaven." It would almost pay the rent and buy the groceries for two people. I quickly adjusted my plans to go for the doctorate.

Immediately upon release from the service, we had a marriage to build and a home to establish. There is a difference between a couple married nearly three years, traversing the continent, writing letters, taking in the sights, and a family making a home. Nona and I had never lived together for an extended period of time. Three months during the summer of 1944 was about the extent of it. And I had changed (more than she). It was more than uprooting that war forced upon us. I was entertaining doubts and facing uncertainties about my future that were unsettling. Nona was at a loss to know what was happening. As I look back on it, it was the result of the rapid-fire changes, opportunities, and disruption that our lives had undergone since my graduation from college. All of my unexamined beliefs, my religious commitments, my life plans were up for grabs. Some of my statements and questions were sacrilege to Nona, but she held steady and believed in me. I found the *Return to Religion* by Link at the Horger's home and it helped in a pragmatic way to settle me down. In a nutshell, Link observed that, after abandoning his faith and seeking to counsel others, he was advising his clients to raise their sights above themselves, work in the YMCA, work to improve their world, live by their principles. In other words, live as a Christian should live and it will solve many of your problems. Meantime, an unusually helpful group of friends in Norman helped me more than they will ever know. Nona got a job at the Naval Air Station and we had enough money to get by. Obviously, we could no longer eat at the best restaurants and spend weekends in the plush hotels as we did quite often during the war years. When apart we had no place to spend our money, now suddenly we had almost no money to spend. Nona had started on her P.H.T. degree (Putting Hubby Through). I am forever in her debt.

NORMAN AND OU

We settled at the University of Oklahoma in Norman. Somehow I had never been able to schedule a course in Economics during my undergraduate days. So I took that in the spring semester at OU. The professor had just returned from General Motors and I found his practical approach very helpful. I had little work in political science so I had enrolled in and finished a course in political parties while in the Navy. I decided to make government my minor on the master's program. American History was to be my major. Dr. E. E. Dale was a cowboy who went to Harvard and became a specialist on the American Indian. I took his class and got to know him. Perhaps the best teacher I ever had was named Malthaner, a man who spoke German as his native language. He had a three-hour summer class in German for Juniors, Seniors, and Graduate Students. We met in an un-air conditioned room at 7:30 a.m. and I believe all but maybe two or three of the thirty-five students who started that class completed it and passed their language exams. Only three hours of credit and we had a "reading knowledge!" It was enjoyable and he made it easy. I would say that, in general, my teachers at Bresee and Bethany were the equal to or better than the teachers at OU but I did not have any who were unqualified. In my minor, I took a course in International Law using the casebook approach. That was quite different.

Coming back to college, I felt so rusty and out of it that I wanted to audit classes in the first semester but the profs laughed at the idea. They assured me that it would come back to me. In a class on World War I, I was mortified when Professor Christian directed a question to me: "What was the cause of United States involvement in WWI?" I was flustered and blurted out "The submarine." To my relief, he agreed. Little by little I regained confidence and my ability to study. As I studied in the reading room of the library, every soul that moved got my attention. In fact I did remember more than I thought. Rebuilding study habits and getting my reading back up to speed was the urgent agenda for that year at Oklahoma.

I also settled my interest in diplomatic and military history (they go together). My adviser was William E. Livezey. He had written a book on Alfred Thayer Mahan, of "Seapower" fame. He even remembered my application for a scholarship before the war and asked why I had not asked for the largest scholarship they had. He said, "You might have gotten it, but, in any case, the applications would have been shuffled down. When an applicant is denied, he will be considered for a lesser scholarship." He took a liking to me. He told of his work as a deacon in the Presbyterian Church. He had a disgust for the task thrust upon him on Saturday nights to get any of their boys out of the bars and back to their rooms if they overindulged. He guided me to my study of "William H. Seward as an Expansionist." Many years later, I received a call from him. "Hey, Willis, are you going to the North Central Meeting at the Palmer House . . . could I bunk with you? The University pays a set allowance for convention expense and that will barely cover meals." Now he was Dean of the College of Liberal Arts at OU and we had opportunity for a lot of "dean's talk." The only argument we had over the thesis was over the use of a comma before "and" when connecting words in a series. I was firm in my belief that the conjunction rendered the comma unnecessary. He was dealing with a committee of readers, so I had to go through my entire master's thesis inserting the commas. Since that time I have been ambivalent and confused about the issue and have to correct myself frequently.

The other professor who helped me in a very important way was Max Moorhead, in Latin American history. He taught a very good course which was my first in that field. He also took students under his wing. When Walter Prescott Webb, author of *The Great Plains*, was to be a guest speaker one afternoon, Max told his class, "This should not be necessary. But if you have to miss my class this week in order to schedule Webb's lecture into your plans, skip my class." Not many teachers say such reckless things. I went to the lecture and to Max's class. But he was right and I remember as much from that lecture as I do from several whole courses. Incidentally, that was a trait of the GI students. We were much more serious about learning something than are younger students. In the fall of 1946, Max approached me this way: "We are building a good department here at OU. We now have twenty-eight doctorates in the history department but we do not use teaching assistants. If you want to get some experience as you move along, you might want to consider the University of California where I did my graduate work. If so, I might be able to give you some help."

The Norman experience was good for reentry into American life as we got to attend every football game, got to the Cotton Bowl, got to visit both the Snowbargers and Horgers, and got involved with the Norman Church of the Nazarene. This was Nona's home church before 1938 so lots of people knew her. E. E. LeCrone was the long time Sunday School Superintendent.

We rented an apartment from them. Willis French was Pastor for a few months before Geren Roberts was called. I had been elected to the church board and we had formed a pretty good male quartet (Ed Taylor, Jimmie Gilbert, Ed Eastwood, and I). Sam and Elizabeth House were there but attended another church in the morning and our church in the evening. The Taylors and Houses were classmates from Bethany days. Jimmie was in a management-training program at C. R. Anthony stores. One fellow wanted me to switch to law and we would set up practice together. Jimmie said, "I can get you into a management training program if you are interested. You can make $30,000 per year." The church was almost overrun with couples enrolled at OU and there was a lot of talent. Maybe that is part of the reason why the District Superintendent decided to start a new church on the west side. There were some older families in First Church who were a bit unhappy. But for the D.S. to begin a new work without talking to our pastor struck us as unwise. Mrs. Roberts spoke to some of us with unusual insight. "It's unfortunate because we expend so much emotional energy on this pending division that we need in order to do our work for the Lord in First Church." Obviously, I remember that statement and have thought of the role of leadership to direct the energies of people efficiently. We have just so much physical and emotional energy in a day: we should try to get the optimum result from it. I was told that Pastor Roberts said later, that never again would he rely on so many students (who were transient) to fill so many key roles in the congregation. They seemed to enjoy us at the time but we were all gone in two or three years. It was not necessarily best for the church.

I completed my master's degree in two semesters and one summer. I had encouraged Max Moorhead to put me in touch with the proper people at California, got my application and transcripts in, and wrote Ted Martin, pastor of the Berkeley Church of the Nazarene about housing. Ted said, "I'm leaving but my brother Paul is following me. Get in touch with him." We bought a '41 Buick from Jimmie and headed west via the southern route in late January 1947. My case was not fully settled at the University of California, we had no place to live, and everything we owned was in the Buick (hopelessly overloaded). But we were young, westerners at heart, and "headed west!" After a stop over at the Wolf's in Arizona and three ruined tires, we pulled in to Berkeley late at night.

BERKELEY AND CAL

Paul Martin had reserved a room for us at the Claremont Hotel in Berkeley "overlooking San Francisco Bay," as they used to say to introduce a radio show featuring the big bands of the 1930's. I had heard of it many times but was not prepared to be escorted to the tower bridal suite. As soon as the porter was gone, we searched feverishly to find the card specifying the nightly rate. There were three or four rooms, a breathtaking view of the Bay and Golden Gate Bridge. We could look down on the tennis courts where some of the pros practiced. I called the desk to say, "I didn't request the bridal suite!" I was assured that after eleven p.m. they had assigned all their rooms and that we would be charged only the basic double room rate. I still do not know, but it would have been Paul Martin's style to cut a deal like that for us and swear the hotel people to secrecy. If he were responsible, it would have been the first of many, many favors he did for us. It was the start of a special relationship that proved mutually satisfying and important to us.

Housing was very tight so we first had to settle for a single room efficiency apartment in a complex built for shipyard workers in Richmond. It was almost twenty miles from the campus but we could afford it and, after the Claremont, it was appropriately humbling. I got registered although certain issues were unresolved about my admission. There were no teaching assistantships open, but after all, we were arriving mid-year. So I settled in to do my best in a new system. It was two weeks after the start of the semester that I was notified to contact the history office concerning their need for a Teaching Assistant. So I was a T.A., got some additional monetary help, and it did not complicate a good start on my own program. About mid-March, I received a notice from the graduate office that they found two deficiencies in my undergraduate transcripts: no foreign language and no laboratory science. When I went in to talk about it, a sergeant type female assistant icily said, "We find no trace of this Bresee College." I told her that it did not exist now; that it had merged with Bethany-Peniel. She had no response nor a suggestion except that I would not have to take these courses until the fall semester since usually one started a language or lab science in the fall and took a complete year of each. I told her, "I have ten hours of French and ten hours of Chemistry. I will write to the Registrar at Bethany, asking him to give you an explanation of the merger and custody of the records." She just threw up her hands, said nothing and I left. Late in April, I received a notice from the Graduate Office: "Your deficiencies have been waived." I was tempted to go in to tell her that I did not ask for a waiver, I had taken the courses. But, since neither Bethany nor Bresee were accredited, and, to the best of my knowledge, only Mattie Bracken had come from BPC to ask admission at Berkeley before me, perhaps I should let well enough alone. This was the application of the lesson learned in the Navy. Ask and good people will often listen to reason. But after all, I had graduated "summa cum laude" and had completed my master's degree before that affront.

I had done another thing that worked in my interest. I noticed that Frederic Logan Paxson had a seminar on Western American History. He was retirement age, the best in his field, and chairman of the department. My presence in his seminar when they found that they had a need for another T.A. made it easy for him to discover me and solve his problem. He knew almost all of my professors at Oklahoma. The departments had mutual respect that made it easy for a transferring graduate student. At Cal, they did not insist on taking any particular courses; you simply had to prepare for your "prelims." They defined about a dozen fields in the history department and we had to pick five in which to write comprehensive exams. The major field and a non-history minor were to be covered in an oral exam near the end of our program. When I thought I was ready, I signed up to take the written preliminary exams. Most of us followed the advice of an advisor who counseled us about the work we had taken and what it would be wise to take at Cal. I took "Historical Method" at Oklahoma and they did not think it necessary to take it at Cal. I audited it because Ernst Kantorowiscz was the teacher. He taught: "Look at history as God looks at history." Later, he would not sign the loyalty oath because he felt it violated his academic freedom and civil rights. But, he explained, "I fought the Communists in the streets" before migrating to the United States. He was a great man. As I started to say, man for man, I found myself in perhaps the strongest history department of those years and their requirements were most reasonable. It is still unlikely that I could have finished in shorter time in any other graduate school.

During these years I needed the counsel and help of Uncle Alvin and Aunt Florence Aller. I had lived with them at Bresee during my freshman year in high school. They moved to Idaho to teach at NNC. He and I went on active duty in the Naval Reserve on the same day in 1942. He returned to graduate studies after the war and they lived in Corvallis during the time we lived in Berkeley. We spent a short vacation with them in Oregon in 1947 and in 1948 they met us in the Bay Area and we drove together to visit relatives in Kansas. I got a newer car in Kansas and we drove both cars back to California where I could get more for my Buick. Nona and Florence were together and Alvin and I were in the other car. There was plenty of time to talk: a botanist to an historian. Each of us was a devout Christian, making our way through graduate school, being intellectually honest, and preparing for careers in a Nazarene college. "What do you make of the biblical record of the Flood? How do you keep the Sabbath when in graduate school? What about the theory of evolution?" In five or six days of traveling together, sharing without fear of consequences, I had the opportunity of a lifetime to refine my thinking on subjects usually left to lonely struggle. Our lives in other dimensions settled into place rather quickly.

These Berkeley years were some of the best of our lives. Foremost, there were Paul, Monica, and Michael Martin - pastor and family. The Berkeley Church of the Nazarene was the second oldest in the denomination. There were some fine families there and I was elected to the church board before many months there. We participated in the music and Sunday School. But Paul Martin was the central attraction. We needed them and they needed us. It took no time to get acquainted and by the General Assembly of 1948, they turned the parsonage (high in the Berkeley hills) over to us to baby sit their dog, Mitzi. Michael was in pre-school, learning French and other surprising subjects. (He was later to graduate from Cal at fifteen and become a professor of composition in their music department.) On Sunday evening after church, Paul would say, "Well, the Sabbath is over," whip out the Sunday paper, and whiz (with us) over to a restaurant. Wherever you rode with Paul at the wheel, you "whizzed." One evening we met them at the parsonage and he drove down from the hills to Richmond to speak at a youth banquet. By the time we arrived, I was as sick as a dog and could not eat. His cars did not last long either. They were lifelong friends of ours. Paul had just finished his Master's degree in philosophy and his ministry was ideal for me as a graduate student. The Northern California District was a very attractive part of the church at that time under the leadership of Dr. Roy Smee. Beulah Camp (near Santa Cruz) was beautiful and had excellent camp meetings.

We moved from Richmond to Albany, to El Cerrito, to Berkeley, finally settling in with the Warrens at 3044 Benvenue, just south of the University. At that time, this was an ideal place to live and Berkeley boasted police force composed of all college graduates. In 1950, Vincent had gotten into some snail poison spread along the sidewalk; we rushed him to the Berkeley hospital emergency room where they pumped his stomach to be on the safe side. There was no charge for emergency services like that. We went to every home football game. Students sat on the east side (with the sun in our eyes), but we also had a magnificent view of the Bay and Golden Gate Bridge. We had Jackie Jensen, a triple threat man who could run, pass, or kick when he got the ball. I believe that Cal went to the Rose Bowl three straight years in that era. Lynn (Pappy) Waldorf was our coach. The fog which rolled in through the Golden Gate at about 4:00 p.m. every day was our air conditioning system. It got quite cool every evening. Nona never got her wardrobe adjusted to the climate in the two and a half years we were there. We did not have time or money for much entertainment, but there were exciting things to do in Oakland and San Francisco. When company came, we always had to take them to Telegraph Hill and Fisherman's Wharf. And so much more!

There were other members of the Berkeley Church whose friendship we valued highly. Harold and Peggy Latham were there and we met again when they were in the suburbs of Chicago before a long tenure as district superintendent of the Georgia district. Peggy's mother was our Sunday School teacher. Henry Smits was an undergraduate student at Cal and after seminary became a teacher of philosophy. The Stu Holcombs were close friends with whom I lived a couple of months after Nona left for Dallas. George Coulter came as our District Superintendent of the Northern California district in the middle of our stay in that part of the country. Eugene Stowe was pastor of the Oakland church and Elwood Sanner was pastor of San Francisco 1st Church. I have had frequent contact with all of these through the years. Through Paul I had numerous reports on Pasadena College but they had no opening for me on the faculty.

We were very fortunate as to a method of financing graduate work with minimal distraction. We were tempted to find employment for me but with the G.I. Bill, four semesters of assistantships, and one as English history reader, we decided to keep a trim budget. Nona got a good job in the Engineering Projects Office, housed just across from the Library (on campus). The office processed the business, contracts, and payroll of the various corporate or government sponsored research projects on the campus. It was enjoyable work and the people were fine. Her boss took off at about 11:50 to go play the carillon bells in the Campanile Tower. I studied in the library a lot so we often had a brown bag lunch together. We would join fifteen or twenty graduate history students on a pleasant hillside. Some wives were usually present. We got to know our fellow graduate students very well. We loved the routine and the people. With about $100 per month from the assistantship, another $100 from the government, and Nona's income, we were set! They limited assistantships to four semesters but the readership in English History was about as lucrative and that gave me five semesters of help. When I had to get to Washington, D.C. for research on my dissertation, I got four weeks of active duty in the naval reserve assigned to the Naval Historical section. I was even able to get free transportation on Military Air Transport Service to and from. The Lord and the government did provide!

At Cal, I was fortunate to work as T.A. for Lawrence Harper and Walton Bean. That routine made me responsible for about 150 students in American History each semester. I never saw an objective test at Cal's history department. We generally had two or three mid-term tests and a two-hour final exam. I was responsible to meet six sections one hour each week for purposes of clarification, quizzes, discussion, and explaining the results of the tests. My duties were to attend the two lectures per week with the entire course enrollment, assist the lecturer, keep order, and monitor the tests. The professor in charge did the lectures, wrote the tests, and gave his T.A.'s guidance. After reading all the tests, we assigned grades and turned them over to the Professor. He was concerned about the grade distribution and the enrollments from semester to semester. Dr. Bean was very sensitive to a drop in enrollment and we told him, "You are out-guessing the class as you write the test questions and you keep them off-balance." Those tests were easy to grade, but the next time his questions were "down the middle - just what they expected" and the grades soared. I found it interesting to see how the profs worried over a drop from 450 to 400, when you would think that they could care less. Not so. George Guttridge had over 200 in his English history class. It was an upper division class and the competition was fierce. In that class, he gave three lectures a week and I graded the tests he wrote. One of my students was Virginia Warren, daughter of the Governor (and Chair of the Regents). I believe I gave her a C- on a first test and she came to see me. Her Dad would let her go on a trip to Europe the next summer if she had B or better in all of her subjects; how could she bring the grade up? We found a way. Really, there was no pressure. She later married the TV personality John Daly. Her dad went on to the Supreme Court! This was good experience for me. However, I began to second-guess myself when one of my buddies applied for (and got) a $2,000 scholarship. There he was in the library working on his dissertation and I was reading stacks of blue books. Mr. Guttridge would take my grades, look them over, and a day or two before they were due at the Registrar's office, he would say, "Don't turn them in until Friday; we've got to keep those fellows humble over there in the administration building."

I took seminars continuously with very fine scholars: Paxson – Western America, Kinnaird -Colonial North America, Guttridege - Modern England, Bisson - International Organization, Hicks - U.S. in the 1920's. I audited Constitutional History with Henry Steele Commager and Civil War with Kenneth Stampp. One of the first courses I took was "Economic Exploitation of Latin America" with Engel Schluiter. I got a B- on my first mid-term test and talked with the Reader. He showed me some of the work of other students and, sure enough, they gave him more complete answers. But I said, "I know this stuff, I just can't write that fast." He had nothing to suggest. So I started taking notes in lectures as nearly verbatim as possible. My writing suffered but, by semester's end, I was writing nearly twice as much in a one-hour test and I got an A for the course. If you know the material, that is one way to cope with tough competition. One of the questions on my prelim in Colonial America was, "Compare and contrast the systems for administration of colonies developed by the French, British, Dutch, Spanish, and Portuguese and the effect of those differences on the colonies in the Western Hemisphere." Why did they leave out the Swedes? I had foggy notions about what to say of the British, French, and Spanish (and just enough time) but how do you fake it when it came to the Dutch and Portuguese? I passed! I'll never know how or why. It was not a case of being unable to write fast enough that time.

John D. Hicks was a Godsend for me. He was writing the volume in the *New America Nation* series on the 1920s and welcomed me into his seminar. I soon asked him to direct my dissertation. After doing research for him on the Navy in the 1920's, I started to review all the literature on Hawaii, Pearl Harbor, and naval bases in the Pacific. After passing my oral exam, that was the only outstanding requirement. Nona and I took a few days to go to Yosemite National Park and then I plowed into the research. I sent Nona to Dallas with Paul and Monica when they were driving that way in early June 1949. Nona was pregnant so a trip with the Martins to her parent's house was a joy. My trip to Washington would separate Nona and I, so why not visit her parents? She also missed two-thirds of my trip to Olivet pulling a trailer that jerked at every bump. I stayed on in the Bay area until it was necessary to leave for Olivet doing all the research I could before plunging into course preparation for my teaching load at ONC. One had to write two or three chapters before approval of the topic was given, so I achieved that before leaving California. Meantime, four weeks of research in Washington, D.C. was made possible through the naval reserve active duty arrangements. Even though my topic was naval history, they still required me to work a bit on one of their projects. They were still trying to locate the exact location of the sinking of the *Monitor*, the Civil War ironclad. So I went to the National Archives, checked the towing vessel's log, and came up with the ten square mile guess that dozens of other researchers had reported. But I got no closer. Only when major sonar improvements were made did they finally locate it.

Along about the end of May, 1949, Dr. Hicks said, "Well, I think we've got a dissertation!" My topic was approved. Ninety percent of my time in Washington was spent on my topic and I made good headway. I needed the records of the meeting in 1903 of the General Board of the Navy. They told me it was still classified and unavailable (even to a navy lieutenant in uniform) but that I could appeal to the Joint Chiefs of Staff. So, I thought that surely someone there would hear my request and see its legitimacy. I appeared at the Pentagon and was received by a colonel who took thirty minutes to tell me "No." All was not lost, however. I learned of Army Historian Louis Morton's article that would soon be published. It gave me the information I needed. Another sidelight of that trip to Washington was that (much later) I submitted my dissertation draft to the Navy department as a courtesy for their help to me. When the draft came back, there was a notation in the margin of one of the pages. "This is not so! I was there D.R.O." The page had reference to some tense relations between the Navy and citizens of Honolulu in the 1920's. There was no mistaking the handwriting; it was Donald R. Osborne's. He was the Captain of the *Duluth* under whom I had served. He had been on a ship at Pearl Harbor at the time of the supposed problem. I had not seen him but apparently he was working in the records section.

I must tell of that trip from San Francisco to Washington and return. While I had business in Washington, I could ride MATS only on a standby basis. So I turned up at Moffatt Field and boarded a four-engine propeller plane at around 8 p.m. By the time we took off and circled over the ocean, it soon was dark. Flying the great circle route, we came close to the Canadian border and it began to get light shortly after 3 a.m. We flew eastward non-stop ten more hours over a patchwork of green, brown, and yellow from the Northern Rockies to the Atlantic on a flight that was the most impressive I ever made. It was like a magic carpet. Such a breadbasket. The prop plane was slow enough that one could take it all in. I got an appreciation for the U.S.A. on that trip that I have never gotten over. Then on July 4th, 1949, I was in Washington for the program and fireworks at the Capitol. Wow! Our flight home was at night. We stopped at Olathe Naval Air Station for fuel and had to wait for two or three hours because we blew a tire on landing. That was my second visit to Olathe.

They say the doctoral oral is like nothing you ever face again in your life. Well, facing a hostile accreditation review team can be as bad but what happened at my oral, should not happen, period. As a candidate, I could not do a thing about it. My chairman, Dr. Koerner, was quite neutral until Mr. Bisson began asking me about the situation in Korea (this is before the North Korean invasion of the south). He objected to Bisson's line of leading questions and tried to fight back by asking me "But what is happening in Hungary?" I could not think of what was going on in Hungary and wondered why he should ask. I should have guessed that his strong anti-communist feelings and accusations of Mr. Bisson being "pink" had something to do with it. It was a case of two professors fighting it out by throwing questions at me. You never want to be in that position. After the time was up, the candidate was asked to wait outside. I heard quite a bit of shouting inside and had to wait more than twenty minutes. Finally, they started filing out smiling and congratulating me but I had been through the wringer. Whew!

The spring and summer of 1949 were singularly eventful. It was most important that I pass my prelims and orals on the first go 'round. They were impossibly tough but I did it. With the Lord's help, with the politics of being known in the department as a T.A., by auditing, if not taking, lots of courses, by hook or by crook (scratch that) - we did it! The short trip to Yosemite was the only immediate reward, then it was back to work. Baby Vince was on the way; no room for error or delay. Others were not so fortunate. It had been a tremendous experience but we must get on with life.

I was impressed about the officing arrangements made for the history department at Cal. They used a room large enough to seat fifty students to locate about twenty desks with a side chair by each. There is one secretary's station and some filing cabinets. Each professor in the department was expected to assign himself three or four office hours per week and give the schedule to the secretary. Students, T.A.s, other professors could all learn when a professor would be in and that would be it. At a busy time, fifteen profs would be talking to a student at the same time in the same room and five students would be waiting. The professor who had no student with him would be reading and waiting. Most of the profs had carels or offices in the library but they met there with only their advanced students or other profs and guarded their privacy well. Also, I was impressed that each professor called the others "Mister." Schaeffer and Guttridge did not hold doctoral degrees so everyone was "Mr." They handled the language requirement in the department. I passed French by translating several pages of the constitutional debates. For the German, I was asked to translate the document that spelled out what we know as the Monroe Doctrine. Mr. Schaeffer called me in and opened my blue book. "For a fellow that knows as much German as you, you should know..." He proceeded to allow me to try again on a half a dozen sentences then passed me. He said, "You had too many errors but you translated three times as much as most of the students translated, so I'm passing you." Thank you very much.

I knew about forty-five to fifty doctoral students in history at Cal. In the intramural softball league, we were the old men but came in second only to the Phys. Ed. majors, whom we thought should have been excluded from intramurals anyway. I played left field and threw a few out at home plate. On weekends we checked out athletic equipment for our own ball game and also had a picnic supper. Most of these fellows were veterans. I think there were three women in the group. This crowd studied seven days a week and drove hard to complete as early as possible. But we all pulled for one another. I shared a T.A. office with Bob Burke (U. of Washington) and Boyd Huff (Gonzaga). Other good friends and the school they went to were: Ed Liewin - New Mexico; Don Cutter - USC; Pinckney - Oregon; Madsen -Montana; Miller- Sacramento State; Clark Chambers - Minnesota; Charles and Barbara Jelavich - Indiana. There were classmates from Pennsylvania, Wisconsin, North Dakota, Arkansas, Florida State, Los Angeles State, and San Jose State. Most of these had put their church relationships on hold but spoke frankly with me about religion. Mrs. Liewin had attended NNC. As my Uncle Alvin Aller observed about his fellow graduate students at Oregon State, we tried to do in six days a week what others had seven days to do. But I faced no adverse discrimination. I saw several of them and several of my professors at historical association meetings in the first few years after graduation.

CH. VIII ON THE JOB MARKET

**"Behind me is infinite power; Before me is endless possibility;
Around me is boundless opportunity; Why should I fear?"
Unknown**

The tradition of graduate schools was that each professor took a few students under his wing as they enrolled in his seminar. In 1948 there were no women on the graduate faculty in history at Berkeley, so I use the male adjective advisedly. In the seminar the graduate student researched a segment of the larger work the professor might be pursuing (in my case, "The U.S. Navy in the 1920's"). When a student finished doctoral work, the professor did his best to place his graduate in a university where, hopefully, he would have a chance to start a seminar of his own, and reproduce after his kind in a scholarly field.

Dr. John D. Hicks was well placed to find openings but, with six or eight GI's finishing at nearly the same time, he had his hands full. In fact, some of them chose to stay at Berkeley another year awaiting a better opportunity. Dr. Hicks suggested that if no university job materialized, a good liberal arts college would be his next choice. He reasoned that teachers' colleges and engineering schools treated history only as general education. Liberal arts colleges offered history and history majors as valuable for history's own sake. He was the first (but not the last) to speak to me of the parallel relationship of Northwestern to the north and Olivet to the south of Chicago. He told of being a Methodist preacher's son who attended a Methodist college (Northwestern) when it was about the size of the Olivet of that time. (This was all the more remarkable when he told me that his father was asked not to return to his Nebraska Methodist post when he failed to preach "holiness.") With this background, he was very

97

encouraging when I aroused some interest from Olivet through my own efforts. But I am getting ahead of myself—I am still in Berkeley.

In February of 1948, Dr. L.T. Corlett had written me about taking a position at Northwest Nazarene College. The position was held by Prof. F.C. Sutherland who was hoping to return to China. My classmate, Ed Taylor, was the second man in the department and he invited us to be their guests for Thanksgiving weekend, 1948. We had a wonderful visit and an offer was forthcoming very promptly. They were pressing for a reply; the Regents even elected me. Sometime in March, 1949, I said "Dr. Corlett, you really don't have a place for me. My friend, Ed Taylor, is offering to go to graduate school next year but he really would prefer to wait another year or two. I would be taking his job." Dr. Corlett replied, "No, you would be taking Prof. Sutherland's place as he returns to China." Then I turned prophet and said, "Oh, but Dr. Sutherland is not going to return to China." I was anticipating the Mao Revolution although I could not foresee the details. NNC's history department remained the same in the Fall of '49 as in the Fall of '48. It was very nice to be wanted even if the pay would have been only $250.00 per month.

Meantime, Dr. Hicks found interest in me at the University of Arkansas, Washington State University, and Southern Oregon College of Education (Ashland), and may have had something to do with a letter encouraging me to apply at the U.S. Naval Academy. I really had about all of the Navy I wanted so I did not follow up on that one. (In retrospect, I should have asked more about what they had in mind; the man they hired at that time was permitted to write the biography of Chester Nimitz. I admired him and would have loved to have the opportunity to write such a book. Nimitz declined having such a book written before his death.)

I believe I might have had the job at the University of Arkansas since one of the groomsmen at my wedding, William Henry Harris, was in the philosophy department there. He was pulling all the strings on that end. Another friend of mine at Berkeley was also after that job. They wanted someone to teach U.S. and Latin American history. The other fellow had more credits in Latin American history and may have known some Spanish so he was hired. If I had gotten myself down there at my own expense, I am quite sure I would have landed that job.

Of Dr. Hicks' suggestions, only Southern Oregon College invited me to visit their campus. Nona and I drove through Northern California, stopped at Humboldt State College in Arcata, California. The Dean there wanted to hire me on the spot but the budget would not permit. At Southern Oregon, we were in the Rogue River valley, one of the beauty spots of the world. They wanted me to come, offered a ten month contract, and wanted an answer within a month. It was a teacher training college, normally they would want me to teach in the summer sessions—that would increase the starting pay to $4,000.00 per year. Since I had to have at least three months in the summer of 1950 to finish my dissertation, it was a long way from home, and would give limited opportunity to do research or attend conventions, I turned it down. Two offers, two turn downs, still no job.

I had written to my former professors like Chester Crill (Pasadena College), John Peters (Oklahoma City University), E.C. Hall (Central State University)—all were making inquiries but not striking pay dirt. Washington State wanted me but could I wait a year (the budget won't allow it this year)? With an uncle on the faculty in sociology at Bethany Nazarene College, I did not contact them and they did not contact me.

Now for the sequence of contacts that brought us to Olivet Nazarene College. Sylvester T. Ludwig, former college president at Bresee College and Bethany-Peniel College, became General Secretary of the Church of the Nazarene in 1944. He was also given the job of Secretary of the Department of Education, a position largely without a history. The educator in him caused him to want to stay connected to the colleges. (This information is interesting to me since I was to succeed him in that office in 1965.) In December, 1948, S.T., whose wife, Clara, was my father's second cousin and who came from my home church, wrote me stating that they had been at Pleasant Hill church the previous Sunday, got my address from my father, and he was interested in compiling a list of prospective teachers for Nazarene colleges. Nazarene college presidents sometimes asked him for leads. In a postscript, he wrote: "Frankly, I would like to see you on our campus at Olivet Nazarene College...." I had already written to ONC and Dr. Selden Dee Kelley, the president, had responded promptly but was unsure of their needs. I wrote a former Bresee teacher of mine, Kathryn Ruth Howe, then head of the Education Department at ONC. She was unsure what Prof. L.A. Marquart would do when his leave of absence was finished. As it turned out, Prof. Marquart did not return for the Fall Semester of 1949 and Dr. James Garner was no longer there in Political Science. Dr. Kelley (January 4) and Dorothy Ellwanger, his secretary (February 7), kept me on the string as Dr. Kelley's health deteriorated. Finally, on April 28, I heard from Dr. C.S. McClain and an offer was wired to me on May 2, 1949. Dr. Kelley had passed away and Dr. Paul Updike, Chairman of the Board, worked with the Administrative Council to make preparations for the coming school year. I was to have no duties in the summer months of 1950 so that I could complete my dissertation, no moving expense reimbursement. The list of courses I was to teach reached me May 31.

Upon reflection, Dr. L.T. Corlett and Dr. Selden Dee Kelley, by contacting me in November of 1948, were ahead of the field and faithfully kept in touch with me. They were trying to persuade me to enter one of the most challenging teaching careers one could imagine. Throughout the 1950's salaries were the topic of conversation when I went to historical conventions and everybody was just getting by. But I had my choice of courses and eager students. The academic community was just what Wahnona and I wanted and needed. When Dr. Harold W. Reed was elected President of Olivet at the Spring meeting of the Board of Trustees, we were reassured. He had been our president at Bresee College so we knew the president better than the administrators or other faculty at Olivet knew him. I reminded Dr. Reed whenever I deemed it appropriate that I was hired one month before he was so I had tenure over him.

A Start at Olivet, 1949

We had been prayerfully seeking God's will; now it was unfolding before our eyes. I could detail extremely tight budgets for our young family, impossible work loads, a very frustrating church building situation, long trips over short vacation times to see our families, but what a start! After two years as assistant Sunday School Superintendent, I was elected S.S. Superintendent at College Church. I was the fifth doctorate on the faculty; that number would soon be ten. Even as the newest and almost the youngest, I was on a study committee to develop a budget, another to state our objectives, and later, a committee to write job descriptions for every position on campus. God had brought us to a place ripe for very rapid development. My experience in the navy and the universities had fitted me for the services needed far beyond my expectations. Others were undoubtedly even more surprised! I took satisfaction from the fact that I was making it on my own without the help of family or lots of connections in that region of the country. Then I realized that, had I gone to Bethany, I would have been in the shadow of my Uncle Vernon, who was six years my senior. At Olivet the sky was the limit.

After the fact, I will make a few observations concerning Divine guidance. I was the product of a Christian home, the youth program of the church, and a Nazarene college. My family, Christian friends, college professors, and church leaders kept me in their prayers and contacts. I was free to try my wings anywhere as I finished my graduate studies. My country had seen to it that I was debt free. That's almost too much freedom; it's almost "no strings attached." Could I deal with it responsibly?

Later, I read Hannah Whitehall Smith's, *The Christian's Secret of a Happy Life*, and found these sources of Divine guidance outlined. We are guided by:

1. **The Bible—a book of principles,**
2. **The convictions of our own judgments (reason),**
3. **Providential circumstances, and**
4. **Clear inward impressions.**

That corresponds to my experience. I was qualified and available. It was up to God to provide a reasonable choice and mine to accept or reject it. God was looking for a person willing to be used. He placed us in the center of developments He planned for Olivet this was the new institution He wanted and needed to advance His Kingdom in Illinois, the Midwest, the United States, and the entire world. While there were anxious moments, it all worked out, just in time. As Smith concludes, when the four above tests are met, "a divine sense of oughtness derived from the harmony of all God's voices" confirms His plan for our lives. Amen.

CH. IX OUR FAMILY

"Two roads diverged in a wood, and I—I took the one less traveled by,
And that has made all the difference."
Robert Frost

We arrived in Bourbonnais on August 10, 1949 after a grueling ride pulling a two-wheeled trailer. Especially grueling for Nona, who was just one month from delivering our son, Vincent. We had so little furniture that we decided to sell in California and buy in Illinois rather than to move. There was to be no moving expense allowance. Our personal effects, books, and mementos fit nicely into a trailer that cost me $25 and which I sold in Illinois for $15. So our moving costs were $10, extra gasoline, and a million jerks on the car owing to rough roads. Nona was in Dallas through June and July, 1949 while I researched in Berkeley and Washington D.C. Then I drove non-stop from Berkeley to Dallas with the trailer and Nona joined me there for the trip to Olivet via Kansas.

We arrived tired but elated. I drew a sharp line between my research and preparation to teach five courses in the Fall Semester. All the month of August, our attention was focused on events in Bourbonnais. The pending arrival of Vincent Keith was as important as the classes I would teach. Thankfully, the pregnancy was uncomplicated. I missed the 7:30 a.m. class on September 16, but was back on duty later that day and accepted the congratulations of students and faculty. It was a big day for us and the whole campus. Everybody shared the news. In retrospect, I think this illustrates the authentic life experiences mixed with academic life in a beautiful way on a small Christian college campus. As I shared with Fordyce Bennett fifteen years later, to allow students to see you performing in the church choir, leading your family in worship, and meeting the problems of your own teenagers, while taking your classes through academic paces—that is teaching through lifestyle.

I celebrated my 28th birthday that August; Nona was 26. We had postponed family until I could take back the responsibility for support. Nona had been our principal support through 1946, 1947, 1948, and the first half of 1949. With the GI bill and assistantships, I helped as much as possible while pressing hard to finish my graduate work in record time. Our strategy was to reject any solution that would divide my time or interests, go to the best graduate school for my field, and minimize the delay in starting our family. It was a strict regimen. It would not be complete until I submitted my thesis in the summer of 1950. And it would be accomplished without debt. Vince, there are three or four reasons why you are not two years older! But, I hope I have made clear that family was as important to us as a degree or careers.

Nona postponed her career as a music teacher. She was truly gifted in music. She had perfect pitch, meaning that she could identify notes by ear and pitch accurately or she could give the perfect pitch to any ensemble. She had been accompanist for the Norman (Oklahoma) High School SATB choir when in her sophomore year. She played the piano by note and by ear and, after college, was proficient on the pipe organ as well. She earned twenty-two hours undergraduate and six graduate hours of credit after Vince was born. She continued her music performance on a voluntary basis but did not begin teaching until after our youngest child started to school in 1958. In fact, small children had her "buffaloed" to a degree and that probably got worse the further she got from her school music training and materials. She and I spoke of her professional training as an insurance policy just in case I were not to be there for the support of the family. It was also the intellectual life of a spouse who needs to keep pace with her professor husband. Her start on a history major in 1940-42 and her accomplishments in music kept her from isolation or an inferiority complex while we lived in Norman and Berkeley. Of course, we also kept together in church activities.

Vincent Keith was born September 16, 1949 and Delia Mae was born September 12, 1952. Faculty young and old liked our kids; so many helped them in innumerable ways. We had an apartment on Convent Street the first year. We gave that up to save rent in the summer of 1950 when we returned to California. Then, Dr. and Mrs. Leist broke their rule against children and rented us one of their nice new apartments. We lived there for two years. Other young faculty neighbors spoiled Vince. Before he could really swing a bat, Butch Ward, the Athletic Director, gave him a cracked softball bat that we taped up; he used that for years. He was in weddings, children's programs at College Church, as was Delia later. Many students as well as faculty from those years still ask about the kids. Two or three of the baby sitters have said, "Oh, I loved to baby sit at your house. I enjoyed those kids so much." We did too! To our chagrin we don't have many pictures of Delia and folks probably gave Vince more attention.

We did a fair job of keeping in touch with our families in Texas and Kansas. Nona's mother, Velma Horger, came to be with us at the birth of each of the babies. Nona's father, J. C. Horger, Sr., and her sister, Frances, visited us only once in Illinois. My parents visited us several times almost always visiting other relatives on my mother's side of the family while in Illinois. The country was distant and cold to the Horgers but more familiar to the Snowbargers, Kings and Smiths. Still, most of the traveling would clearly be up to the young folks. That's us. We drove non-stop with the Hardy Powers family to Dallas that first Thanksgiving (1949). We each had one small child who wouldn't sleep if we stopped. So why waste the cost of a motel room? We went to Kansas for Christmas. Then, Nona and Vince went with the George Moore family to Dallas at Easter and I went to the YMCA in Chicago for nearly a week so I could do research in the libraries there. That was the first time I had gotten to advance my research on my thesis for eight months. Eventually, we settled into a pattern of at least one trip per year to Texas (1,000 miles one way) and at least one trip per year to Kansas (750 miles one way). If family visits like that are not really vacations, then we had almost no vacations. We did learn a lot of alternate routes, some special stop-over points, and how to make it home safely and on time! Most of this was before interstate highways and credit cards. I observed that every time when we arrived at our destination, our children knew their cousins and were at play within five minutes. They still will not miss a family reunion if it is humanly possible. Some of the stop-overs were Roaring River State Park (Missouri), Devil's Den State Park and Hot Springs (Arkansas), and Beaver's Bend State Park (Oklahoma).

Back to that matter of family support. We had stretched out our pay for the first nine months over 12 installments so that we could go back to California, finish my dissertation, and defend it. It was one thing to do the work and finish the degree and another to keep afloat financially. Then, there were the visitors. Uncle Vernon's family came by on their way to the University of Southern California where he would do his degree in Sociology. Then came Chuck and Rosie Oswalt, faculty friends from Olivet, all of Nona's family with whom we took a short trip to Yosemite Park. At about mid-August, all of my family came and we made the trip back to the Midwest (via Nampa, Idaho) with them. Then we returned to

105

Olivet for the start of year number two. How did we finance all that on $3,100.00? I have no idea! But, much as I hated it, Nona had to go back to work, this time at the Joliet Arsenal, driving back and forth with Marge Schoellig, who later married James Ingalls. I think I did heroically to finish a doctoral dissertation as I did. I know Nona was a jewel as we set up a cozy little home and welcomed our first child. We both must have managed our money well to stay within such a tight budget. We wanted the visitors and they were not a burden but it is uncanny how all the plans ripened at the last opportunity to see us in California.

Delia arrived just before Vince's third birthday. Nona had worked two years and helped us regain our financial feet. Fortunately, her health was good but the load was extremely heavy. At times she was on the verge of clinical fatigue. I was pushing myself too. In addition to my regular teaching, I asked for summer teaching and it was directed my way. In the summer of 1952, I taught in the mornings and worked on our house which was being built on Burke Street. The contractor agreed to let me work afternoons on the house for up to $1,500.00 credit at an hourly rate of $1.75. That is a lot of hours. I fell a bit short of my goal but we moved into the new house just as Delia put in her appearance. Now I was as fatigued as Nona! We had a normal Fall Semester and the teaching was becoming somewhat easier as I repeated courses I had taught once or twice before. We enjoyed our young family and the lively college community that was building around us. Our near neighbors were the Walter Larsens, Bond Woodruffs, Clarence Grothaus's, John Cotners, and Ed Brodiens.

In all, we chose to live on a tight budget rather than to have Nona work full time. For all the years of our marriage, Nona worked full time only ten years. She did not have enough quarters of social security withholding to qualify for retirement pay on her own. When Illinois liberalized their teacher retirement eligibility allowing equivalency credit for part time and substitute service to be redeemed, she pieced together 11.277 years of teaching from Kansas, Missouri, and Illinois. It was not until 1980 that my 12-month salary exceeded all other faculty at Olivet when twelve months of income were considered. We led by example which meant less expensive homes, cars, and lifestyle than several families enjoyed. And I had no expense account to cushion the need to entertain occasionally. We were content while living frugally. Who knows to what extent that made me more effective or helped to keep morale high?

Our church home has been very important to us. We generally transferred our membership to the local Nazarene congregation within six weeks of moving, whether it be to Norman, Berkeley, or Bourbonnais. The Olivet situation was different but we stayed with our pattern. Dr. Lloyd

Byron had his office on the main hallway of Burke Administration Building. The sanctuary was the basement chapel for the college. Dr. Byron planned that expansion of the church and the new sanctuary should attach to Burke. The church was thriving and desperately needed a new and separate site. Dr. L.G. Mitten, my division chairman at the college, was Sunday School Superintendent and asked me to be his assistant. Early on, probably in my second year, I was elected to serve on the building committee and on the official church board. One monument to our frustration and folly was a frame building, cobbled together from materials from the dismantling of some GI barracks and placed near Burke. It was built by the church to humor the pastor but we were all ashamed of it. Jokingly, some of us called it McClain Hall. Dr. C. S. McClain, Dean of the College, was also church board secretary. It was his misfortune to record all those silly motions and to communicate the church's request to the President of the college. There was no parking, no room for a sanctuary, no future. While the church used the building for Sunday School classrooms, most of the benefit went to the college Home Economics department. For me this was not the kind of church situation in which I wanted to be an insider.

I remember some wonderful services in that basement sanctuary. When L. Guy Nees came as our pastor, our new church building was finished. College Church was vital in the growth and development of our children. We asked Dr. C.B. Strang to dedicate Vincent at Chicago First Church of the Nazarene. He had been pastor of Bethany First Church while we were in college, he performed our wedding ceremony, and had kept in touch through the war years. After that, we were super loyal to College Church and threw all our efforts into its growth and development as the largest church on the Chicago Central District. I was Sunday School Superintendent for two years and served on the church board all but five (out of the 32) years we lived in Bourbonnais. Nona served in both the music and children's departments. She was very active in the missionary society. We both sang in the church choir for approximately 25 years under the direction of the Larsens, Gerald Greenlee, Carl Greek, Harlow Hopkins, George Dunbar, Harlan Moore, and Dennis Crocker.

By the time we came to Bourbonnais the tension between Catholics, who had lost their college, and the Nazarenes, who had come to stay, was lessened but had not disappeared. Dr. McClain was accepted on the village board and he was appreciated as one who was level-headed and conciliatory. At times, Catholic members, who were factionalized, needed his help to get on with the work of the village. I served at the polls in 1952 to count the votes in the Eisenhower sweep. I was encouraged to run for the school board a few years later and we had as many votes for that race as in the presidential election. I lost but learned a lot about the community. The sore point was a public school board that essentially channeled public funds to the school located in the Notre Dame convent and headed by the Mother Superior who was listed as the principal. By the time Vince was ready for first grade (1955), they had made an offer: Olivet should offer a classroom on the campus and the board would hire a teacher (we could have our own school, but with Mother as the principal). We kept pushing for a genuine public school and, as the community grew, we got increasing support. Eventually four rooms in Birchard Gymnasium were given for elementary classrooms. Our election challenge was finally successful. The new board acted quickly to build buildings, hire a Superintendent, and it was not too late for our children.

These battles showed us that there were many young Catholic families who were progressively minded and who wanted to cooperate with the college people and other Protestants in the community. Two of them asked me to run on their ticket for village board. I did and tried to get Nazarenes to vote for them (not just me). I believe our people did that; their people did not, so I was defeated. But that was progress. Forty years later, Bourbonnais had a Nazarene mayor. By the 1960's, Leroy Wright, an Olivet alumnus, was chosen to be the Superintendent of Schools. The Bourbonnais community is also reasonably united and progressive. Catholic priests on the platform in chapel to hear Dr. E. Stanley Jones and the Reconciliation in the 1980's confirm the great healing that occurred.

The Kankakee community welcomed us, inviting me to speak to Kiwanis, Rotary, County Historical Society, and B'Nai B'Rith. Nona was made a member of the Impromptu Club, made up of wives of older students and younger faculty. Close friends included George and Elizabeth Moore, H. O. and Manie Davis, Ruth Williams, the Reeds, my colleagues in the social sciences (Mittens, Andersons, Humbles, Parrs, Perrys, Esther Roberts, the Oswalts), Demarays, Larsens, Leists, Hendersons, McClains, Ides, Woodruffs, Taylors, on and on. There were also students of those first three or four years who became long-term Bourbonnais residents and were our lifetime friends. That list should be endless but Butch and Lil Ward, Elmer and Doris Brodien, Harlow and Harriet Hopkins, Bob and Mary Reich, Angie Foster, and Marilyn Dewitt, Beverly and Leroy Wright were certainly in the support group. These are the people who took us in and made us a part of the Olivet family when we were uncertain that we should settle in.

CH. X BECOMING A TEACHER

**"Nothing in education is so astonishing as the amount of ignorance it accumulates in the form of inert facts...
Nothing is more tiresome than a superannuated pedagogue."**
The Education of Henry Adams

The years 1949 to 1953 were my chance to build my dream. For at least ten years prior to arriving at Olivet, I had dreamed of being the best teacher in the world. Before the war, I thought I would teach in high school. I thought psychology of learning, possibly principles of teaching and classroom management, might be helpful. In general I thought the other education courses were not helpful. In theory, I thought that student teaching could be the way to prepare, but, in the early forties, it was mostly observation. In neither theory nor practicum courses did we have texts or other instructional resources worth the money to own or to guide us in pedagogy. No wonder that we taught the way we had been taught. The history departments at both Oklahoma and Cal warned graduate students away from Education departments. Study more history, government, literature, or economics—don't waste your time in "Education." Only in 1953, in the seminars of Benjamin Bloom, Ralph Tyler, Norman Burns, and Kurt Lewin, did I find the disciplines worthy of a college teacher's limited preparation time. My formal preparation to teach consisted of an undergraduate major in history, with minors in education, philosophy, and I met certification requirements to teach speech in high school. After the B.A., I took economics, international law, and more American government. I registered three times for American Literature but three times had to drop it due to a conflict. So, considering that a flaw, I have spent a lifetime trying to remedy the lack by reading American literature. In graduate school, I majored in American history at Oklahoma. At Cal, American history was again my major but there were five other fields in which I had to pass comprehensive exams: the colonial period in North and South America, English history, early national period of European history, Latin American history (national period), and international relations (political science). My M.A. thesis, "William H. Seward" as an expansionist, and my Ph.D. dissertation"The Development of Pearl Harbor," both related to diplomatic history and my minor in international relations. So foreign relations and American history are my strong fields. My doctoral oral exam was on American history and international relations.

My teaching experience at the University of California consisted of four semesters of leading quiz sections for the American history course with about 150 students each semester. I met each section weekly, graded all their exams, and awarded the final grades. I was the only "teacher' the student could talk to but the professor was in charge of the course and gave two lectures per week. He also wrote the mid-term and final tests. For two more semesters I was the reader for English history. I did all the grading and student counseling for this course as well. This was excellent experience but I had not been involved in test construction, lecturing, curriculum building, or ordering for the library. I did not know much about the best texts available, so generally chose the one I had last used. My experience included some inside information about department meetings, hiring and faculty in-fighting. My military experience was also valuable for my professional role. Leadership, organization, loyalty, mission statements, objective requirements for promotion, discipline, and courage all have a place on the college campus. I probably underestimated my readiness to teach. Family, church, and dozens of other excellent models contributed considerably to my preparation to teach at Olivet.

All of the above says nothing about the preparing to teach five upper division courses in the Fall Semester, 1949. The *Catalog* listed 80 hours of history and an additional 59 hours of political science. It was up to Ralph Perry, Harvey Humble, and me to teach them or explain when they would be available. Ralph had a full time job as Registrar so he taught only the U.S. history survey. We agreed that Harvey would teach most of the European history but he really should continue with the American Civil War. As of May 31, 1949, no decisions had been reached but I taught American Colonies, English History, History of Canada, Constitutional Law, and World Politics that first semester. All midterm and final exams were essay. Each upper division course required a twenty page paper with no less than six substantial sources, and there were collateral reading assignments. I did not think to set staggered due dates, so all the term papers came in the last week of the semester. As a new teacher my enrollments were large and quite a number of students switched their declared majors to history. I had no reader or student assistant so I was bogged down in January with impossible grading loads (tests and papers). I had to hide that predicament from my students although I think several of them figured it out. I had several future college teachers among that group of students. Earl Ferguson, a Canadian, took the Canadian history course and undoubtedly knew more than I about the subject. I probably had about 125 different students to evaluate, more that one hundred term papers to read and correct, and all those essay exams! There had to be a better way. After all, I was coming off a semester of five new preparations for each of three days per week. And it always took me longer than two hours out of class to prepare for one hour in class, say nothing of grading and counseling.

All of this reminds me of the great change that has taken place in terms of the quality and quantity that goes into a school year. The North Central Association standard for a semester of work was 18 weeks including the week of finals. They assumed that each course would have a two hour final exam. This eighteen week semester generally started after Labor Day so it was January 15 before the semester ended. Many students used the Christmas vacation to write term papers. The tag-end two weeks after New Year's day was a good time for review of the course in anticipation of a true final over the entire course. Second Semester started then on about January 20 and ended on Memorial Day. Much as some students and faculty like to finish before Christmas break and get out in early May, both quality and quantity has been reduced and for no good reason. Now we get 32 instead of 36 weeks of instruction; we pay the teacher for eight months of availability with a nine month salary. Whatever students are doing in the last half of December and the first half of January, with the dozen holidays, breaks, and study days within the September-May school year, the question is still, "How much history did you learn." (That was Harvey Humble's question for every excuse given to him for an absence.) This grade inflation (which is really credit inflation) dates to the 1960's and is blamed on the students but they have ready allies in faculty who did not have the courage to hold the line on quality. I admit I joined them eventually. The hostility of students and parents over F's, D's, and even C's has shaken the integrity of higher education and teachers who feel threatened (endangered) can be excused. They should not, in my opinion, rationalize away the deteriorization. Of course, better instructional materials and delivery systems could off-set some of the loss. But there is so much more to learn and think what an undergraduate could now master

111

if there were four more months of academic effort in the four year span (that ninth month that is now missing from each year).

As these changes were being made several of my colleagues complained, "I simply can't get this all in within the new semester." They had not asked that their work year be shortened. They complained that their students needed this material to do well in graduate school. But they were shouted down. Likewise, the bulge in enrollments from time to time had been used to justify a shift to objective tests even in the humanities. I continued to teach all comers in U.S. History even with a heavy administrative load, but I shifted to objective exams. I felt I had to do it but the test determines the way a student studies. Essays are better for emphasizing the values that I want to instill. I compromised,--right along with the rest of them.

Harvey Humble, F.O. Parr (sociology), and I shared one large room as an office. We had about $40 per year to use for a student secretary. We had no partitions, so there was no private counseling there and the secretary worked as she could fit it in, perhaps briefly three days a week. There were definite benefits to this arrangement. As a new teacher my orientation was well taken care of. We saw one another's tests; argued points of interpretation; talked about departmental issues, such as books for the library, proposed schedules, the chapel speaker, politics, and our families. We even studied there sometimes.

The Business department was on Burke third floor (below us) and Dr. L.G. Mitten was division head. I believe it was my second year that we inaugurated a divisional course, required of all freshmen, "Introduction to the Social Sciences." At the time, the curriculum committee was considering a general education core curriculum to consist of such a course from each of the six divisions (at least five of them). Dr. Mitten was anxious that our division be at the forefront of progress so we began it. Five faculty (two from economics, two from history, and one from sociology) shared the lecture responsibilities. With each lecture went the responsibility to prepare test questions to use on the next exam. All five of us then met a quiz section (university style) once a week. The two lectures per week were held in the chapel. All participating faculty were to attend the lectures (including those given by colleagues) and to read the entire text. The fun started when we disagreed with a lecture given, but it climaxed when we met to approve the wording of the test questions submitted. Harvey said, "Lloyd, that is an excellent question, but the right option is (b) not (d)." Just as we had disagreed with some lecture material, it was very difficult to agree on the foiles (and sometimes the correct answers) based on the text.

Olivet did not go the route of the core curriculum. I don't know how much the students learned in those two years of the experiment. I think it was hard on them. But the five faculty members were very rapid learners. We had interdisciplinary training which was wonderful. It was a rare opportunity to have our test items criticized. We had no bank of test items furnished by the publisher as are now available and the historians were unaccustomed to writing multiple-choice items. I think we all saw the predicament of the students more clearly as we profs disagreed and haggled over the interpretations and test items. Since history is a "granddaddy" discipline, touching many issues dealt with in both economics and sociology, I got a lot of help from the interdisciplinary experience.

There is no doubt that I had to compromise many of my ideals for the teaching content and the methodology of evaluation. I wanted to intersperse literature in my lectures, I wanted to "correct" the exams as well as term papers. There was just not enough time. Later I taught "Historical Method"—a basic library research course. Numerous students would report to me that without that course, they would never have made it through seminary, law school, or their graduate programs. I still think that a well written paper, following an approved manual of style, with proper documentation, paragraphing, introduction, body, and conclusion, should be required for several upper division courses in most of the departments. I had numerous students in their senior year tell me I was the first to hold that line on them. They had always been able to substitute an oral report or had chosen courses in which no paper was required. I believe that there was more "writing across the curriculum" back in 1949-50. I did not achieve my goals for my students but I gave it the old college try. Early mornings, late nights, and week-ends were thrown into the battle to hold the line for "excellence." While enrollments were not my goal, I had lots of students, lots of majors, and plenty of support from my students and colleagues to give me a sense of success.

In a meeting of graduate deans in Chicago in the 1980's, someone raised the question, "Who is the academic conscience on your campus?" The general answer was that the graduate dean was. There was agreement that a campus must have a "conscience." Nearly every student nowadays thinks he must have a bachelor's degree, but not everyone needs a master's degree. So the graduate dean steps in and says "Three tries is enough." It occurred to me that at Olivet, I had been the academic conscience. I had the courage to assign a full plate of work, to set deadlines, and to grade carefully. I used test questions that I knew some could not answer. I divided the sheep from the goats. In many lower division courses I often had a bi-modal curve, more B's and D's than C's. But I feel sure that the ability scores of those students would have followed the same pattern. I counseled, gave extra work, let students redo a paper, tried to coax the work out of them. So I was tough but fair. That reputation was built before I was elected dean and I got the feeling that my selection was applauded by the faculty. They certainly gave me enviable support. And for a rookie age 32, that was important to me. This gratuitous paragraph is inserted here as I built my reputation even though it belongs to a summation rather than to my start.

Another achievement of my first four years was to win the friendship of the head librarian. Ruth Gilley was charged with building the library which was deficient because it had never been funded adequately. That situation was aggravated by the loss of the library in the fire at "Old Olivet" in 1939. Library committees had decided that the book collection should be built around the course offerings for several years and add to periodical and reference collections gradually as a second priority. Ruth mothered the library as if it were her child, but she built it. I used the library quite heavily and she liked that. As a new professor fresh out of graduate school she recognized that bibliography should be one of my strong points. So, while there were departmental quotas for book orders, she fudged and let me order more. So I had superior service from the library all throughout my tenure at Olivet. And, we built a superior library.

CH. XI ELEMENTS OF STRENGTH IN OLIVET'S ACADEMIC PROGRAM

"Don't join too many gangs. Join few if any.
Join the United States and join the family—
But not much in between unless a college."
Robert Frost

This is not a chapter of my "memoirs" except that I will capture some of the oral tradition of Olivet as I remember it. I have written parts of this story in accreditation reports, C.S. McClain has written about much of it in his *I Remember*, and many individuals and prominent families in the Church of the Nazarene carry large sections of it in their family histories (or should). People who sold their farms or residences, moved the family, invested savings or borrowings in a new Christian "university," valued education and gave their sons and daughters to the cause. Like Daniel Burnham advised, they made "no little plans." They drafted a broad, yet specific charter, they hired scholar-administrator leaders, located able and dedicated faculty, and attracted able students. The one minister among the founding trustees was apparently more acquainted with the idea of a university than were the others. All of them may have underestimated the finances required. They probably erred in adopting the university model for organizing their faculty and curricular resources. But, I have concluded that the academic reputation, sullied from time to time by constituents and trustees who meddled too much, goes back to the very beginning. Those of us who came on the scene in the 1950's, stood on their shoulders and deserve only a share of the credit we have received.

115

Illinois Holiness University was chartered by the State of Illinois on May 25, 1909:

> **...the object for which it is formed is to encourage, promote, maintain, and support Christian education in all of its branches, such as ancient and modern languages, science, art, music, philosophy, mathematics, history, including all subjects in colleges and universities, also Bible study and theology, especially the doctrine of entire sanctification as a work of divine grace.**

Quite clearly, this was not a Bible institute. The wording accommodates easily to the category of Christian liberal arts colleges of which there were at least forty in the State of Illinois at the time. The legislature, state department of education, and other educational institutions were familiar with the category. When I arrived at Olivet in 1949, Dr. C.E. Demaray headed a committee that was drafting a catalog statement of "institutional objectives" that would update and elaborate the "mission" statement of the college for that generation of faculty and students. Objectives, purposes, mission statements—there is a faddishness about what we call them, but it is most important that we know what business we are in. And all must know so the language must be clear for every generation and each public. Olivet has enjoyed the advantage of clear objectives.

Olivet had the services of several able scholar-administrators through a period we often see mostly as an era of the "revolving door" to the presidency. The first presidents, Dr. A.M. Hills, Ezra Franklin, and B.F. Haynes, had excellent educational credentials. Dr. E.F. Walker, Dr. J.E.L. Moore, and Dr. T.W. Willingham showed exceptional leadership ability as pastors that translated into good college leadership. Only one of the above had long enough tenure to affect the academic program in an optimal way.

There is another group of leaders (some of whom became president) whose service came in the second echelon of the organization. I refer to the vice-president, academic dean, or, in an instance or two, as a trustee, whose tenure extended much longer and whose influence was effective. E.P. Ellyson, N.W. Sanford, J.E. Hoover, J.W. Akers, and later Laurence Howe, A.K. Bracken, and Carl McClain were the protectors and planners for the academic program for "next year," no matter what might happen in the June meeting of the Trustees. The catalogs reveal a curriculum, a faculty, improved facilities, no matter the uncertainties of leadership and funding. These were high quality people, educated for college work, and setting the example for other faculty. Sanford and McClain took graduate work at the University of Illinois while carrying on their duties. McClain's book (pp.128ff) has pictures of several of these heroes.

While the Board of Trustees was expressing dissatisfactions with one president after another, the core of the academic program was protected. The academic leadership, backed up by Elsie Jenks in the registrar's office, gave the college an academic integrity which benefited the students and laid a basis for recognition later on. McClain credits T.W. Willingham with bringing faculty, students, and alumni together in a spirit of unity that was required to get through the depression years. McClain's tenure as Dean of the College ran from 1931 to 1953—twenty-two years. His proven trustworthiness amidst the uncertainties of the times allowed the autonomy of the office of "dean of the college" and the control of curriculum by the faculty to develop. By 1949, the academic traditions of Olivet permitted the changes proposed by the orderly processes of the instructional branch of the institution to become official policy.

A third element of strength in the academic program was the presence of some outstanding faculty. Most of the administrators mentioned above taught nearly full loads. In addition, Samuel Burkholder (music), T.S. Greer (history), L.B. Smith (philosophy), H.H. Price (mathematics), David Rice (Physics), Clinton Bushey (biology), Kathryn Ruth Howe (education), D.J. Strickler (biology), Naomi and Walter Larsen (music), Laurence Howe (religion), Linford Marquart (history), and Stephen S. White (philosophy and religion) all knew their subject matter and fought the uphill battle to get master's degrees. Those with shorter terms of service like Hugh C. Benner, Esther Carson (Winans), and Della Cain helped establish the traditions of Olivet. They also "stayed by the stuff" and made the college succeed. One must remember that master's degrees were not common during the 1920's or 1930's. There was also a great depression and subsistence level salaries meant that graduate tuition was difficult to come by. Dr. S.S. White finally was the first full-time faculty member at Olivet to earn his doctorate and he earned it from the University of Chicago! Dr. McClain adds a great amount of detail to this story (pp. 54-69 and 189-191).

One could emphasize the use of a number of recent graduates to teach freshman classes, or the turnover rate, or teachers assigned to teach outside their fields of preparation. Those were weaknesses, to be sure. But there were enough qualified faculty, with long enough tenures and enough freedom to develop a curriculum and academic policies that the idea of a Christian liberal arts college took hold. They could describe "The Educated Man." They did a poor job of limiting the number of courses offered, allowing a new Ph.D. too much freedom to add courses without deleting a like number. When I came to the history department in 1949 the catalog listed almost 80 hours of course work, including Victorian England, The Old South, History of Canada, The British Empire, Comparative Government, Municipal Government, International Government, Latin American Governments, International Law, Imperialism and the Near East, and we had all the other regular courses and only two full-time teachers! A history major likely would not take more than 35 or 36 hours so we deleted numerous courses to bring a bit more "truth in advertising." To me, however, even these errors indicated a grasp of the scope and depth of the instructional task.

Dr. White moved on but Dr. L.G. Mitten, Dr. Coral Demaray, and Dr. James Garner had earned doctorates and served in the 1940's prior to Dr. Harold Reed's coming in 1949. Dr. J.B.Mack, a retiree from Wheaton College, had an earned doctorate and taught zoology in the late forties and early fifties. A lot remained to do to build an accredited college but more and more people were becoming aware of the needs thanks to these people of vision, many of whom stepped aside as department chairmen to make a place for younger teachers with less teaching experience but who held the Ph.D. degree. They gave up their own chance to add a graduate degree by teaching 15 hour loads semester after semester. We honor them even if they did take off on "dollar day" in Kankakee, saying "I have to get 50% off on that suit, because I only get a half salary." And it should be noted that one after another of their graduates were getting into some of the best graduate schools, making excellent records, and bolstering the case for accreditation.

The university pattern of organization had been reflected in the *Catalog* and titles quite consistently in the 1940's. There was the College of Liberal Arts, The School of Religion, and The School of Music, each with its "dean." Of course, in some years there may have been almost as many students enrolled in the Bible School and High School units of the institution as in the College of Liberal Arts. By the late forties, the nomenclature was recognized to be a "problem." Dr. McClain's office handled the hiring, contracts, and salaries for all the faculty. His lists go back to 1947; earlier than the personnel records of the business manager. Religion and Music were really "departments," except when the title "dean" might come in handy. It seems that all curriculum issues passed the same obstacle course. Drs. Gardner and Larsen both graciously deferred to the new divisional organization with Dr. McClain as "Dean of the College" when Dr. Reed pressed for it in his first year as President. This organizational wrinkle was, thus, removed while Dr. McClain still served as Dean. While the chart of academic administration was overhauled, the strong support of the President and relative little change in procedures as well as the grace of the individuals affected made for a smooth transition. At this time, student services were vested in a Dean of Men and a Dean of Women. Both of them reported to the "Dean of the College." So athletics, publications, calendar, student government, and student activities,--all came under the supervision of the "Dean's Office." By long tenure and tireless work, C.S. McClain had made the role strong.

Even before Dr. Harold Reed was elected President in 1949, there had been talk of replacing Dr. McClain as Dean. Dr. Reed assured him that he wanted him to continue as dean. Both worked hard to hire more faculty members holding the Ph.D. degree. The faculty was enthusiastic about the drive for accreditation and some of them saw Dr. McClain's lack of an earned doctorate as a handicap. Dr. McClain spoke to Dr. Reed indicating his willingness to step aside and Dr. Reed delayed the change until Spring, 1953. I believe Dr. McClain's account stating that he told Dr. Reed that I would be his choice to assume the Dean's office. I regret to report that some of the faculty became quite disrespectful of their dean in the eighteen months prior to Dr. McClain's resignation. He did not deserve blame. His contributions toward accreditation exceeded the combined contributions of all those detractors. On balance, the best one could say was that the "young bucks" grew impatient and perhaps the experienced administrator had grown too conservative and less enthusiastic for change.

The changes that had been made in the 1930's and 1940's were fundamental. McClain's book outlines them (pp. 127-128). The importance of recognition of the teacher education program led to securing state approval in 1939. In 1940-43 accreditation by the University of Illinois as a Class A college, led to recognition and acceptance of Olivet's credits at full value. This was achieved by following many of the U. of I. curriculum patterns and the help of Dr. G.A. Grossman, the university examiner. In retrospect, these were the crucial forms of recognition and graduates who wished to pursue graduate and professional degrees could overcome lack of regional accreditation—many did. Nearly all of the new faculty hired during the 1950's had overcome that lack. Still there was more to be said for regional accreditation. Only Northwest Nazarene College, among our sister colleges, had achieved it before 1940. When I began as academic dean, there was a card file on each student indicating their ACE Psychological Test scores, three achievement test scores, and a vocational preference score. These were the result of voluntary entrance tests that were a part of freshmen orientation. Olivet had given the Graduate Record exams for three years to see the strengths and weaknesses of our graduates. Data on student characteristics was a solid beginning.

McClain had made another move with Dr. Selden D. Kelly's approval in the summer of 1948. Olivet joined the "Liberal Arts Study" sponsored by the North Central Association. This was a group of colleges (accredited and unaccredited) committed to self-study and sharing a commitment to institutional improvement. Technically, they were studying the place of the liberal arts in teacher education. Summer workshops, packets of self-study materials, and on-campus self-study committees were their stock in trade. Dr. McClain's topic in the 1948 workshop was "The Organization of a Liberal Arts College." As we shall see, these workshop topics and those of subsequent voluntary committees of the faculty were the method of "unofficial," or informal, involvement of a large percentage of the faculty in college policy-making through the 50's and 60's. Eventually I was a member of the NCA committee that guided these studies. I had been helped considerably by this initiative of Dr. McClain. It had been in place five years by the time I took over the Dean's office. Numerous college and church leaders shared with me the unusual potential they saw in Olivet for a strong Christian college (maybe the great Christian University) that was within the grasp of us who were given its leadership in the early 1950's.

Dr. Reed added urgency to the drive for accreditation by inviting Dr. Theodore P. Stephens, a NCA examiner, to visit the campus in November, 1949, to evaluate the college in terms of North Central Association standards. At that time the Association held to quantitative norms. A visit resulted in a "map" showing percentile ranking of an institution on seventy-three characteristics. We knew that we were low in finance, advanced degrees in the faculty, endowment, and library. Stephens suggested that, after diligent effort in the next two years, Olivet apply officially for accreditation.

In his first four years, Dr. Reed set about to install the divisional organization of the curriculum and faculty. Six divisional heads reported to the Dean of the College. Departments were maintained but the chairmanships were less important in institutional policy making. The "Bible School" was closed down. A college budget was developed under the guidance of Dr. Reed and a faculty committee chaired by Dr. L.G. Mitten. An administrative chart was drafted. Dr. C.E. Demaray led a committee in careful study and phrasing of a statement of institutional objectives. Another committee was charged with writing a job analysis for each position in every aspect of the functioning of the campus. The most challenging task for that committee was to separate the duties of the new Dean of Students from those of the academic dean, still called "Dean of the

College." A new self-study report, application, and official campus visit by an NCA team in 1951-52 was processed. Although we were refused accreditation, Dr. Reed returned to the campus and announced, "We have never been closer to accreditation!" Everyone cheered and we went back to work knowing full well what had to be done.

The North Central Association was changing at this very time. There was a movement away from slavish adherence to the quantitative measures. There might be off-setting values. A "living endowment" of church support might be considered. "Contributed services" were acknowledged in Catholic colleges; might that concept be applied to low salaries in Protestant colleges? One way or another, Olivet would make it. Morale was high. We had leaders like R.V. Edmonds of Wheaton, Father Paul Reinert of Saint Louis University, and Dr. Norman Burns, Secretary of the North Central Association pulling for us. But we had not yet been accepted.

To be fair to those who graduated with a bachelor's degree in the thirty years before I came on the scene, consider statements from the 1919-1920 *Catalog* of Olivet University. Admission to freshman standing required a "certificate from an accredited High School or Academy . . . [showing] fifteen units [and including] English 3 units, Math 2 units, and Laboratory Science 1 unit. For description of subjects accepted for admission, see University of Illinois *Catalogue*." Sixty-eight hours of general education were required of all students. To further assure the spread for a liberal education, "Not more than forty hours in any one subject may be counted for graduation." A thesis was required of every senior and to be presented to his/her major professor. A total of 130 semester hours were required for the bachelor's degree. It is true that, with a high school and a Bible School on the same campus, provisional admissions were granted or admission was postponed without trouble from parents and pastors. But the College of Liberal Arts was a place for serious study by qualified students.

NOTES:

Carl S. McClain, *I Remember: My Fifty-seven Years at Olivet Nazarene College*, (Kansas City, Pedestal Press, 1983) is the best source because it is written by one of the principals in the story and most extensive. The self-study reports to the North Central Association of 1951, 1954 and the examiner's reports back to the college (including that of Dr. Stephens in 1949) give detailed information on the history of the college. Memory relating to "Liberal Arts Studies" in which I participated obviously entered into both the facts and interpretation I put on them.

CH. XII THE CHOICE OF A NEW DEAN

"To serve the present age, my calling to fulfill."
Charles Wesley

With the beginning of the year 1953 attention turned to the changing of the guard in the Dean's office. Dr. Reed had postponed the change in academic leadership even though Dr. McClain had offered to resign in 1949. In his annual report to the President prior to the February Board meeting, Dr. McClain again submitted his resignation. This time, Dr. Reed began his search with a plan to recommend a successor for election by the full Board of Trustees.

I do not know which of the list of candidates from outside the institution were interviewed but the list included Paul Culbertson of Pasadena College, Alvin Aller of Northwest Nazarene College, and Paul Gresham of Trevecca. I don't believe that any of them expressed serious interest in moving but I also doubt that an offer was made. Internally, the Olivet faculty might well have expected Bond Woodruff to get the nod. Both he and I had worked hard on the NCA study committees, but Bond had headed the Steering Committee for all the studies. He had contributed to the NCA self-study presented in 1951 more than I. I had chaired the Job Analysis committee which delineated the duties of the Dean of the College and the Dean of Students: separating the Siamese cats! The excitement grew as Dr. Reed said nothing of his plans until January 31, less than a week before board meeting.

January 31, 1953 was the tenth anniversary of our wedding. When Dr. Reed called, asking if Nona and I could come to the President's home that evening, I explained what a special evening that was. He graciously suggested that we come after our special dinner together. We had arranged for the Woodruffs to keep Delia and took Vincent with us. That arrangement was so natural because of our mutual respect and friendship with the Woodruffs which endured through the years. I imagine that Vincent entertained himself while the Reeds and Snowbargers talked business. Dr. Reed knew me from my high school years onward. Likewise, he knew Nona and each family. I remember very few questions being asked but I am sure he spelled out the importance of the position of the Dean of the College not only on campus but to alumni and church constituencies.

To my surprise, the main request was that I remove my wedding band due to the criticism that might come from some members of the Board of Trustees. I will elaborate a bit because some of my readers will not understand the issue at stake. At our wedding we used a single ring ceremony with which my parents and hers agreed. After the wedding, Nona gave me a wedding band which I wore for ten years. Meantime, some of the conservative elements in the Church of the Nazarene, in the name of simplicity, objected to all wedding rings, especially for those in the clergy. Officially, the church permitted the wife of a clergyman to wear a wedding band, but frowned upon the clergyman wearing one. If the dean of Olivet wore a band, there would be serious concern on half the districts of the zone and probably the other half would have been happy to join the battle to liberalize! After all, I had worn my band for 3½ years in the Navy and another 3½ years in graduate school and I had never stood before a Board of Orders and Relations asking for ordination. I certainly could have argued that we were not covered by General Superintendent advices. My feeling was that it was a "non-essential" and not worth making a nasty stand over it. I'm sure many would criticize me for not fighting for my rights but I saw the predicament Dr. Reed was in. I took the ring off and did not wear it again until I retired from Olivet. In retrospect, I am glad I chose the path I took on this issue. I watched as Dr. Reed faced criticism for owning a television set. He waited to purchase a set until the Church gave approval, then openly hoisted his antenna. After all there was a small schism in the Church at that time. His task was to build church support as well as to build a faculty and an academic program. Nona was not upset, rather amused, over the matter.

Apparently, Dr. Reed had made his decision. It was not until 2 p.m. on February 4, 1953, that I heard again from Dr. Reed. He called to ask me to come to Burke Room 307 to meet with the Board of Trustees. As he greeted me, he publicly said, "Congratulations upon being elected Dean of the College." The next morning he presented me in Chapel as "Dean-elect." In both places I was greeted with prolonged applause and just that fast an Associate Professor of History was snatched from his aspiring role as teacher into a whirlwind that scarcely subsided for thirty-three years. If that seems like an over statement, read on.

As I emerged from the Board meeting, the halls were empty but as I walked down the stairs the first person I met was Bond Woodruff. "Congratulations," he said. The word had spread that fast. Then, and later, he pledged me his full support, I took him at his word, and we worked closely together. After chapel on Thursday, Dr. Reed, Dr. McClain, and I met. McClain not only congratulated me but offered to vacate the office immediately. I declined that offer; after all I still had a full teaching load to carry through May. I did agree to edit the college catalog that spring.

I am not asking for sympathy because I recognize what a boost Dr. Reed had given my career. But there are limits of time, energy, and capacity! My teaching had just come to the point that occasionally I was teaching a class for the second time. I was redoing my preparation and notes each time I taught the course. I was Sunday School Superintendent at College Church, where I also served on the Church Board, and the building committee, and sang in the choir.

I was in demand in the community as a speaker. I spoke to B'nai B'rith for Brotherhood Week on "The Universal Declaration of Human Rights," the county Historical Society on "The Fur Trade," and the Kiwanis Club on "Conflict Within the Communist Party," and we are only up to April 1st. I attended one of the first meetings of the Association for Higher Education in March, following media accounts of the death of Stalin while there. The same month found me at the annual meeting of the North Central Association. In May I attended the meeting of the Mississippi Valley Historical Association. Dr. McClain properly brought me into a number of discussions and decisions related to educational policies as well as personnel matters. I was chair of a study committee to revise and strengthen the upper division curriculum and began participating in the President's Cabinet. Nona and the kids certainly got the ragged end of my day. I did not want to give up my teaching but the administrative load clearly was cramping my style as a teacher and scholar.

We decided to make Dr. McClain Registrar and Director of Admissions. He knew both jobs well and graciously accepted those roles. Within weeks of my election, we learned that a brain tumor would require McClain to undergo surgery at the end of the school year. He had been the Director of Summer School but, in his absence, that devolved on me. I had been designated as the NCA workshop attendee to sharpen the report of our committee on the Upper Division Curriculum. This was conducted on the campus of the University of Chicago and lasted for one month. I was exhilarated to go from a seminar with Ralph Tyler on Improvement of Instruction, to another with Benjamin Bloom on Evaluation, to another with Norman Burns on Administration. We had shorter sessions with Carl Rogers and Kurt Lewin. I got a taste of "Education courses" at a genuine graduate level. We could take graduate credit for these courses but I did not ask for it. I made clear to all that as a newly elected dean, I needed all the help I could get. These big name professors took note of my desperation and helped immensely. It was a challenging summer to say the least. Up to that time, I had continued in the U.S. Naval Reserve and had been asked to head a reserve unit in Kankakee by naval authorities. There was no way I could continue in the reserve and be faithful to my duties as academic dean so I resigned my commission and gave up what could have added a nice retirement benefit.

When the contract for 1953-54 came it was for $4,800 for twelve months. I pointed out to Dr. Reed that the new position carried the same monthly pay as the year before while other faculty got small raises. He said, "Oh, but you are assured of work in the summer time!" That was true. So in addition to the extras mentioned above, I covered the Registrar and Admission offices for more than three months while getting ready to begin a new school year as Dean of the College. As the years went by and I had almost total control over setting faculty salaries, I believe there were only three times my salary exceeded the top faculty salaries when their summer salaries were considered. I frequently taught in summer school but without extra pay. That was one way in which I felt I could show the priority of high quality teaching at Olivet.

Another development that took more time, rather than saving time, was the start-up of the Dean of Students office. After my election one of my first questions of Dr. Reed was, "What are my duties?" He seemed stunned and replied, "Well, you have just written them, why are you asking me?" I explained that I had headed a study committee on job analysis and we had submitted our report at the end of the year but that the study committee had no authority to implement the recommendations. He immediately saw my point and assured me that he was then and there placing them in effect. That answered a big question because it had not been clear what would happen to such recommendations. Dr. McClain had not been friendly to the separation of the Office into academic affairs and student affairs. In his book, *I Remember*, he later spoke proudly of the student-centered approach to campus and curricular issues, so I think he did not fully understand the reason for changes in 1953, and almost surely, he saw clearly that the Office of "Dean of the College" might be diminished. As incumbent, he probably felt it necessary to protect his turf. After that became my worry, he could see the benefits in such a change. Dr. R. Wayne Gardner, the first Dean of Students, shared with me the office suite on first floor, southeast corner of Burke, and this change was implemented very smoothly. In fact, the scope and respect given the office of "Dean of the College" was not diminished because the deans of students, drawn from faculty, continued to show high respect for the academic leadership and made sure that both deans spoke with one voice. In at least two years, I was advisor to the Student Council, an indication of the rapport with the other dean.

The calendar years 1953 and 1954 must stand as the most strenuous of our lives. No wonder that Nona had serious health problems. But, we made it through on adrenaline and the support and prayers of lots of people. Dr. Gardner was one of those people. Looking back on those years, they were probably the most productive years at least for setting the direction for the future of Olivet as an academically sound liberal arts college firmly attached to its church roots. Our children were pre-school age and I was not yet 34. A lot of attention for one so young.

Before the war and my military service, I had aspired to be a high school history teacher, perhaps some day a principal. I valued highly the learning and experience in leadership in the Navy. It was a 3½ year lab experience. Attention to duty, personnel training and promotion, inspections, safety, chain of command, characteristics and etiquette of an "Officer and a Gentleman," emergency reactions, even public relations, Orders of the Day, and Officer of the Deck—all had applications to the leadership of Olivet's academic program. But I had aspired to be a teacher and scholar and had done the preparation for that professional role. With four years of full-time teaching, I was coming into my own. My enrollments were high which was a compliment. I had gotten one article published in a scholarly journal. I had refused a request to write a popularized version of the building of the naval base at Pearl Harbor. The invitation to apply at the Naval Academy did not appeal to me. Even after election as Dean, I kept channels open for possible job opportunities as a teacher. I thrived on the work (probably a work-a-holic) but I certainly had not sought the administrative position. Most of my life, I entertained thoughts of returning to teaching. But, could the role of academic dean be "my calling to fulfill?" Looking back forty-five years, --YES.

CH. XIII ACADEMIC PRIORITIES, 1953-1956

**"It is now a commonplace that the dissenting opinions of one generation
become the prevailing interpretation of the next."
Burton J. Hendrick**

The team of leaders that were in place as we began my first year in the Dean's office included C.S. McClain as Registrar and Director of Admissions, R. Wayne Gardner as Dean of Students, John Cotner as Counselor-at-large, and the division chairs: C.E. Demaray in Languages and Literature, L.G. Mitten in Social Sciences, C.E. Grothaus in Sciences and Mathematics, Bond Woodruff in Education and Psychology, Walter Larsen in Fine Arts, and J. Russell Gardner in Religion and Philosophy. I included R. Wayne Gardner and John Cotner because they taught substantial loads and worked hand-in-glove with me as the new student personnel leaders. All of the others were members of the Education Policies Committee. This group had to approve all curricular changes, changes in requirements for graduation, proposed changes in the calendar for a new year, and major regulations concerning academic affairs. Then the recommendations went to the faculty for a vote to give final approval. They could have been obstructionist but they gave approval on the merits to numerous proposals for new or revised programs. J. Russell Gardner finished his Ph.D. degree while he was in his fifties. Walter Larsen had almost completed his specialist degree when an accident took his life. They all worked together remarkably well.

Dr. C.E. Demaray was our "objectives" man. Never quite ready to give a "final" report, he led the committee that produced the document that was discussed and revised by faculty action before it was recommended and approved by the Board of Trustees. The objectives showed three major emphases of the curricular offerings: (a) general education, (b) programs for advanced students, and (c) professional and pre-professional programs of study. The overarching goal was to produce in each student qualities of "intelligent Christian citizenship."

BUILDING THE FACULTY

Among the weakness noted in the first two reviews, was the lack of sufficient numbers of faculty holding the earned doctorate. At that time, the appropriate degree was the Ph.D. degree. In 1949 our faculty ranked at the fifth percentile in doctorates with just four. In subsequent self-studies we showed a gradual increase to six in 1951 and ten in 1954. How can we overcome this deficiency? We argued how many had 30 or more graduate hours of credit beyond the Master's degree. How many had all course work but lacked a dissertation, how many had only the master's degree but ten years or more of experience. Or that those who held only the bachelor's degree were teaching music, a subject in which the normal terminal degree was not the Ph.D. The examiners were convinced that we could do better.

Not to put our faculty down, but the 1949 Institutional Pattern Map showed Olivet faculty at the 20th percentile or lower in graduate study, educational experience, publications, learned societies, leaves of absence, retirement, and insurance. This showed us where to place our emphasis if we were to improve our over-all rating. The same report showed the Olivet faculty above the 60th percentile in master's degrees, faculty committees, teaching load, aids to growth, and even faculty meetings ranked at the 53rd percentile. We concluded that we could do something about the deficiencies and rolled up our sleeves. Apart from the category "publications," we had made substantial improvements by our 1954 report.

The improvement of instruction was undertaken as both doable and likely to produce an immediate benefit for students. Dr. Reed started a President's dinner before the academic year started. This permitted introduction of new employees, giving recognition for achievements of the previous year, pins representing years of service, and a keynote address by the President. A faculty retreat featuring an off-campus speaker and a workshop atmosphere, combined with a weekend of recreation provided another opportunity for faculty to think together and to become acquainted across departmental and divisional lines. A study committee on Conditions of Faculty Service, headed by Wayne Gardner, brought numerous recommendations that were given to the faculty for a vote and then relayed to the President for his approval (and the Board of Trustees where necessary). Remarkably, most of their recommendations were approved. They included:

1. **A system of faculty rank, preserving the right of all full-time teachers to vote in faculty meetings**
2. **A faculty salary scale to be made public**
3. **A system of sabbatical leaves**
4. **A membership fee for joining learned societies**
5. **Registration, room and board at one departmental convention each year**
6. **A system of tenure**
7. **A retirement plan (TIAA-1943, Social Security-1951, CREF-1952)**
8. **Moving expense for incoming faculty**
9. **Group life and hospital insurance**

We were busy. Some of these benefits had been offered to some before. But curiously they were not made public. The publication of the Faculty Manual, announcing the above benefits, as well as the duties of all the administrative officers, duties of division and department chairs, duties of a faculty member, and institutional policies greatly enhanced communication. It also guaranteed equal treatment and made the campus function more smoothly. Gradually, all the added increments of pay for special assignments were eliminated or wrapped into salary contract increases.

In these years the administration of the college encouraged graduate study during the summer by giving a bonus of $20 per semester hour for every graduate hour a faculty member earned beyond the Master's degree. This was not much but it was about the price of in-state tuition at the University of Illinois. The college also subdivided some of its land and sold lots at $750 to encourage faculty to build their own homes. They also built five national prefab homes to rent to faculty. Later, a tract was purchased that had four homes on it and more lots were sold to faculty.

Recruiting the faculty with doctorates was still a matter of finding and cultivation of prospects. Five other Nazarene college presidents were seeking every one we located. Dr. S.T. Ludwig, who was taken from the college presidency to be General Secretary of the Church of the Nazarene in 1944, had another assignment. He was Secretary of Education at headquarters and was, at heart, a school man. He had developed a list of prospects, and as time would allow, he kept in touch with graduate

131

students. He had put me in touch with Olivet. College presidents called each other, deans called deans, all were helpful with prospects they could not use. I contacted Asbury College, George Fox College, Greenville College, Marion College, Malone College, and Taylor University. I called for references on names given me. Of two different names the same Dean told me, "If you want a peck of trouble, hire him," and of the other, "He's just the best man I have. I hope you will leave him alone." Guess who we hired and why we kept calling. It was not until the mid 1960's with help from the Higher Education Act that more adequate numbers of language and science doctorates were available. Later nearly all fields had a barely adequate supply.

In two different departments Dr. Reed laid out to me a strategy that worked at Olivet. The first was music. "To get high quality, Christian faculty that we can count on for a long run, we will have to grow our own. That means graduate them, encourage them to do graduate work, and return to Olivet. In order to recruit the gifted students now, we must go to other Christian colleges for high quality teachers who can cooperate with our rules and theology." With Wheaton and Chicago near at hand we found several, and five or six served full-time for a number of years. One of them could well have been a tenured Olivet professor – Don Hustad. Sure enough, by the beginning of the 1960's, we had strong ONC alumni to take over and build the department to National Association of Schools of Music (NASM) standards. In the 1970's this same plan produced a National League for Nursing (NLN) approved Department of Nursing Education. The strategy in Nursing was less orderly for lack of steady leadership.

STRENGTHENING THE CURRICULUM

The fads of that period in educational history included numerous patterns of general education. It was talked to death in all the conventions and always the reports would be on the flashiest, newest patterns. At the end of the session someone would ask, "Do you have any studies of the effectiveness of this plan on the educational outcomes among your students?" The answer was always, "No, we are just in our third year of developing a program." There was no chance these people would be called back to report on success or failures after five years. They probably had no such desire. But Olivet was ripe for anything our faculty members had observed or imagined. We had six divisions, so why not six general education courses to give the breadth needed at the base of the educational pyramid? So in the 1950's we tried that. Instead of distribution requirements consisting of the broad survey courses in history, literature, philosophy, music, biology, chemistry, zoology, and religion (courses that were required of majors in those departments), we would build new courses that were broader and that could not be counted in a major. Courses like Introduction to the Social Sciences, Introduction to Fine Arts, and General English (communication, 10 hours) were the most audacious of our efforts. These really shook up faculty and students alike. The General Biology course and the Physical Sciences course, while feasible, seriously affected the enrollments in the beginning science courses. Bible and Theology tried to package Old and New Testament and Christian Doctrine to fit the "General Education" feel but that was not easy. We did not get all the disciplines under three or four core courses, as was the goal of many. Several of these courses made a real contribution to the "liberal arts" dimension of our curricular decisions. The late 50's and early 60's was a time of defining our claim to being a liberal arts college. In the 1939 *Catalog*, 71 hours of general education was required, by 1949, it was 68 hours. In any case the general education requirement had been high; but cramming a "liberal education" into four or five core courses proved not to be the pattern for us.

I have mused over this question and I believe there are sound educational reasons why the core approach does not work well on many campuses. The first is unavailability of prepared faculty. Most of college faculties are departmental specialists, with degrees generated out of graduate schools that push for greater and greater specialization. Their focus has been on undergraduate majors, their vocabularies and genuine rewards have pulled them further and further away from the non-majors in their classes. In my own experience, I used the Purdue Rating Scale that showed that my students rated me 10 to 15 points higher, trait by trait, in a history class than they rated me in the Introduction to Social Sciences (mentioned above). I would not have suspected, but they detected the difference even though, by our standards, I was qualified to teach both courses and I believe I am also a generalist. There are more choices in doctoral education now, but there were not enough properly prepared teachers for our general education courses (Harvey Collins was possibly an exception).

Another difficulty is that faculty are enrollment conscious. Suppose you drain off one-half the total credit-hour load and hand them over to your core course, then two-thirds of the faculty has lower enrollments – the college is half its former size to them. And, in their minds, the students are getting watered down courses. Many fewer students are really introduced to their departments as freshmen or sophomores; therefore there is less of a chance to win them as majors. After all why not take a full-force, full year chemistry, history, or economics course. Is that such a waste of time?

One of our study committees went to the trouble of making a matrix of general education objectives. Across the top of the page a title was given to eight columns, titles representing each college objective to be covered in a student's education. Down the left hand side we listed each course required or permitted to be chosen to satisfy general education requirements. Drawing horizontal and vertical lines, we made boxes to list course objectives that matched college objectives. This chart got to be about three by four feet. Teachers were encouraged to help fill in the boxes. I know of no other such study, but I felt that it was helpful. One could see which objectives were completely covered, perhaps too much time required, and some objectives only lightly covered and maybe subject to random election by the student. Not incidentally, teachers were required to write and distribute course syllabi clearly delineating course objectives. These were to be filed in the Dean's office for the convenience of the examiners. It also showed that many faculty were mostly interested in protecting enrollments in their own departments. There is no doubt that our faculty was prepared to discuss general education with any NCA examiner that came along. John Hanson later did a summer workshop project on a "Course Load Matrix," showing how general education requirements affected departmental enrollments. All of this related back to taking our objectives seriously.

When I went to the University of Chicago in the summer of 1953, our NCA Study committee urged me to study the improvements of our upper division curriculum. There were only two or three "centers" for the study of higher education in the whole country although nearly all the large universities have one now. The issue for me was "How can we guarantee the quality of our majors and concentrations?" There are great differences between a music major and a major in business, or teacher preparation and chemistry. What general patterns could be suggested or imposed to be sure that there were not some cheap way through? Some departments were already acquainted with guidelines of specialized accrediting bodies. They were duty bound to do this to guarantee their own currency and quality goals. The more rigidity we imposed either in general education or in structuring a major had to take into consideration the complications we were imposing on departments. Once again, the faculty worked valiantly to shore up our specializations while preserving the strength of the liberal arts college traditions. It became a responsibility of the NCA to protect institutions from the disruptive pressures of specialized accreditation.

We installed a senior comprehensive exam, preferably to be oral, one senior and two faculty from the major field and one from a field other than the major. Some departments asked the senior to take a brief pre-test that would require a short answer on a few absolutely required concepts. The exams were enjoyable (for the professors), friendly, mixed with questions about plans for the future. They most certainly helped in writing letters of recommendation. They required the student to think about the entire field of study as they reviewed in anticipation of the oral and to assess strengths and weaknesses. In a few cases, an additional course was required for the remaining semester. Most of the departments used the plan, liked it, and got into a rhythm so that it was not such a burden. After several years the requirement was dropped. For departments having more than ten graduates per year (business, education, religion, for example) it became almost impossible.

Another bolster to upper division quality was to require a capstone course. Again the purpose, in part, was to pull the pervious experiences together, to segregate the majors to work with the department head to investigate overarching interests. Some made it an introduction to research adapted to one field. Somehow it became an effort to summarize or tie a knot on the major. In one way or another, this change survived in many departments; because many of these classes were small, yet needed to be available every year. I tried to get, for example, one common "Statistics" course to serve at least five or six departments (as I had seen done in several large universities). But not at Olivet! Well then, how about "introduction to research?" If the research were library oriented, maybe; in the sciences, business, education, probably not. One can see that the Dean doesn't always get his way. And we were talking about capstone courses in this paragraph.

Provision for offering and monitoring independent study was implemented. Forms calling for the specifics of the work to be done, deadlines, amount of credit were signed by the student, the instructor, and the department head. Departmental honors at graduation were included under the heading, "privileges open to superior students." With more structure and hands on guidance, "directed study" was encouraged. After all how will the student's education continue after graduation unless he takes responsibility to work alone?

It was the Scholarship Committee that became the committee on exceptions. I believe some safety-valve is required to get the most out of a set of regulations. But it is not good to vest exceptions in the Registrar or the Dean. A committee with representatives from each division can do a lot of things. Each hears what is done for students in the other's divisions. Each can get the approval in advance from the department head concerned. Course substitution or equivalency, changes to make a semester abroad possible, difficulties with the baseball schedule – all require some attempt to shield the student from unnecessary harm due to rigidity. The Registrar can be authorized to deal with a whole "class action" of cases that are not too sensitive. He can be asked to present certain kinds of requests to the committee without fail. For every deviation from the *Catalog* requirements, he should have in writing who approved it and the date. I have dealt with hundreds of so-called "exceptions" and I am convinced that it is the surest way to insure justice for the student while upholding the integrity of the transcript. Many teachers may not know that one task of an on-campus accreditation team is "transcript evaluation," the very thing I have just reviewed. In all the visits during my tenure, we were never once questioned as to deviation from catalog requirements.

The library holdings are important to the examiners too. Each examiner heads to the section in which he teaches. In Olivet's case our main excuse was the fire that destroyed our library in 1939. While that was valid, "How are students to be served now?" Ruth Gilley knew her craft and used her library committee. They did what they had to do: order according to the needs the professors requested. That left out periodicals and reference books. Limited book budgets and the high cost of periodicals and reference materials meant that there was a real crunch when all these new Ph.D.'s arrived, demanded books, periodicals, and reference books and there was neither sufficient stack space nor budget. Ruth handled that pretty well for a short time. She got the committee to release unspent balance from all departments on March 1st, and reallocated the money to departments that wanted to order. She also took care of those professors who put in their appearance at the library. Somehow she thought faculty ought to use the library if they expected their students to use the books.

The obvious need was for a library building and more heroic efforts to build the collection in a balanced way. I watched and listened as the Board of Trustees danced around the question of a new building after the financial crisis of 1949. A library apparently is not the most glamorous project for the trustee to anticipate, but it was a necessity for our bid for accreditation. Another show of unity long to be remembered occurred when the day was set and the construction elevator was in place; the assignment: move the books (in order) from the second floor of Burke to the new shelves in the Memorial Library. Faculty, staff, and students spent a day working, sweating, in a picnic atmosphere, and a giant leap was accomplished for the academic programs.

Many of the academic regulations and practices were modified. We changed from a 3.0 to a 4.0 grading pattern, thus avoiding negative numbers in calculating grade averages. The probation system was refined and enforced, with provision for a hearing before the Scholarship Committee before barring further registration. Previously, ineligibility lists were sent to each faculty member and posted on bulletin boards in the dormitories. They applied to musical groups and athletic teams even the intramural teams (the only kind we had then). We decided against efforts to shame the poor souls. By keeping their predicaments confidential among those who had to know (treating them as adults), we had even better success in finding remediation. There was close cooperation between academic administration and student personnel administration. The calendar, "in hours," athletic schedules (later), and counseling system were jointly developed to facilitate "putting the student in the classroom at his optimum best."

I have condensed the details to a fault. This was a time of unprecedented unity among administration, faculty, staff, and students. The GI's were still around and had a salutary influence. Student leadership, faculty forbearance, as well as support, were vital. We hammered out the details of a Christian liberal arts college for Olivet's region, with strong administrative support, and activity well beyond the call of duty. We were doing this together.

NOTES:

Further details can be found in the 1954 Self-Study Report to North Central Association; Leslie Parrott, *The Olivet Story*, pp. 90-97; and C.S. McClain, *I Remember*, pp.205-209, and his Founder's Day address September, 1959. In addition, the college *Catalog* and Faculty Manual contain the details of the college experience we were building.

CH. XIV ACCREDITATION

"Whoever is in a hurry shows that the thing that he is about is too big for him."
Lord Chesterfield

In 1953 the people of Olivet could pray that the Lord would help us meet North Central standards or that the association would change those standards. Either alternative seemed remote. Every time they spoke of faculty with doctorates, an adequate library, a financial endowment, adequate laboratories, we knew that it was impossible to reach the 50th percentile rating in our generation. From 1895 to 1940, the regional accrediting associations had built a quality control for their "voluntary" members consisting of minimum standards, objective criteria, and precise calculations. Faculty quality was determined by degrees attained. Facility adequacy was measured by square footage per student, no consideration of overall usage. Volumes in the library, regardless how old or useless; size of endowment, hours of instruction. You could "write it on one side of a 3x5 card," as they say. There was little chance for an emerging or "developing" college. But, in reply, they could say, "no one requires you to join the association," then the ubiquitous smile.

Meantime, there were other forms of recognition that served remarkably well for "unaccredited institutions." The state approved charters. State institutions, especially the leading University, gave recommendations as to how credits from private institutions should be recognized. The Registrar's association likewise issued recommendations. After all, students transferred, and common sense told deans and registrars that work already done need not be repeated. At first, the recommendations might restrict credit to "A and B work" and disallow or limit the Bible credit.

Incidentally, Catholic colleges had solved that problem decades before by calling all theology and Bible courses "philosophy." As an institution gained stature in the eyes of neighboring colleges, more and more credits were accepted. The Registrar at Olivet had to go to all meetings of registrars, answer questions, and make phone calls. After a provisional approval, the University of Illinois gave Olivet full accreditation as a Class A college in 1943. Their approval was recognized by most nearby states. Students with lower than a B average at Olivet might have to take an extra semester of undergraduate work in residence before being admitted to graduate or professional schools. Teacher certification was uncertain and, in some states, additional work was required. My generation of Nazarene college graduates nearly all had to battle our way into the graduate school of our choice. It was intimidating. Quality in the individual record was what graduate schools were looking for; and they still do.

There were six regional associations in the United States. North Central, stretching from West Virginia to Arizona and Arkansas to the Dakotas was the largest. NCA, under the leadership of Norman Burns, took the initiative in changing their own approach, and then the other regionals followed. The shift was, in theory, away from quantitative criteria to qualitative appraisal of institutional achievement. It also called for periodic review of all institutions in contrast to "permanent" membership, which had been the result of the previous practice whether intended or not. I heard Norman Burns address the Annual Meeting of the association in the early 1950's calling for "democratization of the accrediting process which would permit the institutions being appraised to play an active role in the process." He mentioned the possibility of errors in judgment on the part of the examiners and how devastating they may be to an applicant. Even overemphasis on objective criteria could lead to an error. But, policing was not to be the purpose of NCA, so much as the stimulation of self-evaluation and self-study as means of sorting out the needs and priorities required to improve the institution's quality. Differences in mission should call for diversity among the member institutions. "What is the institution's educational purpose? How well is it fulfilling that purpose?" (*Encyclopedia of Educational Research I*) Accreditation then is "to ensure:

The fullest possible realization of [the college's] mission and goals

That the goals are soundly conceived and appropriate

Educational programs have been intelligently planned and competently conducted

[The college] is accomplishing the majority of its goals substantially

[The college] has the resources to continue to do so."

As we began our report preparation for the 1984-1985 NCA review thirty years later, the Criteria were as follows:

1. **Olivet has clear and appropriate purposes consistent with its mission**
2. **Olivet has effectively organized adequate resources (human, financial, physical) into programs to accomplish its purposes**
3. **Olivet is accomplishing its purposes**
4. **Olivet can continue to accomplish its purposes.**

From a nearly passive role in accreditation, the institution was now asked to begin the process by submitting evidence that "it has been engaged in a program of self-evaluation." We had to criticize our own operations, stating what steps we were taking to deal with shortcomings. To meld self-criticism with making the argument for reaccreditation was an art. But, they valued the analysis. The visit in 1955 contained a mixture of the old criteria which examiners had committed to memory, and the new, more subjective factors which meant taking administrators on their word and record, especially in matters of planning. So the Lord saw that it was time for Olivet to move ahead to seize the opportunities of the sixties, seventies, and beyond. "Boomers" were to come and education was made available to a much larger percent of the population. Government grants and loans were made available to private colleges as well as to our students. The crucial importance of Christian higher education was becoming more apparent to more and more supporters. We were prepared to move quickly. To their credit, the NCA did not materially change their criteria for thirty years (through the remainder of my tenure). Praise the Lord!

In the 1953-1954 school year Olivet had a number of things in place which would catch the attention of examiners. The president had an earned doctorate in Sociology from the University of Southern California; he had eight years experience as college president, and an excellent record of changes following the guide of several NCA examiners. His new dean had an earned doctorate in history and political science from the University of California (Berkeley). While he was short on administrative experience, he had more than three years as a line officer in the Navy. The examiners could make a judgment call as to his competence. The budding student personnel staff included an older, experienced administrator and a new Ph.D. serving as Counselor-at-large and most of the division heads held the earned doctorate or were near that achievement.

We had standardized test results for all of our students available to faculty counselors. A battery of tests was administered to all incoming freshman. Students actually came one day earlier than would otherwise have been necessary. The ACE Psychological test, three achievement tests, and the Kuder Preference test scores were made available to freshman advisors on registration day, the proud achievement of about six ladies who worked into the night to score them by hand. (This was before any machine scoring was available on our campus.) We added a set of sophomore tests using different forms of the freshman battery. This gave some measure of progression or regression by comparing the freshman record with the sophomore record. Thus, a rough measure of student achievement in General Education. We gave the Graduate Record exam to all seniors, even though the norms available were set mostly on prospective graduate entrants. We knew a lot about our students and their achievement and we were teaching our faculty to make proper use of such information. Giving credit where credit is due, Dr. McClain had set up much of this plan in 1948-1949.

The new order in NCA emphasized "self-study." The self-evaluation and self-study was now the trigger, beginning the process leading to accreditation. Again since 1948, Olivet had participated in the NCA Liberal Arts study. Some seventy colleges had exchanged their studies with us and we reciprocated. Their "coordinators" visited us and offered suggestions. We had those same people at our faculty retreats. Olivet could match any of the colleges in "self-study."

Another asset we had in place was a fine corps of mentors. In the NCA I count Norman Burns (with whom I had a seminar), Manning Patillo, and Alan Pfnister to have been on our side from the start. Father Paul Reinert of St. Louis University was helpful. Our colleague mentors were Lee Furrow of Drury College, John Hollenbach of Hope, Milo Rediger of Taylor, Carl Kreider of Goshen, and John Fadenrecht of Wheaton. Dr. Reed had two or three college presidents he depended upon for advice; R.V. Edmans of Wheaton was the most important. Lewis Mayhew was a big encourager.

Our weaknesses were apparent as well. Getting a library building up and in use was too slow. Finances, although greatly improved since 1949, were still woefully inadequate. Science labs were very deficient. Departmental and book budgets for the library were minimal. Landscaping and maintenance were also minimal. The self-evaluation required us to point out these weaknesses in detail. The responsibility for the self-study was in the academic administration, but we had to probe the institutional secrets of the board of trustees, the business manager, and the president.

(Maybe we do not need to be accredited, after all). A new level of openness and trust was required. Embarrassing secrets sometimes called for a change. For the most part studies of faculty salaries, budget allotments, allocation of special gifts, and percentages of allocation to each function of the college were all finally reported to NCA without ill feeling. Final success in the application for accreditation was enough to erase the tensions that may have developed along the way.

The self-study report of 1954 speaks for itself. In addition to the narrative and 23 diagrams and tables, the various officers were expected to gather records such as audits, enrollment statistics, annual reports, studies of alumni, faculty minutes, and publicity in a place where the examiners could browse them and make notes. Eventually we got expert at that display, covering tables surrounding the entire Martin Board room. We showed honors papers, alumni questionnaires, students admitted to graduate and professional schools, artist-lecture series, debate competitions, student elections, Book-of-the-semester selections, conventions faculty attended, and the President's Dinner Program.

The work of getting this ready (1) to submit the report and (2) for the examiners' visit was assigned to a Steering Committee, of which I was the Chairman this time. There was a chair for each of the principal chapters. I believe that we all worked on the first and last chapters to set the tone of the report. We worked hard for four months. Meantime each of us had our full teaching loads to carry. The steering committee met weekly and got a progress report from the chair of each committee. As soon as feasible I pushed them for written reports. We promptly tore the drafts apart, suggested omissions, and asked awkward questions. It was rigorous. Some of the tables and charts reflect some tough decisions over turf and policy. Nearly all faculty were assigned to one of the chapter committees. If someone was upset or wanted to contribute to a certain chapter, we certainly wanted to hear from her/him. We were getting close to the time when examiners would speak to students and faculty without warning. We must at least be aware of dissent. Finally, we got to the point of agreement on the contents and turned the draft over to the English department for editing. Unless you have seen reports from other institutions in 1954, you might not believe me when I say ours was one of the best. You really should read it!

For the most part, I feel that what the NCA required of us was reasonable and in our best interests. Some of the Board of Trustees would certainly have felt more comfortable if there were not so much openness or that the President should have had a freer hand in promotions and tenure. Tenure was one of the more controversial issues in 1953 and again in 1957. With an average eight years of service on our faculty at the time, we argued that we had *de facto* tenure. We also argued that given the contract they had signed when hired, they had academic freedom to teach their courses as they chose. In turn, they argued that faculty were making such a great contribution to the college that their commitments from the college should not be subject to a whim of an administrator; that the probationary period was sufficient to screen undesirable instructors; and that tenure would be a positive factor in hiring and holding desirable professors. In our case the probationary period was seven years but I had determined to make such decisions no later than the end of the second year. That way, we could get fully behind the teacher in a plan of improvement and a feeling of being a full-fledged member of the team. I had seen administrative indecisiveness which I felt was unfair to the teacher who always got a contract late because no one else had come on the scene. So I could support our tenure system as fair for the teacher with some pressure on the administrator.

Some of our constituents questioned our need for regional accreditation, fearing interference with our true mission. The changes to qualitative criteria answered those questions, but could NCA be trusted. Dr. T.W. Willingham, a former President, was not convinced that it was needed. But NCA said, "You tell us what your mission is and we will judge how well you are accomplishing it." That's fair.

Our admissions standards permitted acceptance of students in the upper three/fourths of their high school class. There were ministerial students who did not meet that standard. The Bible School had been closed and the High School was soon to close. Would Olivet turn down a God-called ministerial student? "No." Those who qualified for College admission could take the Bible Certificate program, convertible to a degree program if they chose later to finish a degree. These students took the courses required by the church *Manual* for ordination. Those who did not meet college admission requirements could audit the same courses, the college reporting annually their progress to the district course of ministerial studies. They had no college credit. This laid the claim for Olivet to be called one of the "invisible" colleges in the 1970s. We became one of the lesser known colleges who knew what to do with marginally prepared students who suddenly were on every campus in the name of equal opportunity. The system of probation, checking loads, employment, some remedial work, and extra counseling was well developed when Harvard and Columbia were just starting to attempt to cope with the problem. It meant serving our constituency, a second chance, the right to an appeal in person before being terminated. Still we avoided the term "open admissions." There were both academic reasons and non-academic reasons why we wanted some restrictions.

There were other concerns about those who were looking over our shoulders and just what might be next on the outsider's agenda. The Board was perhaps tired of being beaten over the head about the NCA and the need for a new library and pressure to pay college "budgets" by October 31st each year. We used the NCA argument to a fair-you-well wherever it came in handy. But there was a changing of the guard in the Board as well. Each year more alumni took leadership roles. The administrators were soon almost "preaching to the choir." I was amazed as I felt the support of the Board that elected me. That support only got stronger as I gained experience and their confidence.

The report was submitted in December, the on-site visit in February, our meeting with the Board of Review, and the action of NCA in late March, 1955. Dr. Reed and I were well received by the Board of Review, answered their questions, and felt that overall the progress was good. But the decision was not final until the membership acted on the recommendation. In our case, we were not on the recommended list and sought an explanation. We were aware that our visiting team chairman had been called out of town because he was under consideration as President of the University of Evansville. The Board of Review did not have his convincing answers to verify our responses to questions. Our library would not be completed for almost a year. Apparently the Board had a few other questions so they deferred our case for a year. They told us that they would send two visitors at Association expense to check us out and action would be taken in 1956. Just like that! And we could do nothing but like it or lump it. I think that I know exactly what happened. We were never told what it was that the Board of Review had questioned. We were not asked to provide another self-study. I think that some adamant member had refused to approve without a word from the chairmen of the team, so we were stranded. Dr. Melvin Hyde, Vice-President of Drake University, was the Chairmen of the visiting team. He was so positive in the exit interview that we knew he would recommend us strongly. He grilled me for two hours or more about how these new plans for tenure, sabbatical leave, and changes in procedure would be carried out. He knew that you could say they were no more than promises in a new Faculty Manual. But, before he left campus, he asked me if I would be interested in being Dean at Evansville. That says a lot when he knew I had been in office only one year and one-half. Had he been in Chicago we would have been in NCA in 1955. He was favorably impressed with Dr. Reed. After 28 years in academic administration and four NCA reviews I am convinced that the team's evaluation of the president and the academic dean are probably half of the battle, unless there were very serious deficiencies elsewhere. The next year two visitors appeared, but we were not told what they wanted to know but we were accepted in 1956. I can't help thinking that Dr. Hyde cleared up the questions probably before June, 1955.

The anxiety over accreditation was extended for a year, so we were able to continue the march toward excellence. "North Central wants this!" It still worked. In anticipation of our Fiftieth Anniversary celebration in 1957, other improvements were undertaken. College Church got a new pastor, L. Guy Nees. When he and his children gave full support to the Bradley-Bourbonnais High School in return for clearing the Wednesday evening schedule for church activities, the death knell rang for the Olivet High School. Along with the district superintendent's two sons, and faculty children in Bradley-Bourbonnais High School, parents pushed the district to go for accreditation.

Now there were enough Protestant parents in Bourbonnais to press the elementary school board to cut off their support of a parochial school with public funds and build a real public school. Several faculty families suffered in silence as Bourbonnais Elementary School had a Mother Superior as principal. Protestant families agreed that this was not good so pressure built for an election to pass a bond issue to build a new school. Eventually, the Board approved and, with the help of ACLU, the old system was overturned. Another milestone was achieved in attracting and holding good faculty.

My role and work load expanded during these same years. I felt it was best to resign my commission in the Naval Reserve. I had seven years of satisfactory service but to continue I would be required to make trips to Joliet for drills or take two weeks per year for active duty. The Naval Reserve authorized me to build a unit in Kankakee of which I would be in command. I did not have time for that so I tried to get the managing editor of the *Journal* to do it. He was in a similar career crunch as I. So we reported that a new unit would be out of the range of possibility. I stayed with my principle of working just one job for pay at a time. I did not say I would not donate my time for other causes. I served as a delegate to General assemblies of the Church from 1956 through 1989. I served on the District Advisory Board of the Chicago Central District for twenty-two years, twenty of them as secretary. In 1957, I was named chairman of the Olivet Planning Commission. I was active in the local historical society, 20th Century Club (a Chatauqua type club with a monthly meeting), and the building committees for church and college buildings, not to mention church choir, Sunday school teacher, and church board member.

The conscientious, self-improvement efforts of the Olivet community continued unabated. We were now a confident lot. The examiners had asked, "What books have you read in the past year not related to your courses." The students and a few professors were asked that question. They asked us to select 10-12 students with whom they could visit for an hour. In that session (no faculty or administrators present) they were asked to name a professor they would recommend that every student on campus should study under. The team reported that there was no unanimous choice, but that several were highly acclaimed and would eventually achieve that status. Qualitative evaluation could take unexpected turns and we had not anticipated that kind of evaluation, nor could we have prepared in advance for it. But the questions were fair. We began talking about "the well round shouldered student" as a new institutional objective.

NOTES:

I have depended on North Central Association articles and addresses, the Olivet Self-studies reports to NCA of 1951 and 1954, the Olivet catalogs, C.S. McClain, *I Remember*, and Leslie Parrott, *The Olivet Story.* My memory still serves me well but readers should remember that an insider's knowledge must bring a certain bias.

CH. XV NINETEEN FIFTY-SEVEN (1957)

"It was the best of times; it was the worst of times."
Charles Dickens

Vince was in second grade. His classes were in Birchard Gymnasium. Protestant students could meet on campus if they chose.

Morale was high among faculty, administrators, and students as we gloried in our recent accreditation and improved standing in the community. College Church was on a roll, gaining recognition from the local High School by clearing Wednesday nights for church activities. Nazarene teens excelled in scholarship, sports, and leadership.

Was it time to celebrate 50 years of Christian Education? When was the university founded? In 1907, with Mary Nesbitt and her elementary school? In 1908, when a board was chosen, a high school added, and several plots of land were acquired? In 1909, when a state charter was granted for "Illinois Holiness University?" Or in 1912, when the University was given to the Chicago Central District, Church of the Nazarene? All through these years, leaders had spoken of starting a holiness university. 1907 was chosen as the founding date. Let's celebrate!

The future was bright; the celebration would be first class. The history of the college (we thought "university" might be presumptuous) was featured in the *Glimmerglass*, talked in chapel, and punctuated by the presence of Mary Nesbitt on campus. A new dormitory was named for her. Governor William Stratton spent the day on the campus. At the faculty retreat, Dean Snowbarger presented a paper on college objectives, comparing statements from the charter and early catalogs to comparable statements in 1957 publications.

The Board of Trustees was brought into the celebration at a joint dinner with the Faculty. They were now solidly behind Dr. Harold W. Reed. A model of how the campus would look in 1982 was shown.

Exceptional student leadership joined in the excitement. The Treble Tone Trio of Linda Luttrell, Frances Richards, and Martha Reed was in demand everywhere. The student newspaper gave remarkable support. Student Council leadership was enthusiastic. The Framis Brothers (Lauren Larson and David Anderson) gave a dramatic presentation of The Olivet Story. The unity and thrust was palpable. There was even talk of Olivet as the "Greatest Holiness College in the World." Dr. Reed approached North Central Association about adding graduate programs.

A tough decision, but one that clarified the institutional mission was the closing of Olivet Academy. Not to deny the importance of a Christian high school, Olivet decided the place was not on a college campus. This was especially true for resident high school students.

In February, 1957, the Board of Trustees created the Institutional Planning Commission. Trustees W.S. Purinton, T.T. McCord, Don Starr, and Paul Updike, were joined by faculty and administration H.W. Reed, W.B. Larsen, R.L. Lunsford, W.E. Snowbarger, Harlan Milby and J.W. Swearingen from the faculty and administration. This Commission was eventually to recommend a 10 year plan to build five buildings at a cost of $3,000,000. (With one substitution, this plan was financed and completed in 1966.)

It was unusual that both faculty and trustees were voting members. Also unusual (and of doubtful wisdom) was the chairmanship going to any one other than the President or Chairman of the Board. The Commission located buildings but built none. Each structure had its own building committee. The Commission dealt with enrollment size and distribution of course enrollments. Acreage, traffic flow, balance between housing, classrooms, laboratories, food service, and chapel capacity—all had to be considered. A campus planner, John Severns, was hired.

Another action of this Board meeting was the appointment of Harlan Milby as Assistant to the President to raise this unimaginable amount of money. Harlan led a huge campaign in the Kankakee community. As he went from one business to another, he sold Olivet as a quality Christian College. He defended our required chapel, our prayer before classes. "Support us for what and who we are," he asked. "We will be a strength to this community." He was a missionary.

Milby also was an economic conservative and wanted desperately to stay away from government money. Dr. Reed, however, said, "We will stretch that government dollar farther than any other institution and the state and nation will be benefited." Both agreed that no government funds should be accepted at the risk of losing our religious character or freedoms. (Eventually, government loans to finance Reed Hall of Science and Ludwig Center were part of the finance package, but all the loans were paid off and there was no infringing on our religious identity.)

Maybe things looked deceptively bright? Guy Nees, the popular pastor of College Church resigned. A flooding rain made a lake of the south side of the campus and damaged College Church. The storm sewer system was inadequate. This added torment to faculty families, still terribly disappointed with the public school situation.

An addendum to the report of the Dean of the College to the President showed turnover of eight full-time and three part-time faculty. With a faculty of 50 to start with, it required considerable effort to maintain a quality faculty. Particularly painful was the loss of two division chairmen, W.B. Larsen and Bond Woodruff; also two department chairmen, Elmore Vail and William Sloan. The passing of Dr. Larsen was a shock to the whole campus. He was like a founding father of the new Olivet.

Two thorny issues in faculty relationships arose in 1957. One was the tenure system. It called for a committee of the faculty to recommend candidates for tenure to the President. In turn, the President's recommendation was required to bring the appointment to the attention of the Board which took final action. Failure to get either of the two recommendations or a negative vote of the Board denied tenure.

In a shameful chapter, the Board wrestled with the issue of men wearing wedding bands. They passed an action requiring faculty to meet the same objective behavioral standards as were being required of ordained elders in the Church of the Nazarene. General Superintendents had advised ordinands not wear wedding bands. The advice stemmed from concerns about simplicity of dress and the wearing of gold. It is likely that the individual in question never learned of the complaint. In time, such regional interpretations and *ex cathedra* solutions were no longer an issue. But the Dean and faculty had to wait it out.

Finally, in the category of dark clouds, was the matter of athletic leadership. Elmore Vail had performed heroically with several student assistants. Students wanting intercollegiate competition, very limited facilities, and volunteer coaches meant discontent. Vail handled it well but he felt he must return to Idaho because of ailing parents. Without a full-time coach or faculty in P.E. in 1957-58, Dr. Wayne Gardner and Dr. Ottis Sayes were asked to be "athletic consultants." Of course, there were the required physical education courses to cover. The competition was spirited but limited to intramural societies. A mathematician wounded in the war and a new professor of Christian Education were pulling leather to keep that important phase of college life moving. The societies with their elected leaders and sponsors kept intramurals going but the purchase of a trampoline, whirlpool, bar bells, and tumbling mats were hardly enough to write home about.

So we operated in the realm of the possible. No student union so the basement of Chapman Hall was made into the "Universe." Refreshments and big crowds! Prophet Food Service was engaged and the food improved for a time. The Home Economics students got a Home Management House. Forrest Nash began a 17 year tenure as pastor of College Church. Butch Ward was hired as Chairman of the Department of Physical Education and coach of basketball, football, baseball, tennis, track and field, and golf on January 31, 1958.

The 50th anniversary celebration finale was the Conference of Nazarene Educators, October 14-17, 1957. Each college sent 4-6 representatives. Dr. G.B. Williamson spoke forcefully. They all celebrated fifty years of "Education with a Christian Purpose."

CH. XVI TOILING UPWARD, 1958-1965

"The heights by [great] men reached and kept,
Were not attained by sudden flight,
But they, while their companions slept,
Were toiling upward in the night."
Anon.

One dean, while congratulating me on Olivet's accreditation, observed that the academic dean's job in the two years before accreditation was sure to be easier than the same job after accreditation. We reached and stretched to make a good showing. Now next year, can we do it again? Can we keep our promises for improved salaries? A stronger library? More doctorates? In part it is a matter of believing we can do it. Then, comes the time to "get it done." To put a positive spin on it, listen to Henry Van Dyke:

The Lord of love comes down from above to live with the men who work. This is a rose that He planted here in the thorn-cursed soil. Heaven is blessed with perfect rest, but the blessing of earth is WORK.

There was so much difference between the institution that elected Dr. Harold Reed to lead it in 1949 and "the best Christian liberal arts college in the world," that his first five years at Olivet were akin to starting a new College. In its first forty years, graduates of the high school and Bible School outnumbered the baccalaureate graduates. Not to diminish the caliber of its faculty nor its curriculum for post-high school students, but many of them did not meet college entrance requirements, or were working off deficiencies, or did not aspire for a bachelor's degree. Some Central Zone Nazarene students simply went to other colleges. Some faculty had feelings of inferiority because other institutions did not recognize Olivet credits.

In 1949 there was a new beginning and we took it seriously. Likewise, College Church looked forward to greater possibilities. Children of faculty and staff personnel changed the public schools of this blue collar community. This was noticeable when the children of pastors at College Church (Nees and Nash) enrolled in Bradley-Bourbonnais High School. The school board began to talk of "accreditation." For Olivet employees with small children, a solid Church, a good public school system, and housing were absolutely necessary. My job was at the college. My home was 365 East Burke Street. My wife and children were my priority. If I failed there, I FAILED.

My partner, Wahnona, and I wanted a Christian home. That meant Christian values and priorities. There never were any questions at our house about attendance at Sunday School, morning worship, and Sunday evening evangelism, plus Wednesday evening prayer meeting. There was no nursery except for babies. So, well before school age our children sat through at least two adult services per week. They must have raised embarrassing situations? No. We sat in the front pews where they could see and hear all that went on. No problem.

My grandparents, maternal and paternal, set that example before me. Our parents were strong churchmen. It was "God First" in three generations of homes. Now how could we pass along the *Santa Fe* (Holy Faith)? Bible reading and Bible story books were part of the cultural diet. The church was the channel for service as well as education. These periods of worship and service were also days of recreation, "rest," and refreshment. We needed very little secular entertainment, no trips to a lake. Those early years of our children's lives were blessed. Our children are our joy. Through the church and schools they met many fine friends.

Nona's life through the 1950's was relatively hard. Finances were tight so she worked at the Joliet Arsenal and later at General Foods in Kankakee. With her help we were able to build a two-bedroom house on Burke Street, Bourbonnais. After the children were both in school, Nona took part-time work at the college with Esther Tripp, she was part-time organist and Music Director at the Disciples of Christ church, and, eventually she taught music part-time. We used baby sitters, the most illustrious of them being Jean Vail, our next door neighbor on Burke Street.

As the village of Bourbonnais came to life, two large houses on Main Street were available to move in order to make way for businesses. Gladys and Al Fletcher took one and we took the other. We moved them to the new Spencer Court circle just north of Goodwin Hall (now Hopkins Alumni Center) on the edge of the campus. The whole town watched, power and telephone lines were cut as the huge houses, one at a time, were moved about three blocks and relocated. We put in an excellent foundation, a new heating system, and a new modern 12' by 12' kitchen. An attached garage and a utility room were also added. Total cost was about $14,000 and we had a "castle." That's what the neighbor kids called it. Our back fence neighbor, Adrian Richard, pointed to an upstairs bedroom and said, "That's my room up there." It had been their family home. Now it was Delia's room. She was ready for 1st grade.

Nona was quite active in the faculty ladies organization, volunteered in the church nursery, and loved the missionary society. She had health problems that were quite serious from time to time. In spite of chronic fatigue, she managed to stay on top. She always had a sweet disposition, lots of friends, and was quietly efficient. Ours was a happy home. The years of the 50's and 60's were defining for families as well as the college and the church.

When Delia was no more than two years old, we took her to a specialist, Dr. Becker, from Chicago, who treated a rash. Meantime, he gave her a thorough examination that guided us through her childhood. He said, "She has an allergy that is manifesting itself now as a skin rash. I will treat it with a 'creosote salve,' it will look unsightly but it will ease the itching. If I use a more intense treatment, I will take away the itch but it will likely break out as asthma, hay fever, or a severe cold." He said, "I can tell you one thing; she will never have any difficulty in school." At about the same time he noticed tell-tale signs of fatigue in Nona. He said, "Your closets are full of clothes waiting to be ironed; there is a backlog of housekeeping chores to be done, and you are behind on your correspondence. Daily tasks that have to be done are getting you down." He was so right.

At about age three Delia was hospitalized with pneumonia. On doctor's orders I delivered her to the admission desk. A nurse had to tear her from my arms. Neither Nona nor I were permitted to return to visit her until the hospital called us four days later. Nona's brother, J.C. (a psychologist), told us "They should be shot for such inhumane treatment." When I picked her up she was white as a sheet, her little bottom was perforated, and she trembled like a leaf. J.C. said, "They gave her those high-powered injections. She already felt strange, now she had those eerie sensations and it scared her to death." She clung to me for dear life. Thereafter, according to J.C., Delia had a "separation complex." Delia's start in the first grade at school was the fall of the year we moved to Spencer Court.

She was inclined to be fearful and often started to cry at about 2 p.m. (at school). Her fear: "That Sheryl (our neighbor), won't wait to walk home with me." These problems were developing as I was beginning my work as academic dean.

Our Family in 1959

Meanwhile, Vincent was a growing, 9-10 year-old and had moved into the Alan Shepard School. Miriam Hall was the fourth grade teacher of both of our children. He was 3 years older than Delia. We explained Delia's problems to him. "We will favor her and try to build her confidence. We love you both alike but we need your understanding and help." He did heroically and has always "looked after" his little sister. Delia doesn't remember this and is skeptical about his heroic deeds. In a playground football scrimmage, he broke a collar bone. Six to eight weeks later, he re-broke the same collar bone. We used an insurance reimbursement check to start his savings account. Just a year or two later, he complained of pain about 9 p.m. The doctor advised immediate surgery for the appendix. I was at his side the next morning when he awoke. I said "Good Morning," and went home to get some sleep. The next day, he accused me of not being with him; apparently he had not been fully awake when we parted. I don't know whether he ever believed that I had stayed by his side. Dr. Hodges complimented us on acting late at night. He said the appendix surely would have burst had we waited until morning to bring him in.

Vince was always with a pack of boys. They stopped by our house going to school and coming home. Vince got four years of French in elementary school with Mrs. Boudreau whom he respected highly. At church he was one of Don Parker's boys. Don had taken survivor training in the service which he taught his boys. Among other things, they swam out-of-doors in each of the twelve months of one year. Several turned out to be lawyers. College Church had no youth pastor during these crucial years but volunteers saw to it that our kids had wholesome activities. In his first two years of high school, Vince got football out of his system after being tackled in practice by Randy Crew who later starred at the University of Illinois.

BACK TO THE COLLEGE

In his first ten years, Dr. Reed put his administrative style in place. It was almost autocratic but there was a reason for that. First to be determined was the difference between the President and the Board of Trustees. The trustees were to set the basic mission. They were to provide the financial support. They were to elect a president. The President was the person who took charge of the operation and managed the details as long as the trustees kept him. Communication from faculty and students must come to the Board of Trustees only through this President There is not to be discussion of a student's discipline or a faculty member's salary in the Board meeting, although questions may be entertained. Decisions on campus life are reached inside the administration, not in the Board of Trustees. After shameful years of numerous short term presidencies, the trustees were ready to support a President on simple principles when Dr. Reed told them it had to be that way.

The President and those he chose to serve him as administrators planned a Board meeting with meticulous care. Each agenda for each committee meeting was prepared in detail and the first motion in a committee meeting was the adoption of the "agenda." Nothing came to the board except with the recommendation of a committee. The President or one of his key administrators was present in every committee session. There would be no surprises.

On December 1, an annual report to the President was due from each administrator. Whether or not Dr. Reed asked for all of these reports, I don't know, but I expect that he received more than he wanted. It was a good way to summarize your year and remind him of what you had been doing with your time. Surely that would justify a few "recommendations." His pattern took this form. In preparation for a February board meeting, he set a series of meetings during a concentrated week in Starved Rock State

Park. Nona and I went for two days, in a beautiful setting, top flight meals, and a roaring fire in the fireplace; I went through the developments and needs of the academic program. Other administrators did likewise. We hammered out our recommendations. We went over the statistics. How did we do? Much can be accomplished just leaning back in the easy chair, watching the fire burn. What will happen next year? The "operation" was going according to plan and the trustees liked the reports they heard at a board meeting.

It was a "buttoned down" administration. One frustrated board member, at about 3 p.m., questioned the chairman, "I want to be recognized. Please give me the floor at the appropriate time. I want to make the motion to adjourn; I want to be able to get something through this Board." They had some bad habits to break, but the meddling board was largely a thing of the past.

In the 50's and 60's, the college refined the system of purchase requisitions and departmental budgets with monthly expenditure reports. Ranks for faculty, salaries by rank, and tenure were adopted. With the publication of each annual catalog there were improvements in standards of scholarship, probation, financial aid, honors, and guidance toward meeting the requirements for a degree. Everything pointed toward the 1964-65 ten-year review by the North Central Association. This was also a time when the Alumni Association made strides through the leadership of Marvin Taylor and Paul Schwada. There were no strings attached to our first accreditation; let us see if we can do it again!

The Planning Commission was at work. John Severns was selected as the campus planner. With input from faculty as well as administrators, Severns made recommendations that were eventually adopted. An enrollment of 1,600 full-time students would be the basis for planning. Curriculum, departmental enrollments, and class sizes would devolve from that total. Campus traffic flow and parking was to be based on peripheral drives. No parking on campus was to be reserved. Five new buildings were to be built in the first ten-year plan: A college center (for students, faculty, and alumni), a science building, a dormitory for men, a dormitory for women, and a chapel-fine arts building. All of these were finished on time except that Chalfant Hall was built as a interim chapel and the Fine Arts building was built separately some years later. The campus plan, encased in a plastic bubble, was presented at the faculty retreat at Springfield. The loss of favorite parking spots got lots of static from the favored few. Often the faculty generated estimates of need that were lower than the campus planner suggested. Considering needs for classrooms, laboratories, housing, food service, student activities, these estimates of need served the college well for over thirty-five years. Put another way, the college has made full use of its capacity.

We owe a debt of gratitude to the heavily loaded faculty who joined the campus-wide self-study culture that characterized Olivet through most of the 50's and 60's. There were three to five topics under study each year. College budget, divisional organization, improvement of general education, upper division curricula, counseling, careers and placement, and faculty development—all got attention. Intercollegiate athletics stirred controversy. While faculty feared overemphasis, most of them saw expansion of wholesome athletic competition as generally worth the risk. This culture of hard work could do with occasional tides of pure enjoyment.

Morale in the faculty was good despite woefully deficient salaries. The Faculty Club (thanks mostly to the ladies) planned social events frequently. Faculty Retreats, with outside speakers, met off campus, while student leaders cared for administrative and teaching duties for a Friday. A Faculty Bulletin kept the announcements coming. A Faculty Handbook published personnel policies, benefits, and academic procedures. It was important to put these policies in writing and to publish them.

COLLEGE CHURCH

College Church of the Nazarene was organized in 1940 when the College moved to Bourbonnais. Dr. J.F. Leist had bought acreage to the south of the original campus then sold it to the college when funds were available. After several years of meeting on the ground floor of Burke Administration building, the college gave the lots upon which the Church was built. Although the church and the college are separate entities, every Christian college needs a College Church for its faculty, staff, and student body. Each strengthens the other.

In my own case, I was elected Sunday School superintendent in 1951. *Ex Officio*, I was a member of the church board. I served on the building committee. I taught a Sunday School class, Wahnona and I sang in the Chancel choir; she was active in the missionary society and the nursery. In the 1950's, I was elected to the Chicago Central District Advisory Board and Delegate to the General Assembly. Eventually, I was selected for two Educational Commissions (1960-64 and 1986-1989), was a member of nine General Assemblies, and served 22 years on the District Advisory Board.

It was my privilege to serve but these posts did take a toll of time. It probably took an average of five hours per week beyond the worship services and Sunday School hour; and beyond my fifty-five hour week at the college. It was especially pressing 1960-64.

FAMILY AND TRAVEL

Our family trips were mostly to Dallas, Texas (1,000 miles) and Sylvia, Kansas (750 miles). Before Interstate highways, that required a block of time but we made it home always once a year and sometimes twice. The parents seldom came our way; the Horgers once, and the Snowbargers three times, over a span of 37 years. Remember how we felt so sorry for the missionaries who were separated from their families. Nona's brother, J.C. Horger, taught two years at the University of Illinois so we saw his family then. We took in the sights along the roads to the South and West. Nona and I made trips to other Nazarene colleges in Idaho, Oklahoma, Massachusetts, California, and Tennessee. We stopped to see friends in Kansas City en route and most of the General Assemblies were there.

In 1961, Nona and I guided our eight week Olivet grand tour of Europe. We left Vince and Delia in Kansas with my parents on the farm. We hated to leave them and it was really sad when we learned while in Italy that our two Manchester dogs had disappeared in Kansas. Apparently, they had strayed out on to the country road and a passer by picked them up. Our tour was super, all thirty-one of those cathedrals!

Our 1963 Expedition, was another gem. We packed a tent in our '62 Mercury, headed to Williamsburg and started northeast all the way to Nova Scotia. We camped about half the time and took motels where necessary to conserve time. Williamsburg, Washington D.C., Philadelphia, New York City, Boston, Halifax, the Thousand Islands of the St. Lawrence Seaway, and home. Those were three weeks well spent, even though the campus was under duress as recovery from the tornado was the first order of business. The 1964 report of the self-study for North Central was due December 1st was not even begun by September 1st, but we were in a better mood to write after a thorough rest.

In 1964 the children went with us to General Assembly in Portland. We played tag with several families as we went through the Black Hills, Yellowstone and on to Portland. We returned through San Francisco, Berkeley, Salt Lake City, Colorado Springs, and Kansas. In 1965 we camped on a trip around Lake Michigan, north on the east side and south on the west. We also planned a trip to Mexico City by car but did not get to take that trip.

COMMUNITY SERVICE

I began my community service in Bourbonnais when I was asked to work at the 1952 election. We had a landslide turnout to elect Dwight David Eisenhower president. Counting ballots was bedrock political experience. I was later interviewed by an ACLU person concerning the local public school situation. We did a door to door inquiry. As we distributed literature we qualified each household pro or con. Our "get out the vote" campaign only called back to those who had been "pro" and proceeded to win the election and we got a genuine public school. This was vitally important for faculty families at ONC. Thereafter, Catholics joined Protestants to bring about community improvements. When Dr. C.S. McCalin took his sabbatical to England, I ran for the Village Board to take his place. I lost. The reason: I didn't get enough votes. I ran a few years later and lost again but community relations were much improved and that project was no longer important to the College. In fact, it was an Olivet faculty member who, as chairman of the Friendship Festival, led the group to reinstate the French pronunciation of the Village name –BOUR-BON-NAIS (NEZ).

THE TORNADO

Thursday afternoon, April 17, 1963, a huge tornado struck Burke Administration Building, raked the entire campus and traveled 70 miles on the ground east into Indiana. Campus, community, families, and church all of us together had our lives complicated. Having glanced out the window I had seen the storm without realizing what I saw, then it struck; our draperies exploded out the windows. The committee meeting in my office made a striking picture. All of us getting our heads under the conference table. Nona was driving Vince on his paper route on Burke Street. They watched the storm as it toppled "Old Smokey" and destroyed "Trailerville." Back in Burke, we ran through all four main floors. We found Joan Noble at the south stairwell with a broken kneecap. Ken Blanchard was outside at the south porch stairway with a concussion. It was just minutes before time for the evening meal or many more would have been exposed to the tragedy of the smokestack. The dining hall was unsafe to use. But remarkably few serious injuries were suffered on campus.

There was a lot of chaos and confusion in the first two hours. In the absence of Dr. Reed I called a meeting of the Administrative team at our house at 8 p.m. Dr. Reed was on his way back from Iowa. There was damage to the fourth floor of Burke, the dining hall, the gymnasium, and Trailerville. There was no electricity. No heat, fallen trees, near panic, but no lives lost on campus. One young man had called my wife telling her "It's dark here in this dorm. We haven't had supper. And there is no hot water so I can't take a shower!" It was tough!

I was Vice-President so I called the meeting to order. We had no electricity so we used candles and kerosene lamps. We thanked the Lord for sparing lives and began our assessment:

ELECTRICITY-We will have it in two or three hours;

WATER-We have our own pumps, it's on now;

HEAT-It will be on when we get electricity;

DORMITORIES-Minor damage only; no need to evacuate;

FOOD SERVICE-It may take two weeks to get the kitchen and dining hall up and running;

CLASSROOMS-Burke will be closed down;

LABORATORIES-All unusable.

Realistically, we were severely damaged. With three full weeks of classes to the end of the year, how could we salvage credits, graduate seniors, and avoid a disaster? Little by little the answers came as we sat around that table. Bradley-Bourbonnais High School offered their kitchen and cafeteria to prepare one main meal each evening. We could arrange a continental breakfast in the dormitories. Maybe we could get sandwiches at noon. Pastor Nash offered the sanctuary, classrooms, workspaces, and storerooms of College Church. Parlors and storage rooms in dormitories were identified.

We broke up on an optimistic note Thursday evening. How close to operational could we be by Friday morning? We called an assembly at College Church at 8 a.m. Personnel from the dean's and registrar's office started at 5 a.m. taking the listing of classes by periods and matching them up with spaces available. A highly "revised" list of room assignments was "dittoed" and posted across campus while we were all in Chapel. No student nor faculty member saw the revised list until after chapel. Dr. Reed and Don Gibson were back and somehow got word of the chapel so they heard with all the rest of us. If you have a class at 8:30, 10:30, and 11:30 etc. go to that class. If you don't have a class, go to one of twelve clean-up stations and join faculty members who will be in charge there. Place burnable trash in one pile, metal, bricks and glass in another. Gather things up so that trucks can carry them away. Go to all your classes and do clean up work when you have no class. Let's put this place back together and be ready to finish the year. Extra effort and the dining hall was back in service earlier than expected. Substitute assignments were made for the labs that were missed. We also found that some classes could just as well meet outside. By the week-end, things were in good order and morale was sky high!

Community crews came on campus almost immediately. Tractors, power saws. Trucks cleared roadways. Administrative offices were relocated to 1st floor of Chapman Hall. Students worked with community volunteers. By 4 p.m. the trash and fallen trees were stacked if not hauled away. The utilities were on. Every one knew where his class would meet on Monday morning. And the campus breathed the Doxology.

A year earlier, Charles Henderson our business manager, had reviewed our insurance coverage with Hugh Pierce, our agent. The campus was covered for replacement costs. Third and fourth floors of Burke were to be replaced. The contractor told me, "I am obligated to replace (a certain number) of linear feet of walls. You can put them where you want them." So overnight, Gardner Walmsley and I drew the fourth floor plan for Languages and Literature. And Leonard Anderson and I drew the plan for Third floor. Faculty offices, classrooms, and labs were included and we squeezed out an elevator for Burke which was long overdue. A million dollar renovation resulted from the storm. It took most of 1964-65 to get every one resituated but it was worth the wait.

The quick recovery from the crisis is to be credited to God's Providences, a college community willing to hold steady and to follow leadership, and tremendous effort on the part of the community, and the church. Several colleges offered help but we really didn't need it. WGN aired an interview with me on TV. It was a case study in social psychology. The miracles of Trailerville were numerous. Gene Braun was on a truck heading to Chicago with Orpheus Choir equipment when he looked south and saw the tornado hit Trailerville where his wife and baby were. Gene turned around, dug his wife and baby out, and both were OK. The choir was to sing in Chicago that night. A week or two later, Orpheus sang in Dayton, Ohio. Gene had the solo lead in one number: "When the Storm Passes Over!" That church almost lost its roof.

CH. XVII TO SERVE THE PRESENT AGE

"To serve the present age
My calling to fulfill
Oh! May it all my powers engage
To do my Master's will."
Charles Wesley

At age 32 (1953), I was handed a tremendous opportunity. I was asked to take academic leadership at Olivet Nazarene College when it was ripe for exceptional development. It was almost intoxicating at times of such accomplishments as the Liberal Arts self-study projects of North Central, regional accreditation, and building the Memorial Library. I had become more introspective asking myself, "Am I in the center of God's will?" Is my life mission in education or in government service? If it is in education, is it teaching, scholarship, or administration? Is it to be in independent or state sponsored institutions? I had not felt a definite "calling" from God to teach in a Christian college. I came to Olivet as my personal choice; Christian colleagues, Christian students in the majority, a small college of liberal arts. My choice of courses to teach, all of that.

Inquiries came from several directions. Elmira College (N.Y.), "Dean of Faculty" at Southern Illinois University, Evansville College (IN), Eastern Nazarene College (MA.), and later three others. A top official at the Office of Higher Education in Washington, D.C. encouraged me to apply. I paid no attention courteously turning these ideas aside before correspondence proceeded or definite offers were made. As for God's leading I assumed I would have been free to take any of these positions. Now as I turned 40, I had to be sure. As numbers of psychologists have observed, adults may experience an identity crisis at age 40-42. What was my true calling, my vocation?

I was tempted by the prospects of broader horizons, more responsibility, career advancement. What might open if I really sought to move? What was best for my wife and children? Would God make it clear to me? In the Bible, Jacob's sons sold Joseph into Egyptian slavery. But Joseph later was to say, "God sent me." Like Joseph, I felt that each new annual contract should be carefully considered and it seemed that God was silent, neutral. Since retirement I feel sure that "God sent me" to Olivet, awaiting further assignment. I stayed "assigned." Now I can refer to "my calling to fulfill, oh, may all my powers engage to do my Master's will."

So my choice/calling was Education; at a Christian college; as an administrator. I had spelled out what it would mean to be "the ideal teacher of undergraduates." I also described "the consummate academic dean." It would be one or the other, not both. I would not conform to the career patterns of historians or university vice-presidents. I would be transformed by the renewing of my mind (Romans 12:2). Building on the shoulders of those who labored before me, I would give my mind and body to the task. I would use the best of new methods to motivate faculty to produce learning experiences and mold the attitudes of students more effectively. Ultimately I would prepare "a strict account to give" at the end of my journey. I would lead by example.

In the process of my searching, I applied for a Fullbright Fellowship to Iran but was turned down. I explored a position with U.S. Aid program. That almost certainly would have made me an "ugly American" and landed me in Vietnam. As I drove past the office in Washington, D.C. in August, 1963, I decided not to apply.

Meantime, as chairman of the Olivet planning commission, I wrote to S.T. Ludwig asking what forward planning the General Church had done relating to higher education. Almost certainly, that figured in my appointment to the 1960-64 Nazarene Education Commission with Dr. Orville Jenkins and Dr. Leslie Parrott. I served on the Research Committee of the Commission and our report went to the 1964 General Assembly, Church of the Nazarene. Thus, my years of pondering, searching, and restlessness converged with developments in the work of the church. I was to have some direct involvement that was totally unanticipated.

Maybe it is rationalization. But there are scripture passages like Jabez prayer, "Enlarge the place of thy tent . . . lengthen thy cords . . . strengthen thy stakes." Or, "Behold I have set before thee an open door, and no man can shut it." And "Your work shall be rewarded." All of these scriptures seem to encourage a Christian in modern times to break the mold and to step out of the box. At least it was an act of courage to face the unknown of the job of Secretary of Education at Nazarene headquarters. Especially so when the six regional colleges vigorously opposed the starting two new regional colleges and a Bible college in the mid -1960's even though this move was voted by the 1964 General Assembly. But when I accepted the position my attitude had to be:

> **Hesitation is a mire –**
> **Climb out, climb up, climb higher,**
> **Fumble, stumble, risk a tumble,**
> **Make a start, however humble!**

The commission report was modified at Portland, Oregon before it was presented to the Assembly. Two new zones were created for regional colleges and a Bible College was to be started. A full-time Secretary of Education was to be selected. Nominees were presented to the meeting of the General Board in February, 1965. Dr. John E. Riley was elected but declined the election. The second nominee was Willis E. Snowbarger and, in a mail ballot, he was elected. My dad was on the General Board and with his ballot, he sent a note begging to be forgiven for voting for his own son. Word of this election reached me in Dallas, Texas where my family was attending the funeral of Dad Horger (Nona's father). I asked for time to consider the call. I assured Dr. Harold Reed that I probably wouldn't accept. But then, I reviewed my previous work on the commission.

At Christmas two months before my election, at our home in Kansas, I had explained at length to my family what the office of Secretary would entail. I spelled out what such a person could do for Nazarene Higher Education and answered all their questions. They too were skeptical about the General Assembly actions but I was putting a positive spin on what could happen. In due time, I accepted the new position. Students humored me by placing signs (Burma Shave Style) along the path I took from office to home. They did not want me to leave. We took a family vacation between jobs camping our way around Lake Michigan. We also stopped a few nights at the Missouri District campgrounds in Fredricksburg. It was there that Delia's asthma became very serious. When we arrived in Overland Park, we put her under the regimen of Dr. Willoughby, the asthma specialist.

We were given a royal welcome in Kansas City. The Willamsons and Benners took us to dinner at the Plaza III. Everyone was very congenial. I was assigned an office across the hall from the Youth Department. I was automatically part of the "Executive Fellowship." We bought a home at

9508 Woodson. We decided to join Kansas City First Church where C. William Ellwanger was the pastor. Gary Moore and Eleanor Whitsett had the music. Jerry Ketner was minister to youth. Nona and I sang in the choir. I taught a young adult Sunday school class. We were immediately deeply involved in the church, we had friends from headquarters, Nazarene Publishing House, and Bethany (dating back to college days).

The children were in the prestigious Shawnee Mission School district and a top notch youth program at church. They had athletic competition, mission trips, work projects, involving Vacation Bible School in South Texas (in Spanish). Both of them went to an international youth institute in Estes Park, Colorado (one in 1967, the other in 1970). Vince was president of his senior high group. Delia had a whole pack of friends in her junior high years. We were constantly driving high school age kids 25 minutes (one way) to youth activities especially on Sundays and Wednesdays. Those trips were to church. Then they had school activities as well. Delia was in band and choir, also Heritage Singers, a select group. Dee Donaldson was a first class Conductor.

Nona taught music at De Soto, Stanley, and Stillwater on the Kansas side and Center District in Missouri. She was active in the ladies group consisting of the wives of Headquarters executives and general superintendents. We were closer to family both hers and mine, so that meant more reunions and visitors to our home. The kids knew all their cousins, grandparents, uncles and aunts. We were with family in their teen years. Millard Reed could have blamed us for not joining, the new Overland Park church of which he was the first pastor. But he understood when I told him we would stay at First Church because of the move from Illinois only a year and one-half earlier has been hard (especially for Vince). In turn, Millard, as District Youth Coordinator pushed Vince and has followed him all his life. We made family trips to Colorado (Green Mountain Falls, Woodland Park, Golden Bell Ranch), to Dallas, Texas; The Black Hills; Portland, Oregon; Berkeley, California; Sylvia, Kansas; Bethany, Oklahoma; Yosemite, Yellowstone, and Nampa, Idaho.

I was blessed with the assignment of Dr. Samuel Young as my General Superintendent sponsor. He had been college President of Eastern Nazarene College so he understood the predicament the Presidents faced when losing several districts of church support in order to form two new zones. He knew their fears for their own ministerial training programs as a new Bible College was to be started. But, he said to me, "Can you support the decision to go ahead with these three institutions? If not, you should not be in this position." That was direction enough. And he was right. I asked, "What are my duties? Could you give me a job description?" He responded, "Anyone who needs a job description is not man enough for the job." But I proceeded to draft my own and showed it to him later. "Is this about what you had in mind?" He sort of nodded and went on to some specifics that needed attention.

It was clear that I was to facilitate the starting of two new junior colleges and a Bible college. But the time table was vague. It was also clear that a great many more faculty would be needed. Boards of Trustees would need to be chosen and organized. Their first task would be to draw up constitutions and the next would be to elect a president. The third step would be to select a site. By that time a Secretary of Education would help in any way possible, but the President of each college would be in charge. The Bible College was the more difficult because they lacked a zone of support. Equally difficult, there was disagreement as to the level of education expected. Was it to be a Bible College as Dr. Williamson argued for? Or, was it a Bible School with little more than a high school diploma as entrance requirements? Three year diploma or four year degree program?

I was flooded with offers of a campus site. I visited a few sites, kept the correspondence until a president could scan the offers and decided which to pursue. One site in Dallas-Fort Worth area eventually became the DFW Airport. Our hosts for that trip were Melvin McCullough and Jerry Lambert. Dr. Strickland was late getting on the job because he was transferring form South Africa. Dr. Cecil Ewell, who was Chairman of the Board, and I did preliminary work with the people in Colorado Springs. I offered some minimal criteria which were met in each of the choices. I feel satisfied in the way that worked out. Also, the constitutions were satisfactory. I accompanied Dr. Curtis Smith and Dr. Stephen Nease to the North Central office of Dr. Norman Burns and they proceeded to "set sail" as prospective members of that accrediting body. Dr. Burns was awestruck at the idea of starting new denominational colleges.

The welfare of the new colleges was one thing, but the effect on the six existing colleges was quite drastic. Olivet lost five districts (two to the west and three to the east). Bethany was hardest hit with the loss of the Kansas district which left them only one hundred miles from their northern zone border, not to mention the loss of financial support and student prospects. Dr. Harold Reed held a fund-raising dinner at Olivet to help the new presidents get a start but that was not very successful. They were working against entrenched Alumni loyalties. But the zonal loyalties were vital to the well-being of the older colleagues.

All of the colleges needed a faculty referral service which Dr. S.T. Ludwig had started even though he was only part-time in Education. Here

I was right again. I felt that there were so many of our alumni or Nazarene members in graduate schools that we could find enough faculty. But it would take cultivation. I published a list of fields where there was a need. I visited the large universities. While there, I contacted the pastors and encouraged them to follow up on Nazarene students. In all, I believe I helped to place at least 25 to 30, qualified faculty in Nazarene colleges in my years on the job. There were more prospects than in previous years and the deans and presidents all rose to these challenges well.

These activities were obviously important since the die was cast and the new institutions were born. My work in support of these institutions was expected. But there were more controversial areas of higher education activity in the church. There were considerable differences in membership and financial strength between the zones. Those with less support wanted "equalization," maybe pooled financial support. All the higher education dollars might come to headquarters and be divided equally or by some proportionate formula; might the effort be thought of as "a system" of Nazarene Higher Education with coordination of efforts? Two or three specializing in health care? Others leading out in graduate programs? Engineering? Does every college need to offer all the special majors? Could one admission office refer prospects to another? Could colleges share faculty on a short-term basis? The presidents were unanimous. These ideas would not work. Loyalties of alumni, consistency of financial support, and yes, a certain amount of competition among Nazarene institutions, was necessary and healthy.

What then could the Secretary of Higher Education do? Find faculty, push for support through higher formulas designated for education. Publicize the work of the colleges. Encourage cooperation between the college leaders. Keep the General Superintendents informed. Connect Nazarene efforts with those of other denominational education leaders. Expand the exchange of information on faculty, finance, and innovation to each of the colleges.

I had thought that one of the new colleges would follow the pattern of work-study colleges in which no tuition was charged but each student owed a specific block of work for the institution. This alternative was blocked by the zonal system which dictated that the new colleges should have to offer the programs that other zones had found would meet the demand of students and parents. So there would be eight alike instead of six alike. My idealistic dreams were not going anywhere. I was not determined to fight for them, because I saw why the experienced presidents opposed them. I was disappointed because I felt that no one was even listening.

On the matter of sharing the educational dollar on an equalized dole from headquarters; I saw an example in the Church of God (Anderson). Anderson College got their church support from headquarters, not from a central zone of support. Their choir tours made a nation-wide itinerary in large churches, not limiting the trips to Central United States. Cultivating a close relationship to Central U.S. was not a priority. Questions where behavioral differences were at issue were resolved in the church headquarters, not by representation from supporting geographical districts. This meant that objections from the pew to college administration were not tied to financial support of the church. Some districts are more attuned to the role of the college and would give more. Other districts do not see the role of a church college as being vital. Sensitivity to the wishes of the district will strengthen the bond. More money will come in. If the money comes from a central fund, that source may be mistaken for a "tax." Freedom for a college leader to develop his own programs and raise all the money he can is a key to the higher levels of denominational support. My colleagues in the higher education secretariat of other denominations were jealous of the success of the Nazarene "system" (which is not a system).

If Nazarene Bible College is an example, my work-study college is also likely impractical. It would have to draw from a nation-wide pool; it would need support other than a "zone." Likely, Nazarene Theological Seminary and the Nazarene Bible College desperately need support above and beyond student tuition and fees. Until that need is funded we hardly can afford to start our "blue collar" college.

There were lines of accountability of the Nazarene colleges to the General Church short of "a system of higher education." The church gave the college its zone of support. The church could take it away. Each college had a general superintendent sponsor who took special interest in the college primarily through the president and the materials he shared (minutes, addresses, financial information). By the 1960's, it was understood that each college owed headquarters a copy of its annual audit. These materials, in time, were collected through the office of the Secretary of Education. Occasionally these data were not provided or the audit was not professionally done. What would the denomination do if one college defaulted? That question was never answered directly. But in practice the answer was, "Go to prayer!" Government and accrediting associations wanted to see complete independence of "one" governing board. The freedom to act independently costs any guarantee of the church offering a safety-net. On three or more occasions, a college has looked to headquarters for a bail out, but to almost no avail. So this is another reason

I say it is not "a system." The freedom to get in trouble is the freedom to find your way out.

On another of my suggestions, promoting Bresee Fellowships, I was overruled but that I would fight for. S.T. Ludwig started the Bresee Fellowships as an effort to minister to Nazarene students on state and secular university campuses. I linked that effort to the cultivation of faculty prospects that were either teaching at these universities or were graduate students for whom teaching at Nazarene college would be a flattering possibility. I found most pastors to be unfamiliar with their own local university. Most of the universities had a voluntary declaration of denominational preference in their registration packets. When I inquired at Wichita State University I was told, "Oh, you'll find the Nazarene names at the Episcopalian ministries office." "Why," I asked. "The university does not sort these declarations. It was the Episcopalians turn to sort and distribute the forms this year. If no one asks for the Nazarene cards, they would still be in the Episcopalian office." My host, the Methodist campus minister, went on to say there must be at least 2,000 students on campus that would not be able to participate in activities he sponsored. So, get a Nazarene over here to pick up those cards.

Likewise, professors and pastors wives were often misfits in the university community; they did not play bridge and were bored with university life. Many times the local church was not anxious to have them. An offer from a Nazarene college was highly competitive when the context for their families was considered. I felt that Nazarene Higher Education needed to mend fences and be acquainted with their counter parts in state universities. Also, Free Methodists produced far more Ph.D.'s than their colleges could hire. We could make common cause with them, the Wesleyans, and Quakers, etc.

We had success with Bresee Fellowships in perhaps 12-15 secular campuses. It took an exceptional pastor or a university professor to guide the project. All student work starts at zero every fall. We sponsored one conference at Ohio State and another at Oklahoma State. A fair turnout and enthusiasm marked each conference. At the 1968 General Assembly, I granted the request of Oklahoma State Student Center for space in Education section of the exhibits. They did a good job of reminding the church that they represented work with 80% of the students. That did it. The college presidents unanimously objected. That exhibit space was for them alone. Nothing could be allowed to challenge their monopoly on the educational dollar. As a result, it eventually became the responsibility the local church or the district to fund any special effort to penetrate the university campuses. Incidentally, Christian Day Schools also lost any connection with the Education Department as they had hoped it might develop.

So, in 1968, my duties dwindled back to: 1) start three colleges (done), 2) recruit faculty, 3) relate the work of higher education to the General Superintendents and other headquarters departments. Other executives began to say "Is that a full-time job?" As for the new institutions, now that they have a constitution, a Board of Trustees, a President, they do not welcome intrusion from headquarters. And I would not want to do that. I expressed my frustrations to Dr. Young who understood fully. I talked with Dr. Eugene Stowe and Dr. V.H. Lewis. Then we had an August meeting in Denver of the President's and General Superintendents. There were other items on the agenda, but my predicament was discussed. All of these men were friends of mine, but there was no hint of an offer until a call from Dr. Reed came in December, 1969.

Meantime, I took my turn at a two-year leadership of the stewardship effort of the church. There was no stewardship department, so other department heads shared the leadership from Headquarters in turns. I hired Terry Reed, a seminarian, on a part-time basis and we learned a lot about how to promote Easter and Thanksgiving offerings. We lived under the fear that in our two year stint, the giving for World Mission would suffer a tremendous drop. And we would be responsible. Each year there was a nice increase, so we could breathe again. We did accommodate to something new – "Faith Promise." Ponder Gilliland started it in California. Instead of funding missionary activities of the church by two large offerings, he took pledges on an annual basis for a wide-range of missionary activity and doubled (and tripled) the amount received. General leaders feared the new categories of mission activities included (such as compassionate ministries, deputation offerings for missionaries, etc.) would diminish the World Mission department allocations. I worked with Ponder to define the package that benefited from Faith Promise and it eventually was adopted church-wide. Giving increased considerably and World Mission share was increased greatly.

I learned a lot in my five years at headquarters. I met often with all of the college presidents. I went to meetings of development officers, business managers, academic deans, deans of students on a regular basis. They all came to share reports. After my leaving, the Minter reports included detailed comparisons of statistics. Nazarene colleges were mentioned approvingly among the secretaries of education from other denominations and in the National Association of Intercollegiate Athletics. The denomination stood by the older colleges as newer ones were built and financed. Faculties were improved in all of the colleges. The departments at headquarters paid more attention to the higher education arm of the church, and colleges improved their relationships to the church.

My family benefited by association with the fine leaders of the Church. Vince and Delia graduated from the finest high school in the nation. The youth program of Kansas City First Church was the finest in our church. Nona got some excellent teaching experience and socialized with the finest ladies. I was accepted among the top church leaders both on the job and in social occasions. I visited all of the colleges, most of them once a year.

Was there anything lacking? Well, salary was virtually the same as Olivet but since pension funds were only vested after five years of service (and I only served five years); I lost five years of pension contributions. And two moves with moving expenses paid, still cost us about an additional $5,000 per move to get settled (another $10,000). So there was no financial advantage. Therefore, these were lateral moves career wise. My children were not eligible for tuition remission at Nazarene schools. All told, three major reversals left me in debt when I returned to Olivet.

The name recognition throughout the church and the good will my family enjoys is priceless. One can bury himself in one location for 40 years and scarcely be remembered. We have been recognized and blessed beyond measure. We have hundreds of good friends.

The one negative factor about working at the headquarters is the isolation or separation from the people where the action is. I complained to the Board of General Superintendents, "I don't have any contact with students, faculty, the people I love to serve. Whatever I do, I do at arms length, through other people." To which General Superintendent George Coulter said, "Willis, do you think that possibly all of us feel that way?" It is lonely at the top.

CH. XVIII MY CALLING TO FULFILL

**"Let us then be up and doing,
We can make our lives sublime,
And, departing leave behind us,
Footprints on the sand of time." Anon.**

While I knew of the faculty changes at Olivet in the fall of 1969, I did not realize the scope of the exodus until it broadened in the spring of 1970. Dr. Harold Reed asked that I meet him at the airport in Flint, Michigan in December of 1969. He laid out the problem of faculty departures and asked me to consider returning as Vice-President for Academic Affairs in the summer of 1970. While I had a job, my unhappiness in it was known. I spoke to three General Superintendents each of whom said, "Do what you want to do, Willis." They asked me not to announce a decision until March first. That would meet Dr. Reed's needs. So, I accepted the offer, I made trips to Olivet primarily to prepare for the 1970-71 school year. Before leaving Kansas City, I participated in the Nazarene Student Leadership Conference at Mount Vernon Nazarene College. My son, Vincent, was there as student body president-elect at Bethany Nazarene College. It was the ninth such conference I had attended.

Professionally viewed, it was a lateral move for me. I was in contact with far more teacher prospects than any other person in the church. I had the confidence of Dr. Reed. He needed me. The prospects for success in maintaining stability in the college were good although it would take some very hard work. Dr. Reed was not ready to step down and probably should not have retired at that time. Olivet students could continue their studies with minimal disruption. Perhaps my day would come later. Delia graduated from High School and enrolled in Mid-America Nazarene College in Olathe. The children helped us move but ours was an "Empty Nest." We took Delia to the Nazarene Youth Conference in Estes Park so we had a small vacation. But I was on duty for Olivet long before I was on the payroll. The enormity of the immediate task was dawning on me. How could we find a Math teacher? Some departments had no faculty. Class schedules were published before teachers were found. David Beaman, as Assistant Dean, had labored heroically. But the students were coming; teachers were not in place!

Due to back surgery, Nona was not able to teach in the fall semester in Bourbonnais schools even though she had a contract. Her recovery was slow. The move was strenuous. We were nicely situated on Gertsam Drive in Bradley. Vince was with us until fall semester started at the University of Illinois in Champaign. We rejoined College Church. I joined Kankakee Rotary Club. Both Nona and I fit back into our church and community roles.

By the way, a word about the college presidency. In the military scheme of leadership, I would have been in line for such a promotion. To accept a lesser position would show a trait reflecting a less than commanding leadership. There was an assumption that I might succeed Dr. Reed, both in Kansas City and at Olivet. But, no discussions were held with me. It was not a condition of my return to Olivet. In a discussion with my son, Vincent, he said, "Dad, there are situations that face college presidents that you might be very uncomfortable with." True. I knew most of the Board of Trustees. They would choose the next president and I was comfortable about that. So the task at hand would "all of my powers engage." Duty calls! One faculty member asked me, "Do you consider yourself to be primarily a faculty member or a member of the administration?" I laughed and said, "When you hire, promote, set salaries, and fire faculty that's administrative. I can't be just another faculty member although I also teach." Not all those who had challenged Dr. Reed had resigned. Generally speaking, the faculty welcomed me back and cooperated admirably in our recovery.

Meantime, Dr. Reed had to recover from a devastating blow. He and Mrs. Reed took a leave for a better part of a semester and went to Australia. He left me, John Cotner, and Ralph Perry *(a troika)* in charge. We would cover the president's office, referring only major decisions to the Chairman of the Board, Dr. Paul Updike. Ralph was to cover the correspondence; otherwise all three of us would consider issues together in a weekly meeting. Individual administrators handled their duties, postponing major decisions if necessary. The plan worked well. Maybe that interlude is a commentary on the influence my return had on the institution. For Dr. Reed, the planning, building, and financing of Benner Library was an all consuming priority.

Dr. Reed had spoken of his plan to retire in 1974. But as that date drew nearer, he began to talk of postponing retirement for a year. The 25 year term was to be a 26 year term. Everyone wanted to be kind to the long term leader who brought the college so far against adverse circumstances. That extra year; however, complicated my existence and many trustees and faculty were not too happy about the delay in full resolution of the 1969 crisis. A nominating committee worked to bring nominees to succeed Dr. Reed, consulting with General Superintendent and faculty.

By 1975, most of the Olivet "system" of curriculum, instruction, scheduling, counseling, and academic administration was in place. The dean's office and registrar's office were able to meet most student needs promptly. Graduation requirements, recommendations for meeting the requirements semester by semester, rules and procedures were in place. At that moment, Ralph Hodges came up with administrative computer programs to fit the needs of a college of our size and budget. Working with Mount Vernon and Point Loma, Ralph used first one and then the others to perfect the system so that Olivet actually led the pack across the nation for a few years in computerized academic administration for small colleges.

Rebuilding the faculty was the major challenge in 1970 and 1971. We had to make several interim appointments in 1970-71. In a few courses we had to cancel the offering and help individual students to find a substitute course, a correspondence course, or find someone to offer directed study. For a two year period we had so many new professors that the whole catalog was open to question. Graduation requirements, major and minor requirements were in doubt if the new faculty did not "own" them. There were interesting faculty meetings when new faculty aired their questions or even called for immediate change. Finding qualified faculty was only half the battle. They had to unite on requirements, curriculum, and rules to develop respect and pride in the Olivet program.

One effort was a self-study titled, "A Vital College: 1980." Starting with objectives, we formed voluntary study committees to take the whole college apart and to put it together again. Standing committees retained their authority for approving actual changes, but every faculty member could air his or her ideas for a change. In a two year perusal numerous changes sponsored by the self-study committees were adopted. Some were not, but the exercise produced a sense of ownership by the faculty (continuing and newly hired). By 1974 the vacancies were filled, some excellent new faculty were taking on leadership roles and it was time to prepare a new self-study for the 1974-75 North Central Association ten-year review. That self-study and campus review brought an extension of accreditation for another ten years. This was the ultimate stamp of approval of my leadership in 1970 to 1975. Of course, it also spoke of the cooperation of at least 90-100 other faculty and staff who saw the recovery through. By the way, Dr. Robert Koenker of Ball State University was our NCA consultant examiner who worked with Olivet through the sixties and early seventies to guide us into graduate work and university status. He was a great booster as well.

The Reed's were very solicitous for the Snowbarger's. It was gratitude for our loyalty and friendship since 1936. He had chosen me as his academic dean when I was only 32. He backed me through the changes and hard work required to gain accreditation in the 50's. During my tenure we never failed to gain a ten year extension of our accreditation without conditions or interim visits. He strengthened the office of academic dean giving more and more responsibilities as the years went by. The only leaves of absence I had were eight weeks to direct a study tour in Europe in 1961 and four weeks the summer following my father's death in 1977 to help my mother get her affairs settled. Dr. Reed was greatly concerned that I get a college presidency somewhere if not at Olivet. The NCA approval in 1975 was special in that the master's degree programs got full approval and we were "cut loose" to add additional graduate programs as we saw fit.

My work in the church multiplied in the 70's. I was reelected to the local board at College Church and to the District Advisory Board (of which I was secretary) for the Chicago Central District. In 1972 I was elected to the General Board, Church of the Nazarene at Headquarters. This post lasted for 13 years, most of that time on the Finance Committee and the Department of Publication. I was chairman of each of these committees for a time.

Vincent took two years of graduate work at the University of Illinois. He got a teaching assistantship in Political Science. In both history and political science his graduate work was very much the same as mine. As he finished his Master's degree he was tired of school so he took a teaching job at Mid-America Nazarene College. His wife was a Bethany Nazarene College graduate and helped him by working at the Episcopalian Student Ministry Center in Champaign. Together they moved to Olathe, Kansas and put down their roots there.

Delia, our daughter, finished her business degree with her husband Garry Pittman in 1974. She took an accounting job with Western Auto stores then later taught business two years. Then she decided to go back to college to complete her B.S.N. degree (nursing). Now both of our children were in Olathe. I haven't said much about our children, but they were a joy to us. They were involved heavily in church youth groups and their college courses and activities. All the way through high school and college we went as a family to reunions and they were enjoying the family contacts. We never asked them to do, or not do, anything for the sake of parents. Do what is right! They really do honor their father and mother.

Back to the college, for that was my life. In 1970-74, I was heavily involved in the Kankakee Rotary Club serving as President 1975-76. I was active in the Rotary Club's initiating the "meals-on-wheels" programs through Riverside Medical Center. We went to the Council for the Advancement of Small Colleges (CASC) meetings until they decided we were too large. I often represented Olivet at meetings of Illinois colleges. We regularly wrote proposals for Title VI grants, federal money channeled through a state agency to public and independent colleges for updating equipment. We continued regular meetings of the Planning Commission. Olivet sent students and faculty to Argonne National Laboratory for study and teaching. This was under the auspices of Associated Colleges of the Chicago Area, of which I was president for a year. Starting the nursing major and searching for faculty was a big job. State approval was mandatory and national accreditation (NLN) was ultimately required. Prospective teachers were experienced in hospitals but not in the classroom. Then, there was a library to be built. It must accommodate a computer center, media services, archives, and radio station. I was on that building committee as well as most of the others built in the Reed years.

By the way, Nona had recovered sufficiently by the Fall of 1971 that she sought a full time teaching job but no opening was available to her. So she did part time or substitute teaching for ten years. She started a music program at Custer Park. Her study showed that three students had some musical experience, one had a violin but couldn't play it; another had a drum set and one had a Jew's harp. Within one year they had a wonderful turn out for a 2:30 p.m. concert with instruments and choir numbers! Eventually, Nona had more than 11 years of teaching experience, enough that she qualified for health insurance upon retirement. She had one assignment teaching French and another in special education which she enjoyed thoroughly.

All of these projects and assignments meant interminable time in committee meetings. I tried to keep these meetings short and to the point. But, no one believed that. My office was often like Grand Central Station and my only exit was through the waiting line. I had remarkably good secretaries and in Dr. Reed's final years, Lora Donoho was my assistant dean. She took the students and I took the faculty. That worked well.

179

With the Registrar's office (adjacent) we took the attitude "This is where your problems can be solved." Even though very busy at times, we were all a cordial team. We loved everybody!

Enrollment had dropped too much and recruitment of new students was neglected. So Gordon Wickersham and I shouldered that task in the spring of 1975. Attention was centered on the choice of the new president and retirement of Dr. Reed. But, Gordon and I produced a gain in enrollment for fall, 1975. This kind of filling the gap occurs frequently when interim arrangements weren't working. That wasn't in the dean's department but something had to be done. By the way, an era had ended.

CH. XIX ALL MY POWERS
ENGAGE (1975-1986)

"The best way out is always through." Robert Frost

When Dr. Leslie Parrott was elected president of Olivet, I immediately offered my resignation. The nominating committee had offered the Board of Trustees only one name. He promptly turned down my offer to step aside. During his visit to the campus in February, 1975, Nona and I took the Parrotts to Sunday dinner and spent the afternoon discussing my working with him and Nona's working with Loralee in the faculty ladies group. Later we spent a whole day together in Kansas City discussing my role, my preferences and about what he expected of me. All of this was very cordial. He asked me to plan an inauguration of the new president.

COLLEGE ACTIVITIES

The year 1975-76 was extremely busy for me and my office. I was president of the Kankakee Rotary Club, the inauguration was a big event, and there were administrative adjustments. I also lost Lora Donoho, my assistant dean. A number of Dr. Reed's materials for transition to a new president ended up in my office. There was uncertainty and at times almost chaos at my end of the Burke Administration building's first floor. My role had broadened to include a revision of the Bylaws, fund raising through applications for Title III federal funds, and implementation of certain dreams of the new administration. Of course, I had all of my former duties plus some of the new priorities. I must admit that the change of administrations kept me off balance.

It should be Dr. Parrot's responsibility to clearly state his priorities for Olivet. I believe he would agree on these (order is random, not an indication of importance):

1. **The campus should have a park-like atmosphere. Beauty, peace, and order would be conducive to study, achievement and maturation. We must brighten our image in publications.**
2. **We should be reconciled to our community. Maternity Church, St. Viator's alumni, Bourbonnais, and Kankakee should value Olivet for what it is; a Nazarene College of liberal arts.**
3. **Expanding and adding new programs such as degree completion for adults, graduate programs in more fields of study, and continuing education in-service for pastors.**
4. **Full adaptation and expansion of the computer functions in administration, instruction and library.**
5. **Recruitment and retention of students should get more attention. Administrative adjustments as well as improved orientation and counseling of students would help to maintain enrollment and graduation rates.**
6. **An enlarged intercollegiate athletic program in harmony with Title IX requirements would help recruitment, retention, and student morale. Building Snowbarger Athletic Park. This came to me as a complete surprise and I was highly pleased by the honor.**
7. **Closer relationship to Nazarene Churches through speakers and services provided by personnel.**
8. **Enrich the chapel program and improve student attitudes toward this requirement to the benefit of the Olivet Community.**
9. **Build Larsen Fine Arts Center and Parrott Gymnasium.**

I had no problem in supporting these priorities. He left the academic priorities much as I had seen them for years. The only problem was the lack of financial support sufficient to do all of the projects at once; so "Which wheel squeaks the loudest?" and, Where do I spend my time and energy? By the way, Dr. Parrott's priorities were nearly all accomplished.

Thus began my eleven year tenure with Dr. Parrott. It was, in a sense, a marathon. After one year, I got my assistant dean back, Norman Moore. Guarding accreditation was an even more demanding task. Fortunately,

Connie Skinner as my administrative assistant stayed with me and saved my life! Departmental accreditation crowded in. First it was Teacher Education (NCATE), then music (NASM), then nursing (NLN), and Dietetics. Social work, Chemistry, and Business inquired and talked about it. The Dean's office had a role to play in each application. The general accreditation by North Central Association was concerned about the institution's strength and viability, whereas, departmental accreditation was to assure that one department got its share of administrative backing and fund allocation. So, one type of accreditation was set up against the other. And another 25 departments must be given their share. Connie, Norman, and I survived all these sand traps. And Olivet grew and improved. Our students were well served – that's what counts. I kept nearly prefect attendance at meetings of the North Central Association and the Association for Higher Education whose meetings were usually in Chicago. There I saw most Nazarene administrators, academic deans, and most of the real experts in higher education independent and state sponsored. Linford Marqaurt took over my roles in Illinois university relations.

Another aspect of change grew in the 70s and 80s. Field service in the 1940's was almost totally "student teaching." By the 1970's there were field experiences added to one field after another until major components were required in ministerial training, social work, consumer sciences, business, nursing, political science, psychology, and perhaps others. In many cases, legal documents were negotiated to guide the relationships between the college, students, hospitals, and businesses. Since the college attorney was a former student of mine, I drafted agreements, he initialed them, and we saved some money. But there was quite a work load to maintain those relationships.

BIG CHANGES COME TO OLIVET

The computer revolution in the 1970's began with very elementary equipment, a FORTRAN course, and a lot of punch cards. By 1975, we had talked to an IBM representative and started talking with Ralph Hodges, a friend from Ohio. By the time of my retirement we had gotten to a fairly adequate system of administrative reports relating to student records, monthly financial reports, and numerous other data in administrative offices. In my last year, we finally had a network of five offices, cable connecting the major buildings to the computer center, and a computer science major. Personally, I began my learning about computers when I audited a FORTRAN course while Vince, my son, took it for credit in a January term (1971). I cannot evaluate our progress in computer as an instructional tool but I feel secure in knowing that Gordon Whitten,

Rogers Cox, Harvey Teas, Ivor Newsham, Richard Wirt, and Virgil Vail provided superior knowledge and skill to get Olivet into the computer game early, without too many false moves. Larry Vail, chairman of the Computer Sciences Department, says that ONU was about 20 years ahead of the wave of computerization.

A federal program for assistance to developing colleges (Title III) was called to our attention by an alumnus, Robert Keyes, who worked with the Mid-continent Regional Educational Laboratory of Kansas City. He was the son-in-law of Dr. S.T. Ludwig who also was an ONU alumnus. Through perhaps five or six applications as a single institution and others as part of a consortium, Olivet received more than three million dollars between 1975 and 1985. It went for computers, graduate work by professors working to complete doctorates, career planning and placement offices, as we described our needs and brought about the improvements promised. Dr. Ivor Newsham was placed in charge of this program during my final years as academic dean. Again a lot of work and a lot was accomplished.

By the Way, we had a pleasant surprise when the Salvation Army Training College in Chicago approached me about a joint program leading to an Associate degree. I had admired their compassionate ministries through the years and rang the bells at Christmas times. The commander of the school visited me in my office and we talked of courses an Olivet professor might teach in Chicago to enrich their programs and their courses, which deserved transfer credit. As we moved ahead, they had access to our library and we built a program that was definitely equivalent to an associate degree at Olivet. Degrees were awarded at a commencement in Chicago. I introduced their leaders to North Central Association officials and they began to seek accreditation on their own. Our friendship with the Salvation Army officers was reinforced by trips to Wrigley Field to see a Cubs game, parking free at the training college nearby.

I read in the newspaper about some small colleges in the Chicago area who were trying to gain for their students access to Argonne National Laboratory. The atomic energy people in Washington had guarded their secrets very well but the Big Ten Universities had been given access to use certain expensive equipment and were granted limited instructional privileges. Why not small colleges? We were within an hour from the lab so we joined "Associated Colleges of the Chicago Area." Certain courses were taught by our professors and use of Argonne's equipment was granted. I was elected president of ACCA for one year. Not only was this a boon to a few advanced students, but our reputation among the Chicago Colleges was enhanced.

Added to the academic program of Olivet was an expanded effort in faculty development. For years, we had a provision for two faculty meetings per month. One was to conduct business. The other was reserved for instructional improvement activities. We had encouraged the sharing of syllabi and visiting the class sessions of colleagues on invitation. Now we went into the process of annual evaluations, recommendations for promotion, sabbatical leave applications and advanced graduate work leading to the doctorate. Title III money assisted. Visiting specialists were called in for the second faculty meetings. Faculty leadership in these developments minimized objections to the extra time required.

Starting the intercollegiate competition in football made for some notoriety for Olivet among the Nazarene Colleges and occupied a lot of our free time. When I was secretary for the Department of Education in Kansas City, I wrote guidelines for intercollegiate athletics passed by the General Board of the Church of the Nazarene. The simple statement "Because of the expense involved, Nazarene Colleges will not participate in intercollegiate football." Now Olivet was planning to start football. The Department of Education in Kansas City cried foul. But the College Board of Trustees had approved and had disregarded the advice from the General Headquarters. Much correspondence and conversation ensued. Eventually, I was asked to present Olivet's case to the General Board. After listening to my contrasting of the birds-eye-view and the worms-eye-view, the General Board gave us the go ahead. Now four of the Nazarene universities think they can bear "the expense involved." Olivet teams did well in other sports so our image was improved and our name was advertised.

By the Way, I have highlighted the additions to my load in the dean's office in the late 70's and early 80's. Believe it or not, the regular duties of academic administration went on. Freshman advising and orientation became more intense and better implemented. The President's Dinner became an institution in its own right with introductions, service awards, and recognitions. Institutional, federal, and state loans and scholarships grew by leaps and bounds. Hiring and promoting of faculty, tenure, library, departmental-budgets, editing the catalog, curricular changes, artist-lecture series, building committees, a more powerful WONU, bylaws, forward planning, and a myriad of details that affect student learning and graduation occupied every waking moment. Jim Tripp and I were the arbiters when a storm threatened. At about 5:30 a.m. we decided when classes should be cancelled. Jim Knight was a mainstay in the Registrar's office. He, the scholarship committee, and I were "the committee on exceptions." We believed in, and practiced common sense in implementing the rules and had an entry explaining our reasons, in writing, for all exceptions granted.

A Crusty Administrator, 1981

One of my chores through the years was to serve on the building committees. We always had an advisory users committee of which I was a part. Then my name was on the Board's committee to forward the users' ideas for final action. The Larsen Fine Arts building was the first major building undertaken after Dr. Parrott became president. Jim Keys was the architect. For Douglas Perry this was his first big project to oversee as Business Manager. The Keys' firm had worked with Richardson, Severns, and Scheeler on several other buildings at Olivet and relied on their engineering department for technical services. Now Keys was associated with another firm for engineering drawings. It is a beautiful building but there were problems. Especially troublesome was the shifting of heating and ventilation equipment from the roof to the basement. It was a very difficult project compared to the Benner Library. The same contractor built the Powers President's Home. I was on the building committee for the athletic complex through the preliminary plans. Later those plans were scrapped and I was gone before the plans for the Les Parrott Center were drawn and built. The Ward (football) Field, the Watson Baseball Field, and the entire athletic park were laid out and built while I was still on the scene. It is one of the finest college outdoor athletic facilities anywhere in the country. I was surprised and pleased to have it dedicated in my honor at Homecoming, 1982.

Graduate programs were divided between Religion and Education. Each of these had a graduate director and accreditation of new programs was separate. When retirement and other personnel changes disrupted these programs, I took on the duties of director of Graduate Studies for a year or two; another example of spreading myself too thin. Through it all, I had excellent support from the faculty. A testimonial to this is the faculty meeting in April, 1986. It turned into "a roast" for the retiring dean and it is on videotape.

CHURCH LEADERSHIP

Upon returning to Olivet in 1970, I resumed my roles as a member of College Church of the Nazarene. I was a Sunday school teacher, Nona and I sang in College Church Choir. I was a member of the church board, and on building committees. I took some ribbing; namely that I was in the choir so I could check the faculty church attendance.

I served on the Chicago Central District Advisory board for a total of 32 years; its secretary for most of these years. That meant that I signed numerous loan applications as the district cosigned loan applications for small or beginning churches. As I considered my risk in case of default, I wondered if the banks knew what they were doing. I was worth less than one percent of the notes I signed for! Of course, it was a district liability. The district elected me to be a delegate to a general assembly. Eventually, I was a member of nine general assemblies.

On the General Church level I was elected Secretary of Education in 1965-70. I was elected to the General Board representing educational institutions in 1972 and served in that capacity until 1985. In that year, I lost the election by a few votes. While I was nominated for reelection, someone had mentioned publicly, "He's retiring." I was 63 at the time, but that seemed to turn the tide and another beat me out. While on the General Board, I served on the Finance Committee and was chairman for several years. I also served on the Department of Publications and chaired that department. In a reorganization of Nazarene Publishing House, I was named director and eventually chairman of its Board of Directors. For one term, I served as president of the General Board and in the capacity signed papers to purchase a complete floor of a skyscraper in Hong Kong for use as a Nazarene Church. Nona and I later visited that church.

In all of my moves, we have transferred our membership promptly and always voted yes for the return of our pastor. My finest friends and my best prayer supporters are in the church. We delight in giving to God through our gifts to the church. It always gives back more than we give. It's a bargain.

COMMUNITY

In the Kankakee community, I got my start in the historical society. We dug up bricks from the foundation of the first house in Bourbonnais as they widened the highway on the corner by Burke Administration building. I spoke in numerous club meetings and we supported the start of Kankakee Community College. We supplied foreign language instruction for their students and they relied on our faculty for some summer teaching.

Nona and I were members of the 20th Century club, a group of community professionals and business people. Our membership included old-timers, doctors, lawyers, and educational administrators. We were a group of some thirty or more, husbands and wives. We were somewhat like a Chatauqua society; we met in the homes of our members, provided our own programs, and had refreshments. We met monthly, generally a paper and discussion.

I joined Rotary in Kankakee in 1970 and I am still a member. I was president in 1975-76. This was a very demanding assignment and one could easily spend full-time in it. Of the service clubs, Rotary is more internationally oriented. Nona and I went to the annual conference in New Orleans in 1976. It was held in the Superdome. One of the rewarding activities for me was the sponsoring of a new "meals-on-wheels" program for Kankakee. We gave leadership and recognition. Churches provided most of the volunteers. Riverside hospital provided the meals.

When the community made a pitch to attract the new plant General Motors was planning for the production of Saturn automobiles, I served as a member of the committee to write the section detailing the educational assets. We described the established programs in the community from kindergarten through college and graduate work. While this chapter painted a favorable picture, the plant was located in Tennessee. I felt I had a role in the reconciliation with the Catholic community through running for a position on the Village Board, working for a genuine public school, and numerous friendships with Catholic neighbors in Bourbonnais.

Largely through the leadership of Dr. Parrott, but not of his planning, a service of reconciliation was held in Maternity Church. He was presented as "a hometown boy." The last president of St. Viator's College was present and referred to Olivet as continuing the educational task of St. Viator's while they shifted to mission work in 40 countries of the world. We returned old home plate, the sun-dial, and theologian's bench to them and we reserved the Viatorian room in Ludwig Center for artifacts and memorabilia of the former owners of the campus.

In general, I feel that I was able to play a constructive role in the eleven years I served under Dr. Leslie Parrott. We had worked closely together through the 1960s. Eventually, our paths crossed through the 70s and 80s, so for 30 years we worked together on a wide variety of projects. I learned a great deal from him although we were different in many ways. His public speaking ability and personality caused the whole community to sit up and take notice. Mary Alice Small and her newspaper tied the community to the college and it all came about through Dr. Parrott's influence. Writing and preaching caused the whole church to take notice. Olivet was to be reckoned with.

CH. XX THE PROOF IS IN THE PUDDING

**"So live that you wouldn't be ashamed to sell
the family parrot to the town gossip." Will Rogers**

By the way, my greatest responsibility in the 1970's and 1980's was to be a husband and a father. In the fast moving schedule of a college teacher and administrator I fear that I trimmed the corners when it came to family responsibilities. I did <u>not</u> get to all of Vince's ball games, or concerts, or Delia's school activities. No regular time alone with each of the children. I did not take Nona out for breakfast every Saturday morning. God had given me a beautiful family. But I spent more time with other people's kids! Who says, "I wish I had spent more time in the office," when you come to evaluate the time you spent with your family? And are you sure that it is correct to say that you can substitute "quality time" for quantity of time?

Nona and my children were so kind to me not to harp on my failings. We always had our evening meal together, and more often than not, breakfast. My out-of-town trips away from them were few. I walked to work while the children were still at home. When I put in my appearance around 5:30 or 6:00 p.m. they came bounding out to meet me. Vince usually had a ball and glove. So we played catch; me in my white shirt. The church nursery was for infants only. So we learned early that it went better if we sat on the second or third row of pews in the sanctuary. They were quite orderly if they could see and hear what was going on. We had very few discipline problems and they loved and honored father and mother. At no point did either of them object to going to church. During high school years, it was the center of their activities.

191

Nona was a beautiful better half of the team. Vince and Delia's responsibility was a product of mothering. She held the fort! They seemed to understand my heavy load. But, I noticed that Vince made more time for his boys than he got from me. Nona was a good cook, kept the house presentable and welcomed the playmates. I had them "help" me with yard work. She gave them cookies. In 1964-65 a pack of five or six boys (Vince's friends) stopped by our house going and coming from school. Home made ice cream was the main treat. We seldom ate out and allowances were of the nickel and dime variety; maybe a quarter. They were paid for major tasks. Somehow, they both learned early to manage their money. When Vince was in college and had an afternoon job and his own money, I received a call, "Dad, I need a new pair of shoes." "I can believe that but why are you calling me?" "Well, I have the money but what brand, style, and price range?" I was amused. A nineteen year old who wants to spend carefully his hard earned shekels! Poor Nona had to put up with penny-pinching and still showed her deep love for me. On our trips as a family to Texas and Kansas it was not unusual for us to arrive in Bourbonnais with less than $2. And this was the era before credit cards. We had wonderful visits with family. Only once did we drive to Dallas non-stop. The excuse was "The baby won't let us sleep if we take a motel." The fact was we couldn't afford it.

Nona belonged to the Impromptu Club which started in the 1950s and is still going strong. These ladies were faithful friends, held monthly meetings, and were a mutual support society for 50 years plus. Nona took her course work to prepare to teach music in public schools. The first jobs helped me through graduate school, in my early years as a professor, then as a stay at home mother. She had been out of college thirteen years before Delia was ready for first grade. Teaching jobs were somewhat scarce, especially if you were looking for a full-time music position. She taught four of our five years in the Kansas City area. Being a top rank musician herself, she gloried in the programs her classes could produce. She was good at it. Her back surgery in 1970 made it necessary for her to lay out for a year. She was never able to find another full-time music job. So she took part-time or interim jobs to supplement the family income and support the children through college. By the way, our kids did not receive tuition remission as did other children of Olivet's faculty. I was not on a Nazarene faculty 1965-70. I was a church administrator! Mid-America did not participate with full tuition grants to faculty children from other Nazarene colleges. Delia got a grant of $350 for one semester. Vince got none from Bethany Nazarene College. They did assist him for a summer of travel on a college quartet and later as student body president in his senior year.

We borrowed on our life insurance policies, squeezed the family budget tighter, and eventually paid all the bills ourselves. Vince graduated in 1971 and Delia in 1974. Their college years were my most stressful in Kansas City and at Olivet. They had beautiful weddings, Vince and Carolyn at College Church (Bourbonnais) and Delia and Garry in Kansas City First Church. All four had bachelor's degrees and a good start in married life.

The empty nest slipped up on us. We had planned a trip by car to Mexico City and the Southwestern United States. Dr. Honorato Rosa helped us plan but it never happened. We still hoped for vacations together but trips to the Snowbarger family reunion were the best we could do. Most of the trips with children and grand children were those to Colorado Springs, at Golden Bell Ranch. They never lost interest but work schedules complicated our getting together. Before my retirement, I made a beautiful trip to the Holy Land while Nona spent two weeks with her mother in Dallas. I was really impressed with Teddy Kolloch, the mayor of Jerusalem. Our group of Christian College deans was entertained at a reception in his home. My travels to Christian college campuses took me to at least 40 colleges and all over the USA. Nona accompanied me to at least twelve of those colleges and several universities. But our travel after 1975 was severely limited except for college or church business.

We have five grand children of whom we are very proud. The last was born in April, 1986 while we were in Olathe, Kansas searching for a retirement home. She is now in college. Angie and Jeff were born in 1977. Scott and Mathew were born in 1980. They were a joy to us as well as to their parents. As the saying goes, "Had we known how much fun they were, we would have had them first." I know I had excellent parents. Nona and I tried to be good parents. Our kids are excellent parents. So why shouldn't the grand kids excel? Each one is different but a joy! They are mine.

By the way, my responsibility to my parents loomed larger in the same period of time that my children were married and my grand children were born. By 1970 my dad was 76 and my mother was 74. They last visited us in our home the first week of April, 1973. They always enjoyed being in our home but 750 miles separated us so, generally, to be with them, meant that we did the traveling. My dad had Parkinson's disease. He said, "It makes me feel like a dummy." I felt terrible not to take him to Rotary luncheon with me. But it took him an hour and one-half to eat. Now it was time for them to move off the farm, out of the house where they had lived for 56 years! My mother told us to come and get what we wanted of the household possessions we cooperated reluctantly July 4, 1975. She was just as brave and strong as when she bid me good-bye to leave for the

South Pacific without a tear. It testified to her trust in God's care for his own. Earthly prospects were certainly fading. In 1977 we visiting them in the nursing home and signed the trust papers which made me legally responsible for the property and my mother's care. I had a lot to learn.

We lived at 1279 Gertsam drive in Bradley from 1970-1986. It was a beautiful home and we had lots of guests. We entertained the history majors nearly every year. In the 80's we invited administrators and division chairmen for a dinner in our back yard. In 1985, we decided to take the group (wives were included) to White Fence Farm. It was our way of saying thank you to those upon whom we depended so much. The weather generally favored us. We did it just as the new academic year was starting.

In the last eight years we were active at Olivet, Nona underwent numerous operations. Two abdominal surgeries, cataract removal on her right eye and lens implantation, and four foot operations were required. In one of the operations she contracted a staph infection. I spent a lot of time just visiting her in the hospital. Especially difficult to manage, were those operations in Chicago. In the eye operation, Dr. Burns told me he had to hold the lens in place by hand because the pupil would not contract normally. Fifteen years later, we learned that the medication used to counteract dilation worked very slowly in cases of Alzheimer patients. We were not aware of that condition until more than 12 years later. Other symptoms of trouble came to our attention in 1982 and following. She did not attempt to teach after that. We continued our church assignments. She was especially interested in World Missions.

By 1984, it was time for me to think ahead. As I reflected on my father and mother's health and vitality as they aged, I felt I was likely to be able to carry a full load with competency up to age 75. If I retired at 65 then what was I to do with the next yen years? Was it biblical to retire? Or should I give of myself as long as I was able? If I am not at Olivet, where should I be? Doing what? So I began casting about for alternative opportunities. There were possibilities. I had done some higher education consulting work while at Olivet. Maybe I could step out on my own and serve their Illinois colleges, perhaps other Nazarene colleges, or other denominations. Five colleges suggested there would be a place for me on a regular basis, full or part time. I was on the short list for the presidency at three Nazarene colleges and one other Christian college. I spoke with John Minter who did comparative studies of small college budgets, salaries, costs, with data coming off the reports given to the federal government. He thought I could help to critique the data and interpret it for his clients. I was in correspondence with Richard Meeth who was using his many connections to start a new International Graduate School in St. Louis. He wanted me but was tragically killed the week before I was to meet him in St. Louis in April, 1986. I narrowly missed the job as head of the Mid-continental Regional Education Laboratory then in Kansas City. Turns out that the man, Lawrence Fish, who was ultimately to name the successor to lead McREL, was my classmate at Southern Nazarene University (class of '42). He told me that, had he known I was available, the job would have been mine. Apparently, God did not see fit to open even one of these doors. As things have worked together for good for me and my family, I am happy and content. I was saved from the Peter Principle!

At first I was concerned about retirement finance but that worked out well. The worst part is losing your work. Are we suddenly worthless? What do you do with your time? Most of my friends of retirement age work for that reason. But is retiring like jumping off a cliff? Yes, and it is no joke. The anxieties are real. So when we have a retirement celebration, don't say, "You deserve a rest." That's a big part of the problem after six weeks of resting. Back in 1982, Dr. Parrott invited me to drive with him to the Illinois Preachers' meeting at Lake Barkley in Kentucky. We began talking about retirement and I volunteered that I should retire before Dr. Parrott because I was one year older than he. It would not be in the best interest of the college for both of us to retire in the same year. So we talked of several options. We met with Dr. Orville Jenkins, the speaker for the meeting. We three had been the Research Committee for the Education Commission 1960-64. We sought his input. On the return trip to the campus, Dr. Parrot offered me several options. (1) Stay on as full-time dean with a full-time assistant dean until normal retirement at 65, (2) become dean of Graduate Studies, or (3) serve as government relations coordinator (state and federal) and teach a part time load.

From 1983 to 1986 nothing opened for me so I chose to take option one which Dr. Parrott offered me which was to stay as Vice-President for Academic Affairs until August, 1986. Then, I would retire and move to another location so as not to complicate the work of the new dean. We still had to undergo a North Central review in 1984-85 and all the work of the office had intensified. The load was getting to be too much and I felt that, for the good of the college, I should step aside at age 65. So I faced a very busy, complicated, and yes, disagreeable two years. There was no choice but to face up to it and do my best.

I started January, 1985 by going with Delia to Topeka, Kansas for the swearing in ceremony of Vince. He had been elected to the Kansas legislature – his beginning in politics. When he took me to the airport for my return to Olivet I updated him on my future plans. We spoke briefly of my working with him in his practice of law and public service. In February we had our NCA visit and were passed for another ten years. That same week Dr. Parrott had discussed the impending change of deans with the district superintendents from the Olivet zone. He talked with me about raising a search committee. My only request was that I was not made a lame duck and that I was only 63½ years old. On March 6 our faculty met and he announced the formation of the search committee. I was in the dreaded lame duck year.

In April, I took the Illinois Life Insurance agent's exam and passed it. In June, I gave the Commencement address at Trevecca Nazarene College. We flew to San Diego for a Faith and Learning Conference, met Vince, Carolyn and their family. We drove to Anaheim for the General Assembly. My former college roommate, Ray Hurn was elected General Superintendent. My service on the General Board was terminated. In August we traveled to Colorado Springs for the Snowbarger reunion. On August 24, I celebrated my 64th birthday and we opened the new school year with a faculty meeting. My diary is remarkably blank until October 6th when it says, "Dr. Ivor Newsham was elected as my successor in the office of academic dean." He was teaching a full load so the calendar year has references to National League of Nursing, C.S. Lewis' Book of the Year, tenure for coaches, Salvation Army, NCHEMS, and a new Allen organ for chapel. My work was finished.

The Olivet community did many things to give us a warm retirement farewell. The college sent us on a four-week, four island tour of Hawaii. College Church gave us a huge farewell reception. The college trustees voted a large gift to bridge our health insurance plans and such uncertainties. Then they invited us and our family to join the trustees at a beautiful dinner. I was invited to be the speaker at the 1986 commencement. That went a long way to erase the horrible feelings of December 30, 1985 when I went alone to empty my desk and turn in my keys so that another could take my place on January 1st.

With little or nothing to do January through August of 1986 except one course, I was quite unhappy. Nothing opened for me or I would have left earlier. As I look back on the last year and one-half I was at Olivet, the college did well, the students were well served, I shouldn't have acted as though any disaster had befallen the college. These changes take place quite regularly and the institution should be strong enough scarcely to miss a beat. If I am the one for whom the time has come, it's up to me (in Barbara Bush's words) to "Get over it!"

CH. XXI INORDINATE
SELF-ESTEEM

"My son, do not despise the Lord's discipline and do not resent his rebuke, because the Lord disciplines those he loves as a father the son he delights in."
Proverbs 3:11-12 (NIV)

RETIREMENT

I am assured of God's love. What a come down from a life of privilege, the service of a wonderful secretary, all of the hullabaloo. From "detached" in the Navy to "retirement," there is something very bad in there.

From 1992 onward we started 50th anniversary celebrations: my graduation from college, our wedding, my naval service, graduate study, move to Olivet, and the list continues. Nona was with me in our home until December, 1995. She was in assisted living care, then skilled care for 4½ years. She passed away quietly February 22, 2000. We donated her remains to science at the University of Kansas Medical Center. The cremains were buried in Memorial Gardens in Kankakee, Illinois. In all I had cared for her nine years. I visited her daily, except a few times when counselors urged me to get away for a weekend or a short trip. We were sweethearts to the end, but she could not speak to me for the last year of her life. Alzheimer's is a sad disease and no medication worked in her case.

When my name was presented in nomination at General Assembly, someone from the floor said, "Oh, he's retiring." Others who were retired served on the General Board but that was enough; another was elected on a fairly close vote. For Dr. Parrott, the 1985 General Assembly was even more memorable. He had run strongly in balloting for General Superintendent in the previous General Assembly and got a considerable vote at Anaheim. But there was a different mix of delegates there and, well before the final election of others, it was apparent that he would not be elected. Age was catching up with him and likely this was his last chance. I had assured him in 1980 and again in 1985 that I wanted to stay clear of any action that would prejudice his chances of election to this highest office in the church. So far as I know, I kept this promise and he appreciated it. But, these considerations seem to have been intertwined in the timing of the Search Committee deadlines and the proposed Board action on the choice of a new dean. Dr. Parrott wanted to choose the new administrator, even if he were not to be president of Olivet after July, 1985. By pressing for action before the General Assembly, my life was complicated and, I believe, my final year was made more difficult.

Maybe all retirement are just as unpredictable and messy, especially if you like your job and like to work. They took my work away from me— prematurely. That was abundantly clear by February, 1986. My "training in" assignments largely vanished. I spent whole days (and many half days) teaching myself to use my new personal computer. I attended team meetings, may have spent ten days assisting with budget and interviewing candidates for the faculty. But these activities were not determinative and I was not in on major decisions. I agreed to give commencement addresses at Olivet and Kankakee Community College. I printed and distributed brochures announcing my availability for consultation. I filed the necessary forms to activate my TIAA-CREF and social security retirement income by September. For eight months, I , who had been swamped with multiple assignments for so long, had almost nothing to do. They paid my salary through August but I was not on leave. I had never had the usual sabbatical in my thirty-two years at ONC and had seldom been able to arrange my full one-month of vacation per year. At the time, I felt the displacement very keenly. Almost as keen was the mystery as to why I had no calls from other Nazarene colleges.

After turning all the stones I knew to turn in pursuit of my profession as a teacher and administrator, I began to look elsewhere. I considered real estate. I talked with Vincent about joint activities to assist his practice. Ultimately, I chose, as had been my life-long pattern, to stay in character and continue to be the educational professional. Eventually (well after the school year was over) Gordon Wetmore, Chairman of the Nazarene Education Commission, arranged an interview and I became a part-time research director. (I think both Dr. Parrott and Dr. Eugene Stowe put in a good word for me.) I had already begun to consult with the

Education Secretary of the Wesleyan Church Headquarters. While there was nothing firm as of Commencement Day, 1986, I was to keep busy at meaningful tasks until General Assembly, 1989.

It is important to record very important support that came to me during these years of uncertainty and impending change. Dr. Edward Mann and Dr. Mark Moore were very supportive and tried to find a different assignment for me. At Olivet, Curtis Brady, Charles Beatty, Ottis Sayes, Forest Benner, Harlow Hopkins, and Joseph Nielson--all in specific ways put themselves out to encourage and support me. The division chairmen, faculty, student leaders, the community college administrators, and lots of ordinary people sent me notes, spoke words of encouragement, and let me know my work was appreciated.

As I reflect back on what happened to me, I conclude that the word "retirement" is poison. I will not recount all the things "I should have done" in 1982 and following. Even though age discrimination is real, I probably should have "resigned" not "retired." Consulting could be both challenging and frustrating. It could save our colleges thousands of dollars but they go on blowing their money on special assignments to faculty members for one-half load credit here ($25,000 with benefits) and one-third load credit there and find that the semester is more than half gone before anything is produced. When Title III funds were not readily available after 1986, the colleges quit hiring consultants of my type and did very little on a contract for service arrangement. I have volunteered my service in some instances and still there were very few calls. Could it be that "retired" carries the connotation of incompetency? I look at some of the photos that were taken of me in 1986. I was tired, I needed rest. A year later I was well rested. My health was stronger at ages 66 to 72 than it was at age 62 to 64. Only three or four college administrators have taken note of that in my case. But, you are on your own in this old world. The word is "cope." I have stirred the pot and some good things developed for me even in retirement.

As we drove south and west an Interstate highways 55 and 70, the haunting song that Peggy Lee made famous, "Is That All There Is?", went through my mind (vamp and all). No matter that I had other calls in due time, the separation at Olivet was "retirement" for us. There was the memorable last faculty meeting. My last chapel talk brought lots of compliments from students. The College Church farewell was beautiful. The dedication of the *Aurora*, autographed baseballs from the team, a half-time recognition and hand-shake at mid-court with Captain Steve Davis, of the basketball team, and dozens of personal letters made for a bold punctuation mark. A chapter was closed with appreciation and warmth, even tinges of anxiety over our leaving. Oh yes, and the ubiquitous plaque--a wall full of them. Without a doubt a major change unlike anything we had previously experienced was taking place. We were pulling up roots, leaving a community where we had belonged for nearly forty years, where our children had been born. It was all very unnatural. It was somewhat like jumping off a cliff; except I have never jumped off a cliff. No, "that is [not] all there is." It just felt that way for a time.

With literally no assignment at all, we were turned loose on the world. Could we manage such freedom? Could we live together in one house twenty-four hours a day? We had never tried that before. We could. We drove to the Gulf Coast for my niece, Rhonda's, wedding. We stopped by Dallas for a week and lived in Nona's mother's apartment so we could visit her in the nursing home. House hunting in the Kansas City area gave a chance to plan with our children. Eventually, it was time to pack the boxes and prepare for the arrival of the moving van. The Education Commission decided on a series of research instruments that included a survey of college, Bible college, and seminary personnel. The time table under which they worked required that such surveys should be administered in the Fall, 1986. Part-time and without a secretary, I felt the pressure to work fast to meet such a schedule. For the second time in our experience, we had to close on one house before selling our previous house. Now the pressure was mounting and I was beginning to feel more normal!

We settled into Olathe College Church and the ministry of Paul Cunningham and Frank Moore's Sunday school class. We began to participate in Prime Time activities. My Bethany-Peniel Class of '42 began alternate year reunions in 1987. We enjoyed our grandchildren and children on a weekly, sometimes daily basis. I transferred my Rotary membership to Olathe and made many new community friends. We enjoyed the contacts with many Olivetians in the Kansas City area including Nashes, Naomi Larsen, Esther Tripp, Paul Cunninghams, Dennis Apples, and alumni serving MidAmerica Nazarene College, headquarters, and Nazarene Publishing House. Incidentally, I had continued to serve as Chairman of the Nazarene Publishing House Board and on the search committee seeking nominees to replace Bud Lunn as Manager upon his retirement. We also renewed friendships with people at First Church where we were members 1965-1970 and headquarters employees with whom I had worked for those five years.

"The paths have fallen to us in pleasant places." We must look ahead, not back. We decided that we must be flexible, bags packed, and ready for whatever opened to us. Meantime, there was free time and we needed to learn to live at a slower pace.

The tasks that I had in 1986 and early 1987 were associated with the Nazarene Education Commission and the Wesleyan Church. Most of the work was done at home with occasional trips to Nazarene headquarters for assistance from the secretarial staff of the General Secretary's Office. To interview and administer the surveys, I traveled to each of the Nazarene colleges in the United States and Canada. Only after a grant was received from Lilly Foundation did we plan trips to the Asia Pacific Regional Conference in Manila June, 1987 and Mexico and Central America November, 1987. It was good to see all of the colleges again and to get to Nazarene Indian Bible College, Asia Pacific Nazarene Theological Seminary, Luzon Nazarene Bible College (Baguio), Korean Nazarene Theological College, Japan Nazarene Seminary (Tokyo), and Japan Christian Junior College (Chiba). Nona accompanied me on the overseas trip and we took in Hong Kong as well. I paid her expense whenever she accompanied me. She also went with me to Mexico, Costa Rica, and Guatemala and to Albuquerque, Colorado Springs, and Nampa, Idaho. But I am getting ahead of myself.

The freelancing life led me to the Theological Conference in February, 1987 where I interviewed Enrique Guang, Elton Wood, Herbert McGonigle, and perhaps one or two other mission college leaders. I did this assuming I would not be able to visit such representatives of overseas institutions and the commission wanted them included in the study. Meantime, the Board of General Superintendents was meeting in the same hotel and attending some of the sessions. One or two sessions were for the college presidents with the general superintendents. The subject under discussion was the replacement for Dr. Mark Moore, who had reached 70 years of age. Dr. Stephen Nease had been elected to the position of Director of Education Services in December but had declined. On at least three occasions the presidents expressed officially their desire to have an elder and former president in this position. In fact, Dr. William Greathouse had discussed nominees for the job with me in 1978, stating that the General Superintendents had decided that the successor to Dr. Edward Mann must be an elder and a former president. Thus, I would be ineligible. So this weighty discussion occurred while I was hanging around the fringes. I was busy at my work, but likely some of the superintendents and presidents must have wondered what this layman was doing at the theological conference. In due time, after Dr. Gordon Wetmore was elected Director of Education Services and declined, they asked Dr. John Knight to talk with me about taking the job, half-time, for one year. I saw the advantage for the church in combining the position of research director and the Education Services office. It would give me office support without additional cost to the church. I would have an office in which to work. On the other hand, I told him that there was no way both jobs could be done in one-half time. It would be full-time until the commission report was completed. He concurred and I accepted the interim assignment. Since it was short term and temporary, I requested and he approved keeping my consulting relationship with the Wesleyans.

On March 16, 1987 I returned to Nazarene headquarters. I surprised myself even though others may have thought it was premeditated. I did not like many of the changes that had occurred in the headquarters structure. Two general superintendents congratulated me on my "half-time assignment." One executive said, "It really can be done on a half-time basis, can't it?" I was a temporary employee, therefore, not entitled to a benefit package. And in September, 1987, I felt it my duty to remind the Generals that my appointment was up in February or March. They would need to set the nominating procedure in motion. It was not until December or January that the suggestion was dropped that maybe I would stay in place until General Assembly, 1989. In February they made it official. The commission report was substantially completed in April, 1988 so I put myself on half-time pay May 1, 1988 through July, 1989. Stephen Nease was elected after General Assembly as the new Commissioner of the International Board of Education. I covered the office without pay from August 1, through October 16, 1989. By under-spending the budget for the director's salary and benefits, replacing two staff members with the hiring of Barbara Najarian, and savings of travel costs that were chargeable to Lilly Foundation, we returned to the Church at least $60,000.00 for other uses. Not bad for a span of two and one-half years? And the salary enabled me to enhance my IRA account which badly needed enhancing.

Before this position opened I had withdrawn a tidy sum (taxable) from my IRA account to square off my debts on moving, a travel trailer and an insurance policy. This made for a horrible tax bill in April of 1988. It looks like poor planning, but I really did not have a clue so that I could anticipate this change of income for 1987.

To be honest the return to headquarters was pleasant and reassuring. The acceptance I was given, the trust shown, the status and travel afforded went a long way towards overcoming any sense of rejection due to the events of the previous four years. My previous service on the General Board was valuable. I was a member of one more General Assembly, bringing the total to ten. The fellowship with other executives and the challenge of general church leadership was both humbling and inspiring. The acceptance given by the college presidents, access to their campuses, and participation in national associations such as the Christian College

Coalition and Association of Independent Colleges was all that I could expect and more. It gave me assurance of the notice and respect given Nazarene colleges, something I feel that I had a part in fostering. It was climaxed with a conference of Nazarene College faculties at Olivet in June, 1989. I was given more credit than I deserved for it, but it was an excellent conference and a nice way to bow out.

My post-retirement career turned out to be primarily this return to Nazarene headquarters. Its compensation was probably greater than consultation would have been. Since it was temporary and part-time, however, I kept the doors open to calls from other clients. I had served as North Central Coordinator in the early '60's, visiting 31 colleges to encourage self-study. I had advised Judson College on retention of student enrollment, Taylor University on self-study, written a proposal that got a key Title III grant for the Nazarene College Consortium, and worked closely with the Christian College Coalition since its inception. I helped Mark Moore set up the Nazarene colleges' participation in the Management Ratios developed by John Minter. I had worked with several other research groups on college studies, making sure that Olivet was included. All of this preceded retirement.

My brochure, mailed to about 200 colleges, encouraged inquiries along these lines. My work with the Wesleyan Church went back to the 1960's when they were studying the Miltonvale-Bartlesville merger. They called again and eventually did a study that paralleled the 1985-1989 Nazarene Education Commission study but it started and ended differently. I had one two-day session with Christian and Missionary Alliance educational leaders. I spent parts of three days with the Assemblies of God education executive. In connection with the teaching of a course at Trevecca, I spent time with Millard Reed and some of his administrators. This involved interviews with all who reported directly to the President and some others. I gave the President a written report as I concluded my work. MidAmerica Nazarene College named me Acting Academic Dean for about four months (July-October, 1992) and Richard Spindle asked me for recommendations on administrative structure, especially in the academic administration. I also was responsible for getting the school year started before the new dean was named. Nazarene Publishing House asked me to do a study of compensation of NPH employees who produced artistic works while employed by NPH. As Chairman of the Board of NPH (and without pay), I was asked to prepare a pattern for the interviewing of candidates for the position of manager. I led out in such interviews before the search committee. These activities were all very interesting but over a five year period following retirement they would not have equaled more than three months work, including the home study of materials and the writing of the follow-up reports. Several tasks were without pay because the time given was so short. This was hardly what I had expected. The response to my brochures was under-whelming.

I had not presented myself as a prospective teacher because my administrative work had pulled me from the classroom and library for too long. With the developments of 1989, concurrently with my leaving headquarters, the Berlin Wall falling, "peace breaking out" all over the world, I began to say, "My course in World Politics needs to be taught." I wrote to about twenty colleges within driving distance of Olathe. One taker was Ottawa University of Kansas City. I taught "International Politics" there during March and April of 1991, 1992, and 1993. With the rapid changes during that time, the course had to be recast each year, but I had plenty of time to revise the syllabus, and finally the text revisions caught up to reality. I taught the same course in Summer Session, 1991 at Trevecca and a course on the Pacific Rim at Olivet Fall, 1992. I enjoyed the teaching but I feel sure I spent twice the time in preparation for each class period as most instructors spend.

FROM THE STANDPOINT OF A SON, HUSBAND, FATHER, AND GRANDFATHER

Retirement gives you time to think more carefully about what really counts. Life is much more than where you work and what you do. People around you seem to care first and foremost about "What you do." Your work seems to define you to other people. But, on reflection, we really know it isn't so! "Being" comes well ahead of "doing." Values and priorities are more important than performance or achievements, direction and destination than speed or efficiency. Our family would not represent radical misfits in Middle West American society, but our lifestyle has been developed around some rather simple principles that are both conservative and radical. It is perhaps curious that before age seventy, I had hardly ever tried to formulate them. I summarized the principles that guided the home life of my Snowbarger grandparents in Chapter IX of *The Snowbarger Family in Kansas*, Volume I.

Here are some other insights that have come to me as I consider how we live out our values. No particular importance is attached to the order:

1. **"Being" is more important than "doing."**
2. **The "micro" is probably more important than the "macro." Personal issues, conscience, character, family obligations, and local responsibilities are more important than humanity, global prescriptions, and trends. It is what**

kind of person am I to those closest to me and what am I doing now that makes me safe to follow.

3. "Out of sight is out of mind." I must take responsibility to support my family and prepare for the future. I cannot rely on a good excuse or blame someone else. The communist system and most collective approaches to social problems are doomed to failure.

4. Saving the world one soul at a time does work. I believe that the Christian church and colleges are effective even though our progress is slow. I feel satisfied to have spent my career, as well as my volunteer time, largely in these efforts. If my children, grandchildren, and students are saved from the ranks of social liabilities and if they can help ameliorate social problems where they serve, I will feel that my efforts were not wasted.

5. To be "used" by others is all right provided the cause is worthy. Why go to a fitness club unless your work is redemptive? My health, talent, and reputation is an endowment to spend on my life mission.

6. Life is always about setting an "example." As an older brother, then an able student, a naval officer, a father, a teacher, an administrator, community leader, churchman, when am I not an example? For good or for ill? What kind of leadership can one have without setting the example for what is expected in followers? What percent of failures in leaders comes from denial of this principle?

7. I believe in life-long learning, but it goes beyond continuing education and elder hostels. God is still teaching me. My prayer is, "Lord, what are you trying to teach me today?" I think He's trying to teach me patience, trust in Him, to see the good in almost everyone like He does, the value of friends, the fragility of life, the beauty of His creation, small things, His grace, my weakness.

8. God's "still small voice," --reading, and listening are still the best learning tools. But solid learning takes lots of time for us slow learners.

9. Wisdom is still to be sought before great riches or flashy careers. Many young students fail to seek out the wisest counsel and the most exemplary teachers before making big academic decisions.

10. People with conventional values like those expressed above are the most successful in their careers. <u>Forbes</u>, October 17, 1988 reports on a longitudinal study begun in 1938 that validates this assertion.

11. Stewardship of possessions and accountability to God are the most profound tests we are put to.

12. I am more convinced than ever of the importance of the work of Christian higher education in the life of our nation as well as the life of the church. This work in our overseas colleges could be even more important than the work in the United States.

13. We all want to be sure that we are not a burden on our children when we grow old. There is no way to guarantee that. How much money will be required? Maybe a bit more than we have. What kind of care? Who can say?

14. Our actions and allocation of time, money, and emotional involvement are more important than right theology or social theory.

15. A true believer in democracy must not ask more for him and his than he tries to deliver to the poorest. I have little respect for those who prescribe for public schools at one level, then send their children to expensive prep schools. I believe in the kind of schools that reflect religious and moral values that may not be possible to espouse in a public school, but not for the purpose of elevating my children above others. And I do not complain about paying taxes plus tuition even when the financial load may seem to be unbearable. Like Dr. A.B. Mackey, I also believe that we could justify sending the complete bill for Christian Education to the government on the basis of value received by the citizens of the state.

16. "Judge not that you be not judged," is good advice because I am a poor judge of people. When that was my assigned task, I did my best but there is so much that we don't know. Understanding and true wisdom is lacking so much of the time when we need it.

17. We greatly under-value leadership in the American society. We are so carried away by selfish, narcissistic, individual rights and indulgences that we have a poor idea of how an ordered social life comes about. We are more in need of

**leadership and owe more willingness to follow than most
of us realize.**

Changes in family responsibilities come with advancing age. I noticed
the difference quite dramatically in 1976 when my sister, Velma, rather
insisted that I would look after the finances of my parents. They were in
a nursing home in Garden City, where she lived. She helped them and
took my mother to church after my father could no longer get about. But
neither she nor her husband wanted to touch their business or finance.
Living trusts were set up and my parents signed over the responsibility to
me as trustee. That was natural in our family tradition and I carried that
responsibility for seventeen years. Two sets of bills to pay each month,
two sets of tax returns each year, gifts, property conveyances, health
care—it was time consuming and required judgment. But my mother,
sisters, and brother expected it of me. I accepted the role, especially when
my father passed away in April, 1977. Funeral arrangements, estate tax
forms, and care of my mother all became primarily my responsibility quite
naturally. Since I took leadership, it was easier for other family members
and decisions to flow in a timely way. I represented the family when that
was necessary. My mother always wanted to know what I was doing, she
always paid her own tithe but lost track of what the income was, since
it came to me. She trusted me and fortunately did not lack for anything
she needed. When she died, it was my duty to distribute the assets of the
trusts to the beneficiaries. Again, that was a large task but I was able to
finish it to everyone's satisfaction and within the instructions of the trust
agreements. I still send flowers or memorial gifts in the name of this larger
family, try to keep a chain letter moving, and see that dates and places are
set for reunions. This change in family status began before retirement but
the heavier part of the responsibility came after I had retired.

We became grandparents in 1977 (our ages were 54 and 56).
Grandparenting was a joy we looked forward to as we moved to Olathe.
Unlike the feeling when we became parents, we knew exactly how to do
grandparenting. We spoiled them rotten (not really). We took them on
a few local excursions shortly after coming to town. We went to their
athletic events, their concerts, and their church programs. We celebrate
birthdays. And we have meals together. We are a part of their lives and
we like that.

Our relationship with our children is different than when they lived at
home. We try to give them space and they take it. Sometimes we don't
see them for a week or ten days even when they lived only a few blocks
away. We ask them how they intend to look after us in the manner to

which we have become accustomed. They are slow to answer, mentioning how their social security taxes are paying for our expensive lifestyle. We help them with their financial emergencies once in a while and thank the Lord that "It's only money." They are still a joy to us and we have been very fortunate. Now comes college and graduate school. They know we will find a way to see them through. We helped Vincent in his political campaigns and Delia get her graduate degree at KU.

As the oldest son and grandson, I felt responsibility. I was showing Vincent some family documents and letters and noticed that his oldest son, Jeffrey, was observing and listening carefully. I said to Vincent, "Some day I'll turn these things over to you to safeguard." When I noticed Jeff's attention, I said, "And Jeff, some day he will probably turn them over to you."

In this regard, I decided one important task that I could do was to write the family history. When, in 1989 and 1990, I had nothing to do, I started to write the story of my Snowbarger grandparents. Lois Snowbarger had done the genealogy carefully and well. I wanted to do a "history." There was very little written. I had some letters in a German script which my friends could not decipher. (These letters, incidentally, were passed from my grandfather, to my father, to me.) So I interviewed my uncles and aunts and my mother, asking the best questions I could pose. Volume I was finished and presented to a reunion. It was well received so I called a meeting of my cousins and proposed a second volume. This time they would finance it, and they would write it. I would edit it and get it printed. They agreed and one year later Volume II was distributed. It took some arm twisting and cajoling but every one agreed it was worthwhile. Some even thanked me for "forcing" them to get it done. In the process, I contacted many distant relatives, especially in Missouri, Iowa, and Kansas, who wanted copies and who helped me in the projects. This is now a part of my role in the Snowbarger family. I can also claim some responsibility for a sixty page autobiography which my mother wrote and which we consider priceless. She was one of those second generation frontier women who were unsung heroines.

A responsibility arising out of the wedding ceremony became a clear and present duty. Wahnona developed Alzheimer's disease. It came not as a total surprise but still I was not prepared for the implications. Her mother's mind had slipped rather badly after she turned eighty. I think I would have been prepared for that. But Nona's disorientation first came to light in August, 1986 as we began to pack to move. She could not pack a box. I had expected to sort and discard as we packed but soon discovered it was all up to me. That meant that we moved more "junk" than planned. Some of those things were not unpacked for seven years.

Nona was near normal for five years after we moved to Olathe, showing only occasionally signs of worsening problems of memory and orientation. Her physical strength was remarkably good, medical bills low, and she was able to keep going. But she became more and more dependent. On July 4, 1991, we had family, Nashes, and McMahons over to our house as usual for a pot luck supper and then to see the fireworks from our front lawn. The time had come, every one was present, but no one got the dishes uncovered or called us to eat. I saw the situation, stepped up, called for some assistance and the meal proceeded. But Nona had not taken her usual role of organizing the buffet. From about that time onward, she did less and less in the kitchen and I took over. She always wanted to help but could not organize the effort. Similarly, she could not "put things away" where they belong. We lost more things that way! Six weeks later, they are found. She lost her orientation especially when away from home. She could not care for her hair, select her clothes, or keep track of time. When some new disability showed itself, I am taken off guard and regret the strain she is under. In general, I tried to keep her active, on the go, and participating in her normal activities. I was assured by others at church that they wanted it that way.

There is no question about "Living By the Vows." I wanted to do my part to the best of my ability. Nona had been faithfully at my side through thick and thin. She had stood by me and put up with me. It is good that I could make up some of it to her. I was blessed with good health. She was mobile. We could travel. A member of a family that has experienced strokes, she had only one and that was largely inconsequential. She had a good appetite, enjoyed the beauties of nature, her children and grandchildren, and liked to go to church. Much of what she once enjoyed escapes her. At her most anxious moments, I didn't know how to calm her. So I simply hugged her tightly and said, "I love you." She responded, "I love you, too." That usually did it. This was the important substance of our conversation. That was a new family role for me—I was learning. At times, I found three dresses with a soiled spot or some flaw. We had to put them on before I saw the problem. And I had not allowed enough time to change that much and still get to our destination. There were even worse problems. And Nona had her preferences too. They were quite pronounced at times, although she was usually very agreeable and wanted to be helpful.

Nona, 50ᵗʰ Wedding Anniversary

We periodically need to count our blessings. In October, 1993, I wrote "we are up and around each day. We have been to church, to Vince's with family to watch a football game, eat a giant Subway sandwich. We sleep well every night, pay our bills on time, made a trip to Arkansas, have good nourishing food, good clothing, a nice car, a warm house, the blessing of God and assurance of his presence and continuing care. Our time is more and more concerned with caring for ourselves, leaving less time for the care of others, but we are not yet a burden on others. In several ways we can still, hopefully, make meaningful contributions to others. We are still trying to lead—by example."

TRAVEL, FINANCE, AND LONELINESS

Many professionals like us hope to travel extensively in retirement. We had also hoped that we could get to many places of interest but had no set plan. The three stages of retirement—"go-go," "slo-go," and "no-go"—was the pattern of our travel experience. The College gave us a beautiful gift in the Spring of 1986. A four island tour of Hawaii, with a group of Kodak employees was arranged for us and we thoroughly enjoyed it. I had spent several weeks in Hawaii during the War but Nona had not been there with me. While it was a guided tour, we had a great guide and lots of free time along the way. One morning, the tour guide said, "Do you remember that this is Palm Sunday?" We sang Easter hymns on the bus for a half hour. After a boat tour of Pearl Harbor, Nona and I took the bus back and spent the afternoon at Pearl Harbor, the *U.S.S. Arizona* Memorial, and familiar spots. So retirement travel was off to a great start.

A flurry of travel surrounded the research director's role I was to play with the Nazarene Education Commission. Colleges are never quite sure what the denomination is up to when big studies like this are mounted, so the director's visit had three purposes: Administer survey instruments, do extensive interviews to supplement the findings of surveys, and reassure administrators and faculty that the results are in friendly hands. This study was to explore the needs of colleges and seminaries under the World Mission Division and the possibility of bringing all Nazarene educational institutions under one headquarters coordinator. We mailed our survey instruments, but got insignificant returns (as we had feared). In the Spring of 1987, I checked the schedule of meetings but made no commitments to travel until we received the Lilly Endowment grant of $20,000 for the study. When that came through, I made reservations to attend the Asia-Pacific Regional Conference in Manila and stops at five institutions in that region. I did not want my travel costs to come from World Missions, even to study the needs of their institutions. On this trip we got to Manila, Baguio, Hong Kong, Guanghou (Canton), Korea, and Japan. On a later trip, we went to Mexico City, Costa Rica, and Guatemala City.

Nona accompanied me on these trips at our expense. My tasks through my career required a moderate amount of travel but I had not mastered the art of combining business and pleasure as some have been able to do it. It always seemed that something back at home base required my attention so I did not leave early or delay getting back home. And Nona had her hands full with the children and part-time employment commitments. Our rule had always been that the employer (college or church) would not be paying a penny more if she accompanied me. I held to this through all my professional career. So I paid her airfare, meals, and the difference between single and double occupancy at hotels. With this kind of understanding in advance, she accompanied me to the Orient, Mexico and Central America, Albuquerque, Colorado Springs, Nampa, St. Louis, Indianapolis, St. Paul, Mount Vernon, Bourbonnais, and Bethany in connection with the Commission business and the Bible College association meetings. She went with me to Nashville, Fayetteville, Arkansas, and Springfield, Missouri as I did consulting work. We had great conversations about life together as we racked up the miles by car in 1987 and 1988. Air travel almost ended by May, 1989. Thereafter, we took a plane only once for the round-trip to nephew Tim's wedding in Houston.

Family related travel has been mostly to Colorado, a tradition that goes back to my parents' vacation haunts. It used to be Green Mountain Falls or Estes Park. Later it was Durango, Ouray, Salida-Bueno Vista, or Colorado Springs-Divide-Golden Bell. A week-end, a week, a month in Colorado at least once each summer became a necessity, no longer a luxury. We bought a used travel trailer, thinking it might help in the consulting work. Let the client pay regular car mileage and a per diem fee for service and I would deduct my costs. Normally, when I hired a consultant, room, meals, and travel about equaled honoraria, so I planned to keep costs low to the client and still take Nona with me at little or no additional cost. That never worked out. But three times, extended stays in Colorado with the trailer added to our enjoyment and that of members of our family.

We spent November, 1990 in Happy Wanderer camp in Indio, California. After Sunday Dinner on the grounds at Goodland, Kansas, we went to Ray and Neloise Stapp's in Denver for Sunday evening to Tuesday morning. Then we stopped at the Arches, Bryce, and Zion parks enroute to Indio. We were at Happy Wanderer with the Louis McMahons for the month in a rented, park model trailer that they helped us to find. This put us in touch with newly made friends in Indio and old friends and relatives, such as, the folks at Pasadena First Church, Howard Wolf's in Banning, and Willodene Marrs in San Jacinto (we spent Thanksgiving Day with them). Evelyn and Allen Hodges came over to see us for a couple of days as did Angie (Foster) and Dan Alger. Having taken our time on the way out, we hurried back to Bethany with an overnight stop at Gallup, New Mexico. We got to Marion's house in Bethany in time for dinner at seven o'clock. We came home by way of Rogers to visit my mother, Velma, and David.

We kept a Ford Van as a towing vehicle as well as for trips with the grandchildren. It made possible a trip to 1993 General Assembly with Velma and David. We went to Olivet so they could see the College and we could visit Kay Sattler and Larry Snowbarger in their homes. Then we went by to see relatives of my mother in Goshen, Indiana. Life in the travel trailer for four people turned out to be quite enjoyable.

After 1987, my brother, two sisters, and I had reunions on January 1st alternating between homes. Prior to that for several years, we tried to get together near our mother in Bethany or Rogers. We had reunions each summer but said, "Why not more often if possible." We also had gotten together in Bethany for Mother's 90th birthday, so we also went to Rogers for her 95th. That was a hilarious time. The highlight was Marion's late arrival and their refusal to go to Janice Hancock's house where they were to sleep. They said, "No, we brought our air mattress." We argued about where it could be placed when seven people already had squatter's rights in a three bedroom house. They insisted that there was space in the entry way. "How will we blow it up?" Marion said that they hooked it up to the rear end of their vacuum cleaner. Velma's cleaner had a different size connection. We began to laugh. Someone suggested a tire pump. That did not work. I began stints of blowing with my mouth. Instead of taking two minute turns, the others laughed on and it was up to me. After about six or eight stints, Kathy tried it out and it curled up around her. More hilarity. Mother got up to see what those crazy kids were doing but they were beyond her control. Finally, I got it blown up before the others had found a better way. Kathy was the one who volunteered to sleep on the air mattress (which closely resembled a "moon walk"). After finally she found a comfortable position, Wilma realized she needed her suitcase which was in the entry closet, and a new round of laughing began. That reunion was memorable because Mother was with us at the table for every meal and enjoyed even the carrying on. That was March 3, 1991. On April 3, 1991 she passed away quietly and family reunions for us were suddenly changed.

In 1980, the President gave me a special increase, indicating that it was to recognize the tax consequences that put clergy administrators at an advantage over laymen on his administrative team. Whatever the reason, we started a Supplemental Retirement Account contributing monthly for seven years. This was a big help on transition expenses and especially with moving and buying a new house in a more expensive area. Finally, the reemployment at Headquarters, messy as it was because it was not planned for, essentially postponed retirement pay schedules by two years. I stopped social security and restarted at a higher level. I was able to postpone annuitizing part of TIAA and all of my CREF benefits so those accumulations increased. I also chose single beneficiary options because I was able to purchase a rather large (for me) insurance policy with Nona as beneficiary. (Joint beneficiary options pay lower benefits, so I have the higher benefits and Nona was still covered if I should die first.)

We had not retired the debt on our home by the time we retired. Sending children through college, a move back to Olivet following a move to Kansas City only five years earlier, ten major surgeries for Nona—all seemed to frustrate our best intentions to double payments and retire the debt. We got a nice home in Olathe. We had watched as it was built for Vince and Carolyn. While we were house hunting, they decided to build again so we made it easy on ourselves and them.

213

Vince, Carolyn, Willis, Delia, Garry

I have had an unusual preparation for financial responsibility. As children, we were never given an allowance and had very few opportunities to earn our own money. For a very short time there was a bounty paid on gopher scalps and jack rabbit ears, a nickel or a dime for evidence of eradication of a pest. We were not paid for chores around the house and farm. Considering how hard it was for them to get cash, we did not expect it from our parents. It was during these years that my grandfather and father were known for their magnanimous gifts to church and college. We knew it was blood money but did not resent it. So, I guess you could say that we were schooled in saving money, and giving it away, rather than spending it. It seems that in church and college work, I was always on the budget or finance committee. It was not that we were among the most affluent, perhaps the more frugal.

By learning insurance, fifteen years as trustee of my parents' trusts, thirty-five years of educational administration, serving on the Board of Publication (later called Board of Directors of Nazarene Publishing House and Chairman for nine or ten years), Finance Committee of the General Board (Chairman for five or six years), and twenty-two years on the Chicago Central District Advisory Board, I became rather sophisticated in church and college finance. There were times that I, as academic dean, had as much to do with balancing the college budget as the Business Manager. A college is so personnel intensive that the size of the faculty, academic support services, and departmental budgets can get unwieldy, especially if enrollment declines. At one stage, I had to cut the faculty size from 102 to 92 in a three year period. To do that without damage to the programs or involuntary terminations is difficult. But I pride myself on the ability to manage through down-sizing. I had thought that there might be some future either in a church or in a college to use these skills in retirement. An opportunity was offered me at Trevecca in 1991-1992, but by that time, Nona's health would not permit that much free time for me to be away from her even if we had moved.

I am especially interested in the Olivet Foundation and we are making major contributions to fund student scholarships. Dependence upon federal and state financial aid sources is the achilles heel of our colleges. We need substantial amounts, like $25 to $50 million, to fund the kind of scholarships it will take to keep a Nazarene college education available to those able to benefit from it. To do what I want to do means I should find a way to earn a lot of money. I have talked to my children about it, and they know that, beyond a modest legacy to each of them, I hope to be able to do something substantial for the Foundation.

The contractor who built our first house told me I was his first customer to limit my demands for the project to the money I could afford. In making a budget, we always began with slightly less budgeted for income than we were sure of, then distributed that budget (no more) over the categories of expenses. That is far different from starting with a list of requests to spend. At home and at the college, we always started with a realistic estimate of income. The college instruction budget finally reached $3,000,000 before I retired. There was no way it would be over-spent.

Applying that financial experience to retirement, there are differences. While college budgets could be expanded by new gifts, now income is relatively fixed year by year. The lessons in frugality all apply. The specter of unbearable medical costs make planning almost impossible. One tactic we have used is to maximize benefits using insurance, single beneficiaries, delayed start of annuities, continued savings, and accepting some risk. We pay very little interest, cut costs where possible, and do not buy expensive services. Our needs are simple. Fortunately, our medical costs are minimal and largely covered by Medicare and insurance. TIAA-CREF plans have been excellent. We take Minimum Distribution Options rather than annuities now that our resources are fixed and other income is minimal. The fifty percent interest in my parents' farm in Grant County is double what I expected due to the choices of a brother and a sister as beneficiaries of the trusts. They preferred cash to land, so I was able to buy their portions and that choice seems good for me. Still, who knows what it will take to keep us from becoming a burden on our children?

The responsibility given me to handle my parents' trusts pushed me to my best efforts to protect and enlarge the trusts so that my parents' goals could be realized. Actually, the value of the trusts was greater when the survivor (my mother) died than when the trusts were created. Both parents were cared for the first year, my mother was supported in a nursing home for eleven and one-half years, and she was cared for by my sister, Velma, for her last two and one-half years (the trusts paying my sister). I learned a lot from the experience and from passing the insurance exam. I tried to see that my giving equaled my income tax. I intend to teach children and grandchildren the virtue of hard work, holding the line on expenses, and the simultaneous joy of giving. And we will still have occasional feasts together, vacations in Colorado, travel, good times, and gifts on holiday and birthdays.

There is a lot of loneliness in retirement. Cut off from your normal routines, it is especially hard at the start of a new school year. It is even worse when you are removed from the community where all the familiar big events come and go without your hearing an announcement. My advice to all who can make your own choice, "Do not move from the community where you have served." If you do move, you invite all your friends to come see you. They do not come. They don't use the telephone, even when the "old man" could save hours of effort. Your offers to be helpful come to naught. So you build a new life. You do not expect people to come or to call. You expect the calendar to be largely blank day after day. You start to build a new circle of friends.

Family, a new church staff and schedule, friends of forty and fifty years ago become important again, and you volunteer for all sorts of things. In our case, children and grandchildren were within a mile of us and that is important in both what we can give and what they give us. Having one of my history majors as pastor (Paul Cunningham), a college religion professor (Frank Moore) as Sunday School teacher, several other former students and Olivet associates in the congregation of College Church, Olathe, helped a lot. A new circle of Prime Time friends was a natural for us. Again, several were former associates at Olivet; others just as fine are new friends—retirees from Minnesota, West Virginia, Iowa, Kansas. An invitation to serve on the Board of Directors of the Kansas City Rescue Mission was a challenge and a privilege. Participation with Heart to Heart in distribution of medical supplies and equipment to Russia and disaster sites was rewarding. Transfer to the Olathe Rotary Club enabled me to know many Olathe Civic leaders. Strangely, we were known as Vince or Delia's Mom and Dad (in the Kankakee area, they are known as "our children"). Since they had preceded us to Olathe by about 15 years during which time Olathe had grown tremendously, they were well known there.

An unusual circle of close friends redeveloped among the Bethany-Peniel Class of '42. We made a special effort to attend the 45th anniversary celebration in September, 1987 at the Golden Bell Ranch in Colorado. We call it a reunion for "Class of '42 and friends" since our class was scattered by the War, some before graduation. We passed around fact sheets and went around the circle telling what had happened since graduation day. The first night we could only tell about ourselves; the second night we could tell about our kids and grandkids. The celebration lasted from the evening of Labor Day through Friday noon. We enjoyed it so much that we concluded, "Let's meet again to celebrate our 47th." So we met in 1989, 1991 and 1993 at Golden Bell and at the Bethany campus in May of 1992 for our 50th. Now there is no guessing about ages and we share about ailments and laugh. Always there is someone who has taken his/her departure since the last meeting, so we have a brief memorial service. What a joy to see how nearly every one of them are winners, great souls! What accomplishments! What great children! Margaret Glen McReynolds Dawson is really the spark plug (benevolent dictator) who kept the group going, and what a blessing. Our final reunion on good old terra firma was in September, 2002.

Many years ago I was told that productive scholars would find time to write with or without financial support or free time given. Faculty members booed when I reported it but I am convinced that it is true. Like many others, I had a list of topics I wanted to research and write about "when I get time." Subjects like "Hoaxes of Democracy," "Middle Management in Higher Education," "The Virtues of Educational Leadership," and many devotional thoughts were on my list. The family history (1990 and 1991) and my own memoirs got attention. But although I have published perhaps thirty *Come Ye Apart* devotionals, another twenty articles, and several twenty page studies, numerous speeches, and a dozen self-studies, I have not been a productive scholar. I am still promising myself, "I will get it done!' I wrote twenty-five pages on the "Reed Years" in *The Olivet Story* (1993) produced by Dr. Leslie Parrott. The University of Hawaii Press suggested that I develop a popularized version of my dissertation to attract a general readership and to furnish lots of illustrations. I could have done it and should have. At the time, I reasoned that only scholarly articles would advance my career. That was correct but I let myself off the hook, did not invest the sleepless nights, and started a pattern of not writing (or "rushing into print" as one of my professors put it) and justified myself in the process.

Our daughter-in-law, Carolyn, gave us the book, *Passages*. Just as there is a child psychology, adolescent psychology, so there is a psychology of adults. *Passages* notes the crises related to approximately forty-two years of age. (Just as I moved to Headquarters at about that age in the mid-1960's.) At age fifty-five my life followed the pattern sketched out in this book. Now in retirement years, the book was right. Psychology and spirituality, related as they are, deserve some space in this opus.

As one who had broad interests, I kept the doors open to pursue a wide variety of activities should this opportunity present itself. I always hoped there would be a chance to own a farm, perhaps operate it on the side. It would be nice to have trees, horses, a dog or two, plenty of space for a garden, maybe forty acres for light farming or truck gardening. I had thought that owning an apartment building, letting the rent pay it out, caring for upkeep, and perhaps living in a double apartment on the ground level would be another estate enhancer. Of course, there were the writing projects that beckoned. I had dreamed of working with Vincent, purchasing an office building, managing and renting it, building a group of professionals who could use pooled services, and refer business to one another (like an attorney, an accountant, a family services counselor, a financial planner). I could assist Vince, hire support staff, maintain the facility and collect rent. From the days of my twenties when all of these were possible, they gradually became less probable. I should admit that I started with a much more ambitious list. Being President of the United States was the first to go. Then, founding and being President of my own university in Los Gatos, California was the next abandoned. But, many dreams continued right into the retirement years. Then as time grew shorter, sure enough, most of them finally sounded very unlikely. Doors began to close. I quit following the real estate ads. I decided that it was best to stay with "the one who brung me," the world of education. With each passing year, other options would seem more risky and, more and more, the question was, "How can I best serve the Lord? What are the open doors left to influence more people to make it to Heaven?"

I thought I might have a chance to teach a Sunday School class, but only substitute work was offered. In almost any other district, I might have been a lay pastor of a small church but not on the Kansas City District with the Seminary and college personnel available. Perhaps I could serve as a church administrator? We had always served in the church choir, but Nona's unsteadiness made that unwise and felt I should stay with her. After age 68 I was not only closed out of the familiar roles in education, I was not needed in the church roles I had known best. Since it had been an issue in the positions I could fill in Nazarene colleges, I began to notice how important ordination was in the minds of some people. I had served the church for my entire career, but there was a major distinction which I had ignored that seemed to circumscribe my service, even if I gave it without salary. At the close of district assemblies, I attended dozens of ordination services, but they began to raise more questions in my mind than previously. When I was a young man, they ordained those "called to preach." I had sincerely considered and concluded that my gifts were in teaching and administration. I had been loyal to the church, served faithfully, and felt it my duty to resolve my own problems of profession, finance, and retirement planning. I asked no church support, housing or car allowance. I worked as a layman for the church. But, somehow I was excluded from certain key positions. Having turned down other non-Nazarene educational posts, my church had no formal roles to offer me (at least so it seemed). Perhaps, the lack of any hint of heading an overseas institution (after it had been suggested to me prior to retirement) fueled these thoughts. I was not elevated to expose the level of my incompetence. Perhaps my experience has had something to do with four laymen having been elected to the Nazarene college presidency shortly after I retired.

I think that throughout life, my career concerns have spawned spiritual problems. Discouragement, frustration, God's silence, lack of a certainty as to God's leading were sure to follow a professional rebuff. Many were the times I went to church on Sunday morning hanging on every word the pastor spoke, marking my Bible, meditating and praying for some ray of hope and encouragement. Considering, then rejecting, the idea of a visit with the pastor about a problem. College and church were too close to discuss some matters with leaders of either organization. In retirement, the isolation was more complete. I had a round of self-doubt but, fortunately, did not slip into depression. I said to Wilma, my sister-in-law, "Can you imagine me in self-doubt?" She said, "No!" That was reassuring. As I overcame the worst of these attacks of wilted dreams and self-pity, Nona's condition and my time required to care for her needs made many of the questions moot. I became more grateful for the pleasant memories. I have stated the negative in full force because I think it might be helpful to others.

Now let me turn to the positive approaches in which I believe, whether or not they have worked out well in my experience.

1. **I have forgiven all the slights and neglects that have disappointed or handicapped me. I have never given in to the temptation to keep a list of hurts. I have lived by the golden rule. I wish everyone well. Maybe we will understand it better by and by; if not, that is OK.**
2. **The Lord is still working on me, so the question now is, "Lord, what are you trying to teach me?" There is lots of room for improvement.**

3. I will keep a positive attitude. I have seen too many older people who cannot but despair of nearly every change, the younger generation, and people who disagree with them. I have too much of a tendency in that direction. I am convinced that a negative attitude is to be fought like the plague. I want to resist evil of all kinds but I need allies in all generations.

4. Of course, my talent and experience is going to waste, but God seems to have an excess of talent He can call upon. Tragic accidents among promising youth are harder to explain than the waning of aged people. Apparently, God needs more examples of patience, stewardship, faithfulness, and love. There is nothing to stop me from developing and illustrating these traits.

5. I must be a friend and support to the "baby boomers" and their children. They have a tough world to tame. I did my best but that was not enough, so they have to tangle with it. I had hoped to pass along my job, insights, and responsibilities to a younger man in 1977. I would have loved to have passed it to my son but, at about that time, he moved away from the academic world. (Was it, in part, because of what he observed in my situation?) Now, I can still encourage others who can benefit from my knowledge and experience and give them what I have learned and the good wishes of one who understands.

6. I am setting an example as I cope with aging. My wife needed me so that was the primary point of action. But there are other areas of life that offer an opportunity for wholesome, courageous, and magnanimous modeling of how to age well.

7. I am finding plenty of things that need to be done. Since energy and free time are not increasing, that ought to hold me! Again, who's to stop me?

8. Older people, like younger, need to keep flexible and seize opportunities when they come. As Nona's neurologist said about travel, "Sure, you should go now. There will surely come a time when you can't go as much." "Now is the time..."

9. I am digging deeply into the Bible and other good literature for nuggets of wisdom. Searching more for wisdom than knowledge. The world of computers is changing too fast

to keep up. Since I can write this on the computer, I need much more than powerful chips. I need to know true wisdom that fades not away (and that will not become obsolete).

10. Being "out of the loop," I am depending more on prayer. I should have used it more when I was in the loop.

11. Fellowship with believers, correspondence with former students and colleagues, making friendships outside my own denomination—all of these things are opening my eyes as to how God is working in His world. Church attendance is still a high priority, but God is working in improbable places and through many in other groups than the ones I know and love.

12. Psalm 46 and others that speak of God's care and our need to put our trust in Him is my greatest consolation. "God is our refuge and strength, a very present help in trouble. Therefore we will not fear..." "Lord, I believe, help Thou my unbelief."

As for the future, I agree with Richard Niebuhr, "By the decades I am a pessimist; by the centuries I am an optimist."

CH. XXII THERE'S MORE

"I love you more, not only for what you are,
But for what I am when I am with you.
I love you, not only for what you have made of yourself,
But for what you are making of me."
Anon.

After retirement challenges one's dignity, inevitably comes the loss of one's spouse. Then you are "alone again." People don't mean any ill but socially this is a world of couples. Tables accommodate six or eight—never five or seven. In Olathe, I always went to the group breakfast at eight o'clock on Friday mornings. After Vince and Carolyn moved to D.C., I invited myself to go to Delia and Garry's house on Friday evening. I went to Sunday School and church and Wednesday evening prayer meeting. Our Senior Adults had at least one dinner per month. But there were lots of days with no human contact except as I made it happen.

We bought a condominium in Sterling Estates in 1994. In 2000 and 2001 I refurbished the house, buying some new furniture and developing one wall of the living room for the state of Kansas, sunflowers, wheat, farms and cattle were the order of the day. Another wall was a collection of family pictures. Delia and Carolyn helped me select some new furniture. I served as president of the Sterling Estates Homeowners Association for a three year term.

I was in my native state, Kansas. I had plenty of time to stop and read the historical markers, to take a day to visit the Cosmosphere, the historical society, Camp Funston, and the air museum in Topeka. I started that series of trips. But, travel alone was not the fun it is to travel with a companion.

I enjoyed 15 years with my grandchildren as they were growing up. Baseball, soccer, basketball, concerts, and plays. Their mission trips, family reunions, scholarships, cars, and jobs. What a bright spot for a seventy year old!

Olathe College church was another joy. The preaching, the Sunday School class, the music, the Victor, Senior Adult trips. Fellowship with wonderful friends—the kind you would love to have close by when you need someone to pray for you.

What really changed my situation for the worse was Vince's run for reelection to Congress in 1998. I had helped in each election campaign and that filled the schedule to some extent. He wasn't supposed to lose but when he did nothing seemed to come together for them in Olathe. In August, 2001, Carolyn took a job in Washington, D.C. September 11, 2001 found them both in Washington with Vince interviewing for a job. I had some feeling of worth as I drove for the County taking older people to doctor's appointments, pharmacies, and hair appointments. Volunteering gave a sense of accomplishment and made for social contact. But, when one-half the family was not in Olathe, I felt keenly the loneliness.

I made the trip to Bourbonnais in August, 2001 for the President's Dinner. August 24 was my birthday—so we celebrated my 80th this time. That dinner was always a beautiful occasion as we marked the start of a new year at Olivet.

I was reasonably well situated in 2001 with lots of good wishes and respect. So many good things. But, there was no real cure for my loneliness. For the first year after Nona's passing I hardly gave a thought to a second marriage. I spoke with Delia about the possibilities of a second marriage. She was non-committal but she knew my loneliness. When I went to the NIROGA in Branson in 2000, I knew that I wanted to go to Bourbonnais from Branson so I could see Laura graduate. Luther and Billie Watson had room in their car and we had good fellowship on the trip. He gave an extensive argument for a second marriage. Even though I said I was not ready to consider that he gave me the name of Ruby Humble. I did not tell him I had already thought of her. Harvey had passed away just one week after Wahnona died. Our families had grown up together: same church, same schools, on and off the campus. Harvey and I had shared the same office from 1949 to 1953. We both taught history.

I contacted Ruby in late November 2001. She sensed my loneliness and invited me to Bourbonnais for Christmas dinner at her house. She had invited other friends. It was a good idea! I stayed at my grandson Jeff's house and spent a good part of Christmas day and the day following at Ruby's house. We had each prepared a list of questions we wanted to discuss, even though it was admittedly "Oh, so sudden." We had so much in common including dissatisfaction with our single, home alone state. After about a month on the phone and e-mail, I wrote the following poem and put Ruby's initials to it. She agrees that it was very much her state of mind at the time.

WHO'S IN CONTROL?

I was doing well without him,
I didn't need all the fuss, I thought,
But he would be receptive
To a meal on Christmas, I ought
To make the poor guy happy—
Fun for me, a variation,
No harm, low risk, a novelty.
Let's do it, sure, for old time's sake.

I didn't see the snare,
Nor detect the dangerous ruse
Hidden in the atmosphere
Of my cozy little lodge.
Our paths had been so parallel,
Our views, our tastes, our goals.
We had some little ripples,
But no differences of note.

What would our kids think?
What about timing?
I just need to see him,
We can work it out.
It will never work,
I love my status quo;
Will that letter ever come?
How long before he calls?

We really need to talk
What are these strange feelings?
In my head—or in my heart?
Am I beginning to love this guy,
In spite of his clumsy start?
We need to get acquainted, let's travel.
Be together, "Best Friends,"
Nothing wrong with that.

But all these thoughts, these questions
'Twill take us months to cover.
How, when, will we ever be together?
Is heart dominating head?
The fever, it's rising!
Shouldn't there be an Ibuprofen?
A visit will be no cure.
I may be losing control

If we ever are together,
The fever will rise the more.
Love will grow in the hothouse
Down on Biloxi's shore.
We've got the rest of our lives
To let the heads catch up.
Dear Lord, Dear Lord save us
Was this your plan all the time?
RJH

Ruby and Willis

Curiously, Ruby's oldest son, Jim, and my son, Vince, became our marriage counselors. With one voice they said, "What's the hurry? You don't really know one another. Dad you are putting pressure on Ruby. Slow it down!" They were right but we ignored them. Our minds moved in the same channels. We did not know details of tastes, preferences, but we may never know or understand all of those traits. That's where genuine love smoothes over any differences. We enjoyed being together. Sure, we should read books and note problem areas in other second marriages, but we already share values, patterns of behavior, church membership, loyalty to Olivet, deep roots of friendship and community. It will work! And daily conversations will weld together our personalities.

The two principle areas of possible trouble all agree are children and finance. Our children were obviously as surprised as we were. But it was a matter of time. When they saw us happy and fulfilled, there was no resistance. Also as to finance there was even surprise at how simply those questions were settled. Ruby was elected to the Alumni board, kept active in her book clubs and birthday groups. I continued in Rotary, in writing, and gardening.

The wedding in the Prayer Chapel on the Olivet campus was a beautiful 45 minute ceremony. About 100 guests were present. The reception was in Hopkins Alumni Center. It was light-hearted, with beautiful music, humor and love all around. Friends of 40 years and more were there. Many from our families made the trip to be there. We were on the campus where our children grew up. A beautiful day, April 20, 2002.

Essentially, we were on our honeymoon until July 12 with trips to Branson, MO, Bethany, OK, Georgetown, IL, Lake Barkley, KY, Nashville, TN, and Olathe, KS. In Nashville, we attended the Nazarene Layman's Conference at the Opryland Hotel. What a wonderful week! And I introduced my bride to dozens of friends and family at all of these stops. At that time, we were thinking of keeping my home in Olathe and Ruby would keep her home in Bourbonnais. That didn't work out too well so in August I sold my condominium and moved my things to Bourbonnais. That made for a rather sudden exit from Olathe. The Olivet community welcomed me back home.

While we always want to see and talk to our grandchildren, our loneliness was cured. I was not alone. Our calendar filled with church activities, concerts, ball games, plays, and some service opportunities. It was still more **being** than **doing** as our strength waned. But we have a flower garden landscaped in the back yard. I planted a vegetable garden that produced surpluses to share with neighbors. Ruby got her 4' by 8' raised garden. We planted eleven rose bushes. Tending the lawn and gardens (annuals and perennials) proved to be farm like chores. Ruby and I were both raised on a farm.

We added a railing on the front porch complete with spindles. Ruby had a spacious deck built at the back of the house then we had it screened in to make it into a patio room. We revamped storage areas. She squeezed me into her limited space and we had a cozy home. We had numerous guests. All of our children have been in our home for overnight visits. I was eighty when we were married and Ruby was seventy-nine. We feel like we are doing remarkably well as octogenarians.

In no aspect of life are we more active than in travel. We have traveled Interstate 10 from Florida to Arizona. We flew to California and Washington, D.C. Otherwise, we have traveled by car to Lake Geneva and Door County, WI; Gatlinburg and Nashville, TN; Bridge City and San Antonio, TX; Alexandria and Morristown, IN; Norway, Champaign, Arthur, Starved Rock, and Springfield, IL; Branson and Hannibal, MO; and Columbus, OH. We have found several key restaurants on the way that are worth a return visit. If we set a limit on our day's travel of about 350 miles we can keep rested and enjoy our evenings. Ruby wants to go to England. And we will see our family members each year. Companionship in our travels makes a big difference.

I was asked by a friend how I could do the gardening work that was strenuous. I replied that I had quit that kind of work five years ago. "But," she said, "you are doing it this year." "Oh, but I was older five years ago."

CLOSING PRAYER
PSALM 90

[1]*A prayer of Moses the man of God.*
Lord, you have been our dwelling place
throughout all generations.
[2] Before the mountains were born
or you brought forth the earth and the world,
from everlasting to everlasting you are God.

[3] You turn men back to dust,
saying, "Return to dust, O sons of men."
[4] For a thousand years in your sight
are like a day that has just gone by,
or like a watch in the night.
[5] You sweep men away in the sleep of death;
they are like the new grass of the morning-
[6] though in the morning it springs up new,
by evening it is dry and withered.

⁷ We are consumed by your anger
and terrified by your indignation.
⁸ You have set our iniquities before you,
our secret sins in the light of your presence.
⁹ All our days pass away under your wrath;
we finish our years with a moan.
¹⁰ The length of our days is seventy years-
or eighty, if we have the strength;
yet their span is but trouble and sorrow,
for they quickly pass, and we fly away.

¹¹ Who knows the power of your anger?
For your wrath is as great as the fear that is due you.
¹² Teach us to number our days aright,
that we may gain a heart of wisdom.

¹³ Relent, O LORD ! How long will it be?
Have compassion on your servants.
¹⁴ Satisfy us in the morning with your unfailing love,
that we may sing for joy and be glad all our days.
¹⁵ Make us glad for as many days as you have afflicted us,
for as many years as we have seen trouble.
¹⁶ May your deeds be shown to your servants,
your splendor to their children.

**¹⁷ May the favor of the Lord our God rest upon us;
establish the work of our hands for us-
yes, establish the work of our hands. (NIV)**

AMEN

Printed in the United States
29906LVS00001B/145-198